Love, Duty & Sacrifice

Love, Duty & Sacrifice

Nicola Webb

Copyright © Nicola Webb 2023
Produced in association with

The right of Nicola Webb to be identified as the Author of this Work has been asserted by her in accordance with the Copyright, Designs and Patents Act 1988.

All rights reserved. No part of this publication may be reproduced, stored in a retrieval system, or transmitted, in any form or by any means, electronic, mechanical, photocopying, recording or otherwise, without the prior permission of Words by Design.

ISBN: 978-1-914002-34-2

Typeset in Cambria and Century Schoolbook

Printed and bound in the UK
www.wordsbydesign.co.uk

For Mary Anne and all women who toil hard and succeed magnificently, whilst never quite feeling they 'made the grade'.

This work is based on actual people and events but with some scenes and dialogue created for dramatic purposes.

Contents

A History Uncovered	1
Mary Anne: Our First Glimpse	4
The Chaworth-Musters: Landed but Aristocratic?	6
The Victorian Family Begins	13
John And Lina At Leisure	18
Work and Good Deeds	26
Patrick's Early Years	40
Mary Anne: A Simple, Rural Life	43
The Sharpe Family: 'Precious Little Comfort'	49
Mary Anne's Journey Begins	54
'Polly': A Life in Service	61
'Seen But Not Heard': Polly's Typical Day	66
A Chance Encounter	74
The Big News	81
John and Lina's Latter Years	88
'We Have To Return': Patrick Inherits	98
'Learning the Ropes' at Annesley	106
'Great and Good': The Couple Blossom	119
The Edwardian Family at Its Height	128
'Over by Christmas': War Breaks Out	149
The Home Front	157
1914: The Western Front Takes Shape	168
1915: Stalemate and Despair	184
1916: The Deadliest Battles	204
1917: Gas, Tanks and Skirmishes	213
Malaria and Dysentery: The Middle Eastern War	223
1918: The Tide Turns	232
A Nation in Mourning	240
A 'Perfect' Economic Storm	246
The End of an Era	263
The Story Ends	275

* * *

Acknowledgements	277
Reading List	279

A History Uncovered

The stables and gatehouse

On a chilly Autumn morning, I walk down Dog & Bear Lane – a deserted, muddy track in Annesley, Northwest Nottinghamshire. Dripping trees fold over me, forming a secret tunnel. All is quiet, apart from the squelch of wet leaves and the chirp and whistle of a solitary Blackbird. The lane opens to reveal a long sweep of rutted tarmac drive, leading to a two-storey stone gatehouse, arch and clocktower.

　I walk up to the security fencing surrounding the house, strewn with a prickle of signs – 'Danger – Keep Out', 'Private' and 'Strictly No Entry' – and peer through. I see acres of overgrown garden, broken-down stone balustrade and unkempt terraces surrounding an imposing Victorian mansion. Three storeys high, with tall, dark windows, I feel the house watching me.

The side and front of Annesley Hall

Ruined rear of Annesley Hall.
Photo courtesy of 28dayslater.co.uk

Walking around outside, I see one wing to the rear is mostly demolished, its stark interiors on view, and the house is missing its roof for the most part. Surreally, a small iron grate hangs high up in the air, scraps of wallpaper can be seen flapping in the breeze. Later I discover this was the nursery wing, once home to childish squeals and laughter.

My journey to Annesley was sparked by reading a few sentences on the family in a book by Jeremy Musson,[1] and him sending me an extract of a memoir, which prompted me to contact several family members.

Belonging to the ancient Chaworth-Musters family, the house was sold in 1973 and never again inhabited. Within five years it was subjected to two major fires and has been decaying ever since. What had caused this prominent family to go from its peak in the 1870s, to this derelict mansion only 100 or so years later? I was intrigued.

This story introduces the family at the height of its wealth and status when John (1838-1887) and Caroline (Lina) Chaworth-Musters (1832-1912) headed the family. However, the primary focus is on the late Victorian period and beyond, when their son Patricius, known as Patrick, (1860-1921) and his wife, Mary Anne (1863-1930) were at the helm.

---

1. Jeremy Musson, *Up and Down Stairs: the history of the country house servant*, 2009.

MARY ANNE: OUR FIRST GLIMPSE

Mary Anne stared dully at the silver breakfast tray on her lap. She was 51; her dark hair threaded with grey and a tired, drawn face. It was 27 July 1914, a few days after the county's social event of the year – the wedding at Annesley Hall of her and her husband's daughter, Lina to Captain Hugh Pattinson.

Mary Anne had dreaded the event and the planning it entailed. Would the weather be kind? Would the food be to standard? Would her guests approve? Straightening her pillow, she picked up a letter from Lina, written from her honeymoon in France. Frowning, she read:

> Dear Mama, I hope you have recovered from all the fuss of the wedding before starting the Norwegian packing?
>
> I want to hear all the different accounts of the wedding, which I thought was a huge success. I've had several letters saying how well it was done. Mrs Pattinson thought it was awfully well done. We got the Nottingham papers with the amusing photographs!
>
> We are looking forward to the Norwegian trip and are sailing a week after you. Do write with the accounts when you can.
>
> Your Loving Daughter, Lina.

Mary Anne placed the letter back on the tray. Pushing aside her uneaten breakfast, she leant back on the lace pillow, eyes closed. She must gather herself – there were the travel arrangements to finalise and the household to put in order before the family left for Norway. Yet her mind wandered back to the wedding party and why, over 25 years after marrying into the Chaworth-Musters family, she sometimes still felt like a cuckoo in their nest.

* * *

Lina's letter was kind and thoughtful, seeking to dispel her mother's anxieties. This was a theme that was to run throughout Mary Anne's life, as we shall see. The words Lina uses in relation to the wedding: *'recovered'* and *'fuss'*, clearly highlight Mary Anne's feelings about the event. Her daughter also takes pains to reassure Mary Anne about how well she had succeeded. Even then, she senses her own reassurances were not enough, so she includes those of her mother-in-law, Mary Pattinson – the wife of a very successful Newcastle manufacturer and daughter of a noted solicitor, JP, Deputy Lieutenant and High Sheriff. Mrs Pattinson was therefore the 'right sort' in the family's view, and her opinion on the success of the wedding would have counted.

Mary Anne appeared to spend her life striving to please and, whilst she succeeded brilliantly, it may have had a high personal cost. So, why did she sometimes feel like an imposter? We'll examine her family background soon but, first, we look at that of the Chaworth-Musters.

The Chaworth-Musters: Landed but Aristocratic?

In 1903, Patrick's mother, Lina Chaworth-Musters wrote a lengthy article for the Thoroton Society (a local history group she co-founded) tracing all the main branches of the family's history back to 1063 or so – Viscounts and Peers included. Outlined below is a quick summary of the family's properties at the time of this account.

Annesley Hall, the main seat, and home of the Chaworth-Musters family had long-established origins in a 13th Century medieval hall. In Henry VI's reign, in the 1400s, Lord Chaworth, an Irish Peer, inherited the Annesley estate through the marriage of one of his family with Alice de Annesley. In the 1600s, Annesley had a Viscount Chaworth but the family appears to have lost the title in the late 1690s, due to a lack of male heirs.

Annesley Hall, circa 1880s

The Hall was extended in the 17th century but fell into disrepair when the family favoured Colwick Hall as the main residence. This changed in 1838, when Annesley was extensively remodelled, and the family once again used it as their principal residence. It was further extended in the 1860s (the photo shown left is from around this time). The house was a grand Victorian residence with separate wings, tiered and landscaped gardens, its own church, stable block, and servants' quarters (which included a bake house, smithy, laundry, and brewery), a substantial arched entrance and various nearby lodges for senior house and estate staff.

The Chaworth-Musters rose to become significant landowners in Nottinghamshire in the mid-1800s, owning nearly 8,000 (largely agricultural) acres and several fine houses in addition to Annesley Hall: Colwick Hall, Wiverton Hall, Edwalton Manor, and Bridgford Hall.

Sir John Musters of Hornsey, who was knighted at Whitehall in 1663, purchased the **Colwick** estate. It passed in time to another John (Jack) and his wife, Mary Ann Musters. In 1831 the Hall was sacked by rioters, enraged at the failure of the Second Reform Bill. Mary Ann hid from the rioters in the gardens but was so traumatised by the event, that she died soon after, in 1832. From

Colwick Hall

that point, a heartbroken Jack rarely used Colwick, preferring to stay in his house at Grosvenor Place, London. Lina Chaworth-Musters wrote in 1888 that, despite his prolonged absences, *"everything was kept in the most perfect order by the old servants, Mr and Mrs Ward."*

After Jack's death in 1849, the family still rarely used Colwick, preferring Annesley or Wiverton Hall. Lina reports that in 1850 there was a family disagreement over Jack's will between his son William and his sons-in-law, Robert, and Anthony Hamond. William offered £4,000 (over £427,000 today[2]) for its contents, which was not accepted, so the heir John Chaworth-Musters (Lina's husband) sold most of the contents and let the property to tenants. Among the items sold, was a portrait of Mary Ann Musters painted by Thomas Phillips RA (a leading English portrait painter), which fetched £5,000 (over £533,000 today) at Christies in London. John's son Patrick sold Colwick Hall and estate to the Nottingham Racehorse Company in 1896 and it is now a smart hotel and conference centre.

Wiverton Hall

---

2. All financial conversions use the Bank of England's inflation calculator, converted to 2023 prices.

Wiverton Hall was formerly a house of considerable size and importance and became the family's property in the reign of Edward III in the 1300s. It was largely destroyed in the English Civil War in 1645 and rebuilt in the Tudor Gothic Revival style in 1814.

In the 19th and early 20th centuries Wiverton was mainly used by the family's adult younger sons or its widows. Lina Chaworth-Musters moved there in 1888 once widowed, and lived there until her death in 1912, then in 1923 it was let to tenants. It was finally sold in 1938 to the Crown, along with its estate of over 2,000 acres.

Edwalton Manor

Edwalton Manor was held by the Chaworth family since the early 1200s. The Hall, as it later became known, was used by the family as a residence at times, but mostly let. It was finally sold by Patrick Chaworth-Musters in 1887 to local brewer, Thomas Shipstone, and later became a hotel, before being developed into a private residential estate by Crosby Homes.

The family came into the **West Bridgford** estate by somewhat unorthodox means. Around 1675, Sir John Musters' daughter-in-law, Millicent Musters won the estate playing cards with Henry Pierrepont, Marquess of Dorchester. Her son Mundy Musters Senior inherited the estate in 1697. Bridgford Hall was built by Mundy Musters, Lord of the estates of West Bridgford and Colwick in 1768 and was tenanted for around 100 years.

Bridgford Hall

In 1827, Jack Musters became Lord of Bridgford Hall through his marriage in 1805 to Mary Ann Chaworth. It was largely let, and one tenant was the notable Nottingham lace manufacturer, Lewis Heymann, who lived there from 1840 until his death in 1869. In 1883 John Chaworth-Musters sold the Hall (but not the Lordship) and the immediate surrounding land to Heymann's son Albert. Albert philanthropically sold the Hall's gardens to West Bridgford Urban District Council in 1923, which led to the creation of the public Bridgford Park.

The Hall was extensively renovated in 2017 and now houses the Council Registry office and a series of smart hotel apartments (many of which are named after the Musters family). The family name and associations also live on in West Bridgford through several roads: Annesley Road; Chaworth Road; Musters Road, Court, and Crescent; Colwick Road; Edwalton Avenue, and roads named Patrick, George, Henry, and Millicent, plus Hound Road and Fox Road, which captured John and Lina's main interest!

The Family's Status

We can see from this brief review that the Chaworth-Musters family was ancient, and landowning. But where did they sit in society in the Victorian period – both in terms of wealth and status?

In 1873, the *New Domesday Book* listed John Chaworth-Musters as owning 7,826 acres in Nottinghamshire and five in Derbyshire. This placed him in an elite group. According to Bateman's *The Great Landowners of Great Britain and Ireland* of 1876, there were fewer than 1,500 English landowners who held more than 1,500 acres – and this group held a total of 43% of all the land in England.

In 1876, the *Spectator* calculated that only 710 people owned more than 25% of the land in England and Wales – a calculation based on the person holding more than 5,000 acres in any one county. John Chaworth-Musters fell into this elite category with over 7,000 acres in Nottinghamshire.

Bateman's 4th and final edition of *The Great Landowners* published in 1883, most accurately places the family in the social context of the time. It covers those with more than 3,000 acres and/or £3,000 pa income (around £300,000 pa today. Income, at the time, was based roughly on achieving £1 per acre). By then, a reduced number of 1,363 landowners held 41% of England's land. Around 39% (525) of those were titled but the majority (61%) were commoners. Bateman's classifications were "great landowners" – those owning over 10,000 acres, who were usually titled, nationally wealthy and often held Government positions; "greater gentry" – those owning 3,000 to 9,999 acres, who were mostly untitled, but wealthy in a specific county and holding regional positions of power and/or status, e.g., Lieutenant of a county; and the "squirearchy" – those with 1,000 to 2,999 acres and untitled.

The Chaworth-Musters would have come under Bateman's classification of "greater gentry": recognised, ancient land-owning families, with a large estate, and county status but no title. This puts the family in context in the 1870s and 1880s but what about beyond that? It is fair to say that the fortunes of the Chaworth-Musters from land were set to diminish, as they would for many UK landowners at the time.

In the 1870s, the mass transportation of cheap grain to Britain from the Canadian prairies drastically undercut domestic prices. In the 1870s and 1880s there were also a succession of bad harvests in the UK. Coined as 'The Great Depression of English agriculture' (1873-96), these factors combined to depress farming rents, as tenant farmers gave up their tenancies and landlords struggled to replace them, often at lower rents or had to take land in-hand themselves. And, just as incomes dropped, many large landowners had gone into debt trying to mechanise their farms and increase production levels, to compete with the 'industrialised' farms in North America and Australia.

The worsening economic situation (from the landowner's point of view) was compounded by the repeal of the Corn Laws in 1849 (import tariffs designed to keep British arable prices high), together with new laws favouring tenants: The Agricultural Holdings Act 1875, and its amendment in 1883. In addition, in 1880, the Ground Game Act came into effect, which allowed tenants to kill game trespassing on their farms. It was clear that the power was shifting from the landowner to the tenant.

Between 1870 and 1914, land values fell by 66%. From 1870-1896, estate-owning families rapidly declined, and many estates were broken up over two to three subsequent generations.

Economic commentators note that increased patronage in the local community by Victorian landowners was perhaps a final attempt to reassert the well-established feudal nature of rural society. As greater gentry, John and Lina Chaworth-Musters played their part in this paternalism – donating land and money to finance the village free school, build a new church and numerous other improvements, such as the building of a pub and post office.

Matters were somewhat alleviated for the Chaworth-Musters. Whilst income from their 7,000 acres would have reduced in the 1870s-90s, they were experiencing a rapid and significant growth in wealth from mining on their estate at Annesley. At the same time, they also enjoyed the social cachet of being a long-established landowning family. So, the answer to the question 'landed but aristocratic?' is that the family was no longer titled, but were classed as elite, 'greater gentry' and treated as such in the county and beyond.

The Victorian Family Begins

Whilst this story principally concerns itself with Patrick and his wife, Mary Anne, it is important to first know about his parents, who were largely responsible for creating the modern-day Annesley Hall and for shaping Patrick into the man he became.

John Chaworth-Musters (Patrick's father) was born at Wiverton on 9 January 1838. Sadly, his parents both died of tuberculosis; his father, John George, passed away in 1842 and his mother, Emily, in 1845. Orphaned at only seven years old, John was brought up by two uncles, Robert and Philip Hamond, and lived in the small country village of Gayton, Norfolk, around seven miles from King's Lynn, possibly renting Gayton Hall (home of Lord Romsey).

John enjoyed a country lifestyle with all its traditional pursuits, which became a lifelong interest and one that he shared with his son, Patrick. Whilst living in Norfolk, John and his siblings regularly visited Annesley Hall in the holidays, so were familiar with the estate and nearby village.

In 1849, John's grandfather died, and John (still aged only eleven) inherited Annesley and the family's other estates, which were held in trust. He was granted an annual allowance by the Court of Chancery, until he came of age at 21. John moved to Annesley Hall with his siblings

John taken c. 1887 (aged 49)

in 1850, under the guardianship of his Uncle Philip Hamond, who managed the estate.

Annesley was then a largely agricultural community with the only industry being local cottagers working on home looms to make hosiery. However, these sole traders couldn't expand as they did in the northwest, as there were neither streams to drive the machinery nor, at that time, easy access to coal.

But times were changing, as the Great Exhibition in London in 1851 proved. It showcased a new world of technology and innovation, involving the development of land-based industry, such as quarrying, mining, and forestry. In addition, there was an urban manufacturing boom – driven by the effective mining and easier distribution of a now cheap source of power – coal.

In keeping with this march of progress, in the nine years from 1850-1859, when John inherited, Philip Hamond and his wife Anne undertook a significant redevelopment of Annesley Hall. They demolished and rebuilt the Eastern side of the courtyard to the house, created a grand entrance archway to the estate, built a new lodge on Derby Road, and a farmhouse. We have no record of the expense, but it must have been significant.

John was sent to Eton, but it was not a success and he left soon after joining the school. The Hamond's perhaps then realised he needed a good but practical education to later run the estate. So, from the age of 14, John was schooled in Devon by Reverend Joseph Lloyd Brereton (1822-1901), rector of West Buckland, Devon (1852-57). Reverend Brereton was seen as an educational reformer; he established a fee-paying boarding school to provide a liberal, 'low church' education to middle class farmer's sons, with an emphasis on the practical and outdoors life, and at a fraction of the cost charged by English public schools of the time. He effectively created the county – rather than diocese-based educational system, and later linked it to universities – starting with a college at Cambridge.

John's guardians made an astute choice, as his senior education probably better fitted him for the 'Lord of the country manor' role he was to take on. It also suited John well. Lina reports that Reverend Brereton's pupils regularly rode about his estate in Devon and John saw his first fox hunt in 1855. He developed a lifelong affection for Dr Brereton, as noted by his wife Lina in a family memoir. John came home to Annesley for holidays with his uncles and extended family, where he continued to focus on his key love – nature and, especially, hunting.

John met his future wife, Caroline (Lina) Ann Sherbrooke, in 1855, when he was just 17 and she was 13. She lived at nearby Oxton Hall, and the families knew one another. Lina retells a sweet story of their meeting. John lifted her onto her pony to ride home and said to his cousin Sophie Hamond, *"Well, that is a pretty little girl, if you like."*

Lina pictured in hunting garb, probably in her fifties

Lina reveals how family-oriented John's upbringing was. She states that she *"envied his large circle of cousins"* and that his uncle, Philip Hamond *"had a great dislike of society and rarely invited anyone in the county to Annesley"*, but Lina's family were an exception and received regular invites. John kept a small pack of beagles at Annesley, which he regularly took over to Oxton Hall for him, Lina, and her brothers to go hunting. However, despite his love of the outdoors, Lina reports that he was a *"very delicate boy and never had good health throughout his life."*

John's happy home life was interrupted briefly when Uncle Philip sent him to Christ Church College, Oxford. John matriculated (enrolled) on 15th May 1856, aged 18, and came down (left) in the summer of 1857. College records[3] show that in the Michaelmas term (October-December) of 1856, he studied some Xenophon, Cicero, and mathematics. In the Hilary term (January-March) of 1857, he looked at the Iliad and the Aeneid, studied a bit more maths, and some theology. Lina met up with him once at Oxford. But the following term, Trinity (April-June) of 1857, John was granted leave of absence for health reasons, and never returned, so he didn't complete his degree.

A keen traveller, John travelled to Egypt for a winter on the Nile in 1857 to aid his health, accompanied by his brother George and his tutor, Dr Brereton. He returned home in June 1858, and by that Autumn 20-year-old John and childhood sweetheart Lina, (then

---

3. Judith Curthoys, Christ Church, University of Oxford's Archivist.

aged only 16) were engaged. The families were of similar wealth, status and close, so it could have been classed as an 'arranged' marriage, but it is generally thought that John and Lina made a love match. This is highly likely to have influenced his son Patrick, who later sought to have the same enduring affection and shared interests with his own life partner.

In 1859, when John came of age, he inherited the Annesley estate. It is notable that he settled the generous amount of £5,000 each, (over £498,000 in today's money) on both his sister Mary Ann and his brother George at that point. This was in addition to the direct inheritance they received, meaning the siblings were very comfortably off, John especially so. It is indicative both of John's generous nature, and of how wealthy the family was in mid-Victorian times, solely from their land and estates.

Wicked Lord Byron

To celebrate John's 21st birthday on 9th January 1859, the family entertained tenants from all their estates at a grand ball at Colwick Hall, which was, once again, let soon afterwards. The party is noted for a reminder of a tragic event in the family's history.

In January 1765, William Chaworth was involved in a duel with his cousin and neighbour, William Byron, 5th Baron (Lord) Byron – who was great uncle of the poet, Lord Byron. Having been drinking heavily for hours in the Star & Garter in Pall Mall, London, the pair got into a vicious argument over which of their estates contained the most game, or the most efficient methods of preventing poaching (accounts differ).

Lord Byron challenged William to a duel by sword, which took place in a poorly lit anteroom. Byron struck William in the stomach, and he was taken to Hanover Square, where a doctor treated him and conscious, though in great pain, William made a Will. Sadly, he died the next morning, aged only 39, of his wounds, his chief regret seemingly that the duel had not been fought in the *"best of conditions"*.

Lord Byron was tried for murder and found guilty of manslaughter but got off on a technicality, on Appeal, pleading a statute of Edward VI, which extended the 'Benefit of clergy' to be exempt from punishment, to the Peers of the Realm. He was freed, having only to pay a small fine. This caused great scandal at the time, and he gained the nickname 'Wicked Lord Byron', which he allegedly enjoyed.

William Chaworth's sword was taken from the tavern by a fellow diner and, in a kind gesture, was presented to John Chaworth-Musters at his coming-of-age party by a descendant. The sword hung for years in the central hall at Annesley Hall and the story often recounted – no doubt as a lesson to the young men of the family of the possible consequences of hard drinking and duels!

Having come of age, John married 17-year-old Lina as soon as he was able, on 15th March 1859 at her family seat of Oxton Hall (near Southwell, Notts). They honeymooned in Italy, France and Switzerland, arriving home to Annesley in June 1859. As a wedding present, John bought Lina a pony carriage and a pair of dark chestnut ponies, with which she was *"greatly delighted"*. They travelled to Whitby to stay with friends in the Autumn, and by then Lina was six months' pregnant. Returning to Oxton Hall to live, they continued their sporting pursuits, and John broke his collarbone on his 22nd birthday in January 1860, whilst hunting.

The couple's first child – a son – was born on 13th January 1860 at Oxton Hall, having been conceived just one month after the couple married, and was baptized on 11th March. His name was registered as John Patricius (a popular name throughout the family's history), but he was known as Patrick. To commemorate his birth, John and Lina commissioned a stone memorial (which became known as 'Patrick's stone') within the new plantation of trees in their deer park. Their brew master, Thomas Whyler created a commemorative ale in the Hall's own brew house, which was laid down until Patrick came of age.

John And Lina At Leisure

Lina was a Victorian woman of outstanding energy and ability. Possibly unusually for the time, John encouraged Lina in all her interests, which included philanthropic works, social history, and creative writing (she published several books). She was also the driving force behind many of the changes to Annesley Hall.

Lina is referred to as being *"amiable"* and *"warm"* in newspaper reports of the time, but she was only human and didn't get on with everyone all the time. Writing to her daughter Emily (Kitty) in 1842, she talks about an exchange of letters with John's sister, saying that Mary Ann wrote to her in an *"angry and evidently proud spirit"* and signed off *"totally devoid of anything like affection."*

The Hunters

The couple had similar interests, especially foxhunting. In 1860 John spent time and money assembling his own pack of hounds, which Lina described as *"a most uphill task to begin hunting on an estate that had been without hounds for sixteen years."* It involved great expense and labour: corresponding with neighbours about boundaries; planting groves and copses of trees and gorse; and erecting bridle gates and bridges.

In 1861 John oversaw the rebuilding of the stables and had kennels built at Wiverton for his hounds. He generally managed three days of hunting a fortnight on his estates in Annesley, West Bridgford, Edwalton and Wiverton, which he had stocked with foxes. Lina joined in and, from accounts, was probably a more accomplished rider than John.

John was made Master of the South Nottinghamshire hounds from 1861 to 1868 (an ancient family-related hunt that he had re-established). In 1868, the Master of the famous Leicestershire Quorn Hunt (reputedly the oldest) resigned, and John *"offered to take his own pack and hunt the county at his own expense"*. He rented a house in Loughborough and spent much time there in the hunting season for the next two years, but gave up the Mastership in 1870, deciding it was too expensive and too much hard work to keep a second hunt going in another county.

Photos of John at this time show a stocky chap (aged around 32), bearded and side whiskered (in the fashion of the day), sporting shiny leather riding boots with polished brass spurs, top hat, white breeches, and a smart hunting jacket, from which peeks a small pewter or copper huntsman's horn. John looks every inch the country gentleman.

John in hunting garb

By the 1870s, John had become an imposing, heavily built man with a beard, balding and with light brown hair. This photo, thought to be taken around 1870, shows John in full hunting regalia, complete with a hunting horn tucked inside his jacket. A painting commissioned in 1879, (when he was aged 41) to mark his being made Master of the Hounds and now part of the British Museum's collection, shows him with his beloved horse and hounds.

Sold by the family in 1973, it was passed on and eventually realised £19,000 (around £34,000 today) at a Christie's auction in 1996. In 1875 John published a 200-page book of 'Hunting Songs and Poems', showing his love of the sport.

However, the strain of running both hunts took a toll on John's health and he visited a spa in Carlsbad in Germany in the summer of 1870. Lina reports however that the *"waters [at the spa] were too strong and he never really had good health"* from that point. This was sad in a man of only 32 years old. John continued with the South Nottinghamshire hunt from 1871-76 but ill-health forced him give up his hounds, much to his dismay. He sold them in 1877 for £2,000 (a staggering £184,000 today), to a huntsman named Theodore Talbot from Glamorganshire.

In 1880, the author Leonard Jacks wrote about John's sporting career:

> *A thorough sportsman and an English gentleman; that is how I should describe Mr. Musters, of Annesley Park. One of the best riders across country he has been in his day, and every sportsman in the county was sorry enough when he withdrew from the chase, now some years ago, as the tenant farmers of Nottinghamshire felt sorry when he severed his active connection with the Chamber of Agriculture, because he could not conscientiously lend himself to a course which that body proposed to pursue.*
>
> *As master of the Quorn, a post which none but a wealthy man and a sportsman versed in every movement of the chase could possibly undertake, with any hope of success, he won that peculiar and enviable popularity which attaches to a successful master of foxhounds, and later as master of the South Nottinghamshire, a pack which, under his sway, became scarcely less famous than the Leicestershire one, he gained the esteem of every lover of the hunt in the county.*

A 'Salmon Lord'

John also enjoyed coarse salmon fishing, having been introduced to the sport by his uncle, Anthony Hamond, with whom he was close. Anthony died in 1869, and Lina wrote a moving tribute to him in her 1893 memoir:

> *Uncle Anthony Hamond [was] a very clever man, a practical farmer on a large scale, a great reader and politician, as well as active in county business. He was one of the best and wisest friends I ever had, or John either, and he was a great loss to us when he died.*

John took Lina to Norway for the first time in Spring 1861, with baby Patrick, and a college friend, and rented a stretch of the Aaland River, in Sognefjord, southern Norway. In other years he rented stretches of the Maudal and the Quinisdal rivers, near Kristiansand, in west Norway. Lina reports that John *"never missed but one year after that, as long as he lived."*

Like mountain climbing and hunting, British aristocrats introduced angling to Norway in the 19th century. Well-off adventurers, officers and other upper-class gentlemen were impressed by the wild, beautiful, and unspoiled countryside and plentiful rivers. For a salmon fisherman, Norway was a dream.

The first British anglers to Norway no doubt provoked merriment. Even though a few locals fished with a rod and line, the local farmers regarded the foreigners as eccentric, wondering why they used a stick and string, when nets, fish pots and traditional traps were easier and more productive.

These well-heeled British visitors became known as the Salmon Lords and their numbers increased rapidly by the mid-1800s. Hundreds of travel books were published, filled with superlatives, sketches, and photographs of the countryside. These accounts tempted even more tourists to go, and by the 1880s, Norway witnessed the early days of mass tourism, which lasted until the First World War.

The tourism led to several major changes in poor, rural Norway. Thomas Bennett, an Englishman who had moved to Christiania (now Oslo), started the country's first travel agency, the roads were greatly improved, the steam ship companies ran regular services and luxurious hotels were built in the most beautiful surroundings.

Most of the Salmon Lords, however, were quite happy living in rougher conditions, to be close to the rivers. Sir Horace Rumbold, a diplomat and ambassador to Sweden, wrote this after a fishing trip to Norway's Lågen river in 1884:

> *Our quarters at the farmhouse at which we put up were about as rough as they well could be. Farmer Hannevold and his belongings being thoroughly untidy and slovenly in their habits and household arrangements. The food they gave us, too, was coarse and unappetising. Fortunately, we had brought with us an ample supply of tinned things, which, with the fish of our own catching, broiled fresh from the river, and the great wash-hand bowlfuls of fragrant wood strawberries and the delicious cream set before us, made a menu fit for a King.*

Because of this sub-standard accommodation, it was quite common for more frequent and wealthier visitors to buy or build their own fishing lodges. For years, John and Lina rented a lodge in Surnadal, not far from Kristiansand in northern Norway. John wrote to Lina (usually every week) over the summer months from Surnadal in 1860-1865 and spoke excitedly of the quality of the fishing and hunting, detailing the visitors he had met. He often listed the exact weights and type of every fish he had caught but he missed hunting, saying: *"There's plenty in the water but nothing to shoot."*

As with many Victorian couples, they would spend weeks apart, but the fact that theirs was a love match is clear from his letters. He always addressed her very fondly: *"My dearest Lina"*, *"My darling Lina"* or "Linny" and signed off equally affectionately, wishing love to their children:

> *I shall be so glad to come home to you very soon.*
> *Goodbye my own, sweetest love.*
> *Your ever-loving husband.*

He ended one letter that was full of news of fish caught and those that slipped away, with a PS: *"This is a most stupid letter, but I cannot help it Dear."* The family left their mark in some small ways,

The Laerdal river, Norway. Photo courtesy of Espen Schive.

as today the main hotel in Surnadal has a restaurant called 'The Musters'.

John and Lina visited Norway so often that in 1877, they bought a farmhouse, converted to a fishing lodge on Sognefjord near the Laerdal river in southern Norway and called it Lysne Lodge. Sognefjord is nicknamed the King of the Fjords, as it is the largest and deepest fjord in Norway. The area remains unspoilt with idyllic, dramatic granite and forested scenery.

John and Lina would have seen Laerdal at nearly its busiest – though still sparsely populated – its population decreased from 3,900 in 1855 to 2,400 in 1920, due to emigration to America after the Great War, and it now stands at approximately 2,200.

The whole family would visit the Lodge for four to six weeks in the summer, with John staying for longer periods. The journey, via The Bergen Steamship Company, would have taken around four days in total, ending with a carriage and train ride from Laerdal to Bergen.

When not fishing in Norway, John spent time visiting his shooting box in Senlis, in the province of Aumont, 40 km north of Paris, where he increasingly went in his later years, as an antidote to his failing health.

John also took an active interest in the South Nottinghamshire Yeomanry (a volunteer cavalry unit of the army) and Lina writes of annual reviews of the Yeomanry at Annesley Hall, with mounted drills, followed by lunch in the park estate, where her husband presented the prizes.

The 'King of Patagonia'

When not abroad, John and Lina often hosted family visitors to Annesley Hall. John's naval commander brother George saw action in the Crimean War, receiving the English and Turkish Crimean medals. From 1861 to 1866 he served in the sloop HMS Stromboli off the coast of South America but took half-pay in 1869 to go off and explore the region.

He travelled with a tribe of Patagonian Indians for around a year and published a book: *At home with the Patagonians: a year's wanderings over untrodden ground from the Straits of Magellan to the Rio Negro* (1871; 2nd edition, 1873). This led to his being awarded a gold watch in 1872 by the Royal Geographical Society and gaining the nickname *'The King of Patagonia'*.

In 1872 George went to Vancouver in Canada and travelled around parts of British Columbia with native tribes. Sailing home, the following year, he met a Mr Williams, a British merchant in Bolivia, and his daughter Herminia. George and Herminia were married in 1873. Lina shows her sensibility and empathy when she wrote in her memoir of their *"uncomfortable"* wedding at Nottingham's Roman Catholic chapel, where the *"protestant guests behaved ill in the chapel."* The Chaworth-Musters family was protestant but clearly Lina found this behaviour unacceptable.

George

The couple then returned to Bolivia and the results of George's explorations were published in the Journal of the Royal Geographical Society in 1877. Returning home from Bolivia in 1876, they settled quietly, dividing their time between Annesley and Wiverton Hall. Much to the amusement of the family George brought back a massive stuffed Anaconda (one of the world's largest breeds of snake), which lay curled up on a table in the family's great hall. But George reportedly found it hard to adjust to life in the UK and servants often found him wrapped in a blanket, sleeping under the stars on the lawns near the house.

In 1878, travelling again, George was appointed as British Consul to Mozambique, but later that year he became ill with an abscess in his side. Coming home, he was nursed by Herminia, whilst Lina looked after their three young girls, Emily, Theresa, and Rosita. George sadly died from blood poisoning in Aumont, France (his brother's retreat for convalescence) on 25th January 1879, aged only 38.

Falling unconscious a few hours before he died, his last word is reported to have been *"Annesley."* His brother was also abroad for his health at the time, so his cousins stood in for him at George's funeral, where he was buried in the old churchyard at Annesley Hall.

On his return, John commissioned a striking memorial in George's memory in the shape of an anchor. Herminia and her three girls stayed at Annesley for a time before she moved back to live

Memorial to George Chaworth-Musters

with her family in South America, and later remarried. Commentators of the time described George as *"A fearless explorer, and a man of unfailing tact and winning manners."*

WORK AND GOOD DEEDS

In April 1861, the family had moved to Annesley Hall. The area was known to be rich in coal, as there had been a modest amount of surface mining, so in 1864, after being approached, John leased land to William Worswick of Coleorton in Leicestershire (a former coal merchant and now mine owner) for test mining. The tests were a success, and The Annesley Colliery Company was formed, with John as one of the Directors. The first sod was removed to sink the mineshaft, with great ceremony, on the bitterly cold day on 1st January 1865.

Annesley Colliery 1907. Photo courtesy of David Amos

By law, coalmines needed two shafts to draw a flow of air through the workings. Shaft sinking continued throughout 1865 and 1866 and, on 5th October 1867, the shaft reached the Top Hard Seam at 1,419 feet. Much work was still required to open out the tunnels, and, in total, 473 yards of rock were removed – by hand. It was not until 5th February 1868 that the first coal was raised for sale. Among that first load, 15 tons was sold to John Chaworth-Musters for 10 shillings and 8 pence per ton. The Annesley Colliery Company was now in business and the Top Hard seam formed the bulk of the colliery's production for the next 50 years or so. Because of the demand for coal in the First World War, in 1914, the shafts were deepened to reach the Deep Hard and the Deep Soft seams, which were worked until 1950.

Apart from being coal-rich, the family's land had the essential benefit of lying close to the Midland Railway, Mansfield branch line, which was in place when the colliery opened. It was much improved by the mid-1870s, when Annesley had three railway lines and two stations nearby, including a connection from London to Nottingham. Mostly funded to carry coal, it meant the ACC could move its coal faster, further, and cheaper, thus reaping greater profits.

Those that invested in coal mines generally sought profit above all else and were often City investors who never saw their mines, let alone met miners. Working conditions were mostly poor, the job highly dangerous and pay low. Nor were miners protected by Guilds of Middle Ages, unlike many other trades. Annesley Colliery was perhaps a little different from many mines of the time. For a start, the main investor William Worswick was no faceless investor. He had a strong mining background and was personally involved, as he came from a neighbouring county.

Secondly, John was a director of the company (as was his eldest son, Patrick, and then his heir, Jack) and he and Lina took an active role in the mining community which lay only a mile from Annesley Hall, and helped it flourish. The Directors and the Chaworth-Musters contributed to build miner's housing, with large private gardens, a church, sports facilities, a school, shops, pubs, and a post office. Word spread about the 'perks' of the job (especially housing, which was rare at the time) and large numbers of miners and their families relocated from Yorkshire, Durham and Leicestershire.

As with most mines of the day, Annesley was not free from tragedy. In May 1877 there was an underground fire at the north intake, a short distance from the Top Hard pit bottom. The roadway was sealed with stoppings to try to extinguish the fire but on reopening it a month later, on 27th June, an explosion occurred, which killed seven miners. Four men died from carbon-monoxide poisoning, with a further three killed whilst bravely attempting to rescue their colleagues. The Chaworth-Musters erected a memorial for the dead in New Annesley churchyard, which can still be seen today.

Annesley Village Flourishes

Annesley colliery boasts several famous alumni. Arthur Lawrence, father of the famous Eastwood author, DH Lawrence, was based at Annesley for a short period in the early 1870s. And there was a strong cricketing connection. Locals in Nottinghamshire were proud of saying that any England cricket selector seeking a new opening bowler need only peep down one of the county's pit-shafts. The famous 'bodyline' Ashes test tour of 1932-33, saw the pace-bowler Harold Larwood rise to fame. He mined the Deep Soft seam, 1,400ft below Annesley, then did his bit for England. Copies of Larwood's birth and wedding certificates once adorned the walls of the Cricketers Arms pub in Annesley.

Lina also took an increasingly active interest in village affairs. In the 1860s, the village population was 300 and the school catered for 50 boys and girls – most of the children present at the time. But the increase in demand for free schooling meant the Church of England village school was now too small. John paid to turn the schoolmaster's living accommodation into an extra schoolroom, which allowed up to 100 children to be taught religion and morals, spelling, reading, writing and arithmetic, plus sewing for the girls. In

Annesley Row houses, circa 1914. Photo courtesy of David Amos.

1867, in line with national policy, the village free school was taken over and run by the local Government.

Lina oversaw the construction of a post office and general store. She also had a hand in the design and construction of two rows of terraced housing (160 cottages in total) or 'Annesley Rows' as they are locally known, which were built between 1869 and 1873 (photo above). The houses were of a standard colliery design of the time, with a living room, kitchen and three bedrooms, but no bathroom – miners washed in a tin bath in front of the kitchen fire.

The Annesley Row houses had larger than average gardens, enabling families to grow much of their own food, build pigeon lofts, greenhouses, or sheds for the men to play dominoes and cards. As with most mining communities, they were close-knit and looked out for one another. If a wife were sick or in childbirth, neighbours would do her washing, feed her children, and cook and bring dinner round to her husband until she was up and about.

Home improvements

In contrast to this hand-to-mouth life, by the mid-1860s, the Chaworth-Musters were well and truly wealthy – with over 7,000 acres of land, plus earnings from the colliery. The family's wealth and status meant that John was made High Sheriff of Nottingham in 1864. But, though wealthy, they were also spending heavily. The couple had three children (with more to follow) and decided to extend the house. They commissioned a leading country house architect, most likely Anthony Salvin (1799-1881), to remodel Annesley Hall. The aim was to accommodate a schoolroom and children's nurseries, so Salvin designed the extension to match the rest of the Hall, incorporating a courtyard with access to the Derby Road for deliveries.

They flattened an existing butchery, bakery, and washrooms, and added the extension on the North side, cutting into a bank of land. A plaque set into a chimney stack commemorates the finish of the work in 1865.

Ahead of their time and with plentiful coal, John had buildings built around the courtyard to house a central heating boiler and fuel storage, with a ramp inside a tunnel for coal delivery straight from the Derby Road, down a chute, and into the store.

In 1861, the census recorded a staff of 18 house servants. With a growing number of staff, the couple created new servant's

The servants' quarters, viewed from the old churchyard

quarters above the large stable block that formed an arched entrance to the estate, a few hundred metres from the main house. They also added a stone wall and steps between the church and main house.

By 1880, the proliferation of and interest in large country houses in England was reaching its highest number. Annesley Hall was no exception and in 1881, author Leonard Jacks included Annesley in his book, *The Great Houses of Nottinghamshire and the County Families*. It paints a vivid picture of this typically Victorian house at the time; one which is not grand but rather 'lived in' and bearing witness to a family and sporting life:

> *Annesley Hall is now the abode of a 'prosperous old family' of one of the largest landowners in the county; a genuine sportsman, and a true gentleman, who now, having given up at a tolerably early age all active participation in the national sport, still takes the liveliest interest in everything concerning it. The desolation has long since been dispelled by the going to and fro of friends*

*The front of Annesley Hall, c. 1874.
Photo courtesy of Nottinghamshire Guardian.*

and dependents, the happy voices of children, who are rapidly growing up into manhood and womanhood, and by the sunshine of home life.

The stonework of the fine front is concealed by ivy of many, many years' growth, and at the side over-looking the park, a gigantic Virginia Creeper stretches wide-spreading, sturdy trailers, bearing a profusion of dark red leaves in autumn. The approach to the Hall is through a spacious park, with whose grand old trees and fine herd of deer many people who take their walks abroad are familiar. To get to the hall you have to pass through the portals of the 'massy gate' which stood there in Byron's day, and there is no cause to be afraid of a great handsome staghound, which comes bounding towards you in playful curves. There are several of these beautiful hounds about the house, and they enjoy special privileges.

The central hall is full of objects of interest. It has an unmistakeably ancient look. The furniture is old, the pictures on the walls are old, the deerskins which cover the floor are getting the worse for wear, the great jack boots which hang over the ancient fireplace, were made by no modern shoemaker, and the jerkin which is suspended beside them is evidently the work of a mediaeval tailor. The great boots and the old garment with the ancient weapons, which are hung up here are said to have belonged to that eccentric outlaw whose existence has never yet been satisfactorily established – Robin Hood.

On the walls are some family portraits representing ancestors, in the costumes, which marked different periods, including Mr. Mundy Musters. In this apartment is kept the delicate bladed, finely tempered, handsomely mounted sword with which Sir John Byron is said to have killed Mr. Chaworth in a famous duel that has become a matter of history. The picture of that unfortunate gentleman, with his pale face and melancholy expression is hung in another part of the house. The strong quaint looking iron rails, which guard the staircases, were not forged in any existing furnace.

The Oratory at Annesley, circa 1924.
Photo courtesy of Illustrated London News.

Ascending the staircase and passing Ward's picture of Lord Byron to which attention has already been called, and some more family portraits, one obtains access to the old drawing room. Two great staghounds are enjoying the comfort of this very comfortable apartment; one is curled up in canine ease upon the sofa and the other is studying the figuring of the Dutch tiles which ornament a fireplace of gigantic proportions, and which on this chill autumn morning contains a bright, warm fire.

The massive doorway contains one of those rare specimens of woodcarving, which are sometimes to be met with in old country mansions, though there are few houses hereabouts that can boast such a specimen as this. It was executed by some clever carver in the reign of Charles II at the instigation, it is said, of Lord Chaworth, the then Lord of the manor. The ceiling is panelled and made dark with cornices of carved wood. The carving is evidently of the same date as that about the entrance. The huge fireplace with its Dutch tiles furnishes further evidence of the antiquity of this chamber.

There are in this old drawing room, besides a large and somewhat faded picture of John the Baptist preaching in the Wilderness, which occupies a considerable space over the fireplace, some family portraits in an excellent state of preservation, for the colours are almost as bright as when the pictures came from the easel. They include paintings of Lady Mary Byron who died in 1703, daughter of the Earl of Bridgwater, of Frances Lady Byron, daughter of William, Earl of Portland. The beautiful little collection of miniatures, the most interesting of which I have already mentioned, are carefully preserved, together with other small things each possessing some particular interest of its own.

The modern drawing-room downstairs is a very different apartment. It is furnished and fitted as the reception room of a great country house should be; with luxurious settees, and chairs and couches set upon a downy carpet.

Its broad casement commands a view of one of the prettiest bits of park scenery in England. Such delightful grassy undulations; hills rising gently in the distance, grand old trees, the growth of centuries, and the gleam of water down in the hollow.

There are some watercolours of Eastern cities on the wall of the drawing room, a portrait of Lord Chesterfield,

Annesley drawing room

the man of fashion and celebrated wit, in court dress, and one of Lady Howe, which bears the one just named close company. The dining room is a large and handsome apartment, containing several hunting pictures the figures in which are family portraits. The large one over the mantelpiece shows the present owner's grandfather on horseback, with two other gentlemen fully equipped for the chase, and the dogs look anxious to be off.

In the corner near the window is the portrait of Mr. John Musters, a handsome man, who died in 1842 at the early age of thirty-four, and near the door one's attention is called to the portrait of a lady – very beautiful she must have been too, who by a single game of cards won a fine estate of several thousand productive acres. [The West Bridgford estate]. The room is lofty and light as are all the other principle rooms in this old house.

The speediest way of getting to the gardens is by traversing a grand old, flagged terrace, flanked all along by a high wall covered with creeping plants which grow in the sweetest confusion. Here it is said Lord Byron used to practice pistol firing, probably to the terror of Miss

Annesley Hall and grounds, 1973. Photo courtesy of AP Nicholson.

Chaworth. The terrace is ornamented by a balcony of stone, coloured in many places by lichens and mosses, and bearing in the centre of its length a stone urn on which is carved the escutcheon of the Chaworths. Two broad flights of steps terminating the terrace, bring you into the gardens where there are little paths leading into the most delicious solitudes.

It is worth a visit to Annesley to be allowed to wander amongst the splendid shrubs which so thickly stud this portion of the estate; masses of bright green – sturdy bay, and lusty laurels, which latter look like so many leafy wigwams. It is very quiet in these garden solitudes, on this still October morning, when the only sound to be heard is the crackling of the crisp reddish-brown leaves, which strew the paths, and the occasional shrilly note of the robin.

Leonard Jacks' description of the hall omits many oddities that reveal the family's love of hunting, shooting, and fishing. A photo of the hall from the period shows the walls lined with around 15 stuffed stags' heads and antlers; glass cases of stuffed birds and animals; George's stuffed Anaconda coiled on a heavy wooden refectory table draped in an ancient tapestry; a selection of animal

The hall at Annesley, c. 1900. Photo ChM-Ph-2-2, courtesy of University of Nottingham Manuscripts and Special Collections.

skin rugs and wool runners covering the floor; an old wooden sleigh (possibly Norwegian); a spinning wheel; a marble bust; and a large, brass ship's bell on the floor under the table. It has the look of a country museum of curiosities.

Spending continued unabated in the 1870s, with John and Lina keen to look after their tenants and miners. The 1870 Elementary Education Act came into force, making free state-funded education available (although not compulsory) to children between the ages of five and 13. Perhaps because of this, a new and larger school was built in 1870, costing John £1,400 (today's equivalent of £129,000). After school hours, the building was also used as a reading room, library, and savings bank. This growth continued over the next 25 years and in 1895, the Kelly's Directory showed that the village school had grown to teach 200 infants and a further 200 boys and girls.

A New Church Is Needed

John donated more land to create a public cemetery, plus built a further cottage in The Grove and three large houses, one for the pit manager and another for the vicar. The old parish church next to Annesley House was both too small and remote from the enlarged village, so John decided to have a new one built (although family services continued in the old church until the early 1940s). The family donated the land and funded half the £5,000 cost (a total of over £461,000 in today's value), the remainder being funded by various coal merchants, and private subscribers, including the new vicar (who came from a wealthy family) and gave generously.

All Saints Church, Annesley. Photo courtesy of Rob Howl.

The site was chosen carefully, with the church being built on a small hill, surveying the village, and providing great views across to Newstead Abbey. Started in 1872, the church was consecrated in 1874 and a spire added in 1876. Patrick Chaworth (1635-1693), 3rd Viscount Chaworth of Armagh had 'The Achievement' designed in 1686, which was a stone heraldic display of the importance of the family. He died without male heirs, so the title expired with him. Located originally in the old parish church, The Achievement was moved to the new church in 1976.

Tragically, the new Annesley church was almost destroyed by arson in 1907, and the fire could be seen from miles away. Contemporary newspaper reports state that there were three fires on three successive nights in the area, although the perpetrator remained unknown. A fire truck pulled by horses came to the fire, but it couldn't get up the short, steep hill to the church. In desperation, the vicar organised local miners and women to form a human chain, moving buckets of water up from the Grove. Sadly, there was not enough water to put out the fire, which burnt all night. The roof, most of the interior and the bells were destroyed in the fire but fortunately, the church was insured for £8,000 and rebuilt for a cost of £4,000 (over £372,000).

Apart from the building works, staff costs were increasing. John and Lina, followed by Patrick, their heir, would have found it harder to recruit domestic staff and may have had to search further afield and pay higher wages, to compete with other sectors. The proximity of a main railway line was good for distributing Annesley's coal, but every benefit can bring a downside. Mobility, for women especially, meant they could travel into Nottingham, Sutton or Hucknall to work in hosiery factories or in retail for better pay than as domestic servants. There was also a rapid rise in large grocery chains at the time, with Sainsbury founded in 1869, Lipton in 1871, and Marks & Spencer in 1894, all of which lured women away from domestic service.

Men, instead of undertaking dangerous mining, could travel to Mansfield or Nottingham to work in the growing number of factories – principally cotton spinning, hosiery, lace, tobacco, and bicycle manufacture. Overall, the population in Annesley peaked around 1881 at 1,474 (having grown from only 288 in 1861), dropped to 1,271 in 1911 and fell further still after the First World War, when the demand for coal fell away.

Despite the difficulty in recruiting and retaining servants, Annesley estate servant numbers show some consistency. The census shows numbers ran at 30 servants in 1881 and perhaps to raise further income to pay for this large staff, John sold the first plots of his West Bridgford estate for housing development in 1880. In 1891 the Annesley staff was 19 (significantly lower than before, probably due to a concerted effort to reduce expenses on the heir,

Patrick's part). In 1901 it had risen again to 31 (reflecting a much larger household of children) and dropped to 14 in 1911 (most of the children had now grown up, left home and the hunting had ended). The composition of servants also changed in the 1900s, with nursery staff reduced and grooms, blacksmiths and gamekeepers disappearing as Patrick moved away from hunting, with a chauffeur appearing on the payroll for the first time in the 1911 census.

Whatever the number, treating their servants well was a trait that seemed to run in the family in the 1800s. In 1820, Mary Ann Chaworth engaged a young country girl, Rebecca Wright, as her lady's maid. She served the Chaworth-Musters faithfully for 67 years, and when she died in 1887, aged 87, she was still with the family, living in a tied cottage. John erected a gravestone in her memory recording her as a *"friend and faithful servant in the family."*

Patrick's Early Years

Eldest son and heir, John Patricius (Patrick), was educated briefly at Eton, like his father before him. College records[4] show that he joined as a boarder in the Lent Half (the Easter term) of 1874, when he was aged 14, and left in in the Michaelmas Half (Winter term) of 1876 (aged 16).

His housemasters during his short time at Eton were the Rev. Henry Daman, Oscar Browning, and Evelyn Shirley Shuckburgh, a noted classical scholar and translator. Oscar Browning was a vocal and active opponent of the school's traditional curriculum and teaching methods. He introduced progressive techniques to the classroom, to the general approval of his pupils but the dismay of the Eton authorities.

Patrick photographed in his early thirties

Patrick's other tutors were Reverend Duncan Crookes Tovey, a classicist and expert on the poet Thomas Gray, and Herbert Hailstone, a classical translator who sadly committed suicide in Regent's Park, London, aged 46.

---

4. Joshua Insley, Archives Assistant, Eton College Library.

There is no mention of Patrick for any academic or sporting achievements in the *Eton College Chronicle* – the fortnightly school magazine. However, it is likely that he participated in Eton's many sports and, especially, took an active role in the Beagle Society. One contemporaneous entry about the Beagle Society in the Chronicle reports:

> *The Eton College Pack has commenced this season very successfully; they have had more than one good run, and having invested in several couples of new hounds, they have been rewarded with one days' sport at least, which has seldom, if ever, been equalled in the annals of Eton hunting.*

Maybe this great run out was helped by Patrick's experienced hand, as both before and after leaving Eton, Patrick was home tutored and enjoyed long summers with the family, where he could hunt and fish to his heart's content. With Patrick's love of country pursuits and the outdoors, it is perhaps not surprising that he lasted only 18 months in the academic 'hothouse' of Eton and was then tutored at home.

Again, like his father, Patrick was sent to Christ Church College, Oxford. He matriculated (enrolled) on 25th January 1878, shortly after his 18th birthday. Neither he nor his father took a degree. Patrick was evidently a poor student and failed his first examinations three times in three consecutive terms[5] – Hilary term (January-March 1878), Trinity (April-June) and Michaelmas (October-December). As a result, he left Oxford, probably at the end of the same year. His formal education now over, Patrick was instead schooled by his father and senior servants in the business of managing the large estate that he would one day inherit.

The census taken on 3rd April 1881 showed just how big a concern the estate was. Quite apart from the business affairs of the Colliery, there were the many tenant farmers to deal with and a total of 30 household and outdoor servants. The census lists the household as being John and Lina; Patrick, aged 21; Mary, his sister, 17; sister Catherine (Kitty) 16; and Geoffrey Charlton (a visitor, aged seven). Patrick's brother George must have been absent at the time

---

5. Judith Curthoys, Christ Church, University of Oxford, Archivist.

of the census. In addition, there were the 30 house and estate servants.

Among the servants were the elderly Rebecca Wright, housekeeper; William Batcock, butler; two footmen, including Charles Parr (whose loyalty to the family was rewarded when he later was promoted to butler); six grooms, a kennel man, and his assistant – these being testimony to John and Lina's love of hunting. Also appearing for the first time in 1881 is Mary Anne Sharpe, aged 18, listed as a housemaid, but whose actual role was junior nursery housemaid.

Patrick's early life was one of privilege but also, relatively humble. He was largely home schooled, didn't stay long in further education and showed a strong preference for running the country estate, rather than take a job in the city or enter the army. His leisure pursuits were entirely countryside focused – hunting, shooting, and fishing – and holidays were spent simply with his parents in a modest lodge in Norway or with family in Norfolk. Whilst wealthy and lacking for nothing, the descriptions of the family house and their lifestyle show the Victorian Chaworth-Musters family had simple tastes and didn't live 'the high life'. That said, Patrick and his siblings lacked for nothing, and their future well-being and income was secure. This was in great contrast to his future mate, as we shall see.

Mary Anne: A Simple, Rural Life

A cloistered kitchen bubbling with chatter from the dozen seated girls. Toddlers, four- or five-years' old move among the older girls, clutching small scissors. Around them hangs a strong smell of the stable, tainted breath, unwashed clothes, and the sharp smell of straw. All this is overlaid by the acrid smell of sulphur, the straw fresh from the bleaching vat in the backyard.

The girls work in unison, the younger ones softly humming a tune to keep themselves on track: 'under one and over two, pull it tight and that will do.' Their rosy lips, cracked and raw, parted to reveal the sweet smell of rotting teeth. After a long day plaiting, their mothers will rub lavender oil into their sore fingers and lips, to try to ease the pain.

* * *

Mary Anne was born in Newtown, a hamlet adjoining Henlow, a small village in rural Bedfordshire, in 1863. Her parents were both born locally and married in Henlow on 26th June 1855. Her father, George Sharpe (1832-1901), who died aged 69, was a wood sawyer, and her mother, Mary Daniels (1831-1915), who died aged 84, was a straw plaiter.

Mary Anne had four older siblings and three younger – a total of eight children in the family: Emma (1856-1882); William (1857-?); Lizzie (1859-1905); Eliza (1861-1946); Mary Anne (1863-1930); Rose (1864-1960), Minnie (1866-1948); and Frank (1873-1931).

Henlow was largely agricultural, as the 1881 census showed for nearby Wilstead (where her father was born): 98 (50%) of the men with jobs were registered as agricultural – mostly farm labourers and three (1.5%) were carpenters/joiners (as were her father, George and brother, William). Of 207 women with occupations, 118 (57%) were working in the lace trade and 14 (7%)

Mary Anne photographed c. aged 22

worked in straw manufacture (the hat, bonnet, and straw plaiting trade), as did Mary Anne's mother and several of her sisters. Overall, there were estimated to be around 30,000 people (mainly women and girls) employed as straw plaiters in England in 1871.[6]

After Mary Anne was born, the family moved to live at 2 Paynes Cottages, Clifton, Bedfordshire, which was likely to be a two-bedroom cottage and small for this family of ten. Conditions would have been cramped, with little privacy and not much money coming in. The 1871 census gives a household of nine, with Mary Anne listed as a scholar, aged eight, so we know she had some education. But, by the time of the next census, aged 18, she had moved to Annesley Hall. In the 1881 census, George is listed as a sawyer still, William, Eliza and Mary Anne have left home, and the remaining three girls are all listed as straw plaiters.

The Straw Plaiting Life

It is likely that Mary Anne and her sisters were educated at the plaiting 'school' and they pursued the same trade as their mother. Straw plaiting was hard piecework, for little reward, but the cottage industry was particularly important – supplying the thriving straw-hat manufacturing industry of nearby Luton and Dunstable. Luton Town Football Club is still known by its nickname, 'The Hatters'.

As with many cottage industries of the time, child labour played a significant role. Commentators of the day reported: *"A well-ordered family [could] obtain as much or more than the husband who [was] at work on [a] neighbouring farm."* Mary Anne's father was a sawyer, probably for a neighbouring large estate owner, and her elder brother was a journeyman carpenter (with work likely to be

---

6. Editor, Hugh Chisholm, *Encyclopaedia Britannica*, 1911.

hard to come by) so, with a mother and, eventually six girls plaiting, the women could well have materially contributed to the Sharpe family finances.

To make a straw hat, special straight straw had to be selected, trimmed, and bundled. The straws were then plaited into long ribbons, which could be made in a variety of patterns. Like lacemaking, women learnt the craft when young, at their mother's knee or, often, they were sent to plaiting 'schools' from the age of four to twelve, typically, so their mother was free to work at home without distraction.

Small children of four or five four years old were taught to clip off the loose ends of straw, with scissors tied to their bodies, so as not to lose them. They also had to sweep the floor clear of straw clippings – crucial to their safety, as sparks from the kitchen fire could ignite easily. Plait schools often ran pre-school classes on Sunday mornings when girls under five years old were taught to

A straw plaiting 'school'. Image from Cassell's Family Magazine, 1882. Artist unknown.

make 'widdle waddle', which was unsellable plaits made from old pieces of string, so they could learn the technique.

Most 'schools' in rural areas were held in a small cottage kitchen into which up to 20 children were crammed. A news report in 1867 described the rooms as:

> Low, small and close, where the atmosphere in winter becomes intolerable, fetid and unwholesome.

The girls would gather in the kitchen and work for up to nine hours a day, six days a week. Parents paid two pence a week for each child to attend and supplied their own straw. This outlay was recouped from the completed plait the girls made – provided it was saleable – for which they were paid sixpence a day (around £1.57 in today's money, so a very modest £9.42 a week). Older children could earn four shillings or more a week, supplementing the farm labourer father's income of around 10 shillings.

Starting at 8.00am, the girls usually sat on stools around a kitchen table or range, a bundle of straw under their left arm and a wooden box on their right to hold the completed plaited lengths.

The work rate was governed by their age and experience but, typically, at five years old, children were expected to complete 10 yards of plait a day; at six to eight years, 15 yards; and over eight, 17 to 20 yards a day. The plait was sold onto a wholesaler in scores – a score being 20 yards.

The straw lengths had to be bleached before use with sulphur (brimstone), kept in the backyard, which created a pungent smell. Most straw plaiting families kept a vat containing this stinking mixture of charcoal and sulphur, which was used to fumigate and preserve the straw and produce a whiter plait. After bleaching, the straw required several hours of soaking in a washtub, followed by a long drying process.

One of the worst aspects of plaiting was the girls had to wet the lengths of dried, bleached straw by drawing them through their lips, to make it more pliable, otherwise it would snap when plaited. The taste was awful, and the residual bleach and sharp edges cut and split the children's mouths and fingers. The friction and sulphur also wore away their tooth enamel. Women in the straw plaiting trade were known for having poor front teeth, red sores around their lips and red, raw hands, so their mother would go through a nightly ritual of rubbing lavender oil into the children's hands to ease the soreness. It is noticeable that in the few existing photos of Mary Anne she never smiles or shows her teeth, so maybe they were affected by her straw plaiting work, and she tried to cover her embarrassment in later life.

The girls sang ditties as they plaited to help them learn the patterns. Everyone picked up five strands of straw and softened them in their mouth. They would sing *"Under one and over two, pull it tight and that will do"* to create a simple flat plait or *"Criss-cross patch and then a twirl... twist it back for English Pearl"* for a more elaborate design. If they had a problem, they had to raise a hand, stop plaiting and the mistress overseer came to help. Every hour the overseer would check the yards in each box, to ensure the girls were on target.

By law, those employing children had to stop at midday for lunch, which the children had brought with them. This was usually just a slice of bread and dripping, accompanied by a soft drink the plait school owner gave them – hot in winter and cold in summer.

After lunch came 'schooling'. The term should be used lightly, as although reading and writing were supposedly part of the school's provision, they were not high on the agenda. Many parents did not want their children's work to be side-tracked by such economically unproductive activities, so the children were often illiterate. An adult of the day commented:

> *I never knew any of these plaiting schools where writing or arithmetic was taught, probably for the simple reason that these old ladies [the plait school owners] knew nothing of it themselves.*[7]

At most, the schooling comprised repeating a few Bible verses, maybe some reading practice, doing simple sums, and practicing their letters (writing). However, by the late 1860s, the local Boards were starting to shut plait schools down and encourage children into local council-run free schools.

In the afternoon, the overseer collected the plaits from each of the girls, checked the quality of each length and pressed it. She also ensured it was the right length (it was a fraudulent act to sell short measures), using a wooden measuring stick. This same 'formidable stick,' would be freely used, if needed, to keep the children at their work.

---

7. P Wray: http://www.prestonherts.co.uk/.

At the end of each week, the local hat manufacturer or his agent would send a cart round to collect the order, again, checking the contents of every box. He paid the overseer and confirmed the required order for the following week.

After plait school finished at 5pm, the girls went home but most, even the younger ones, were expected to continue plaiting in their own homes well into the night – making plait to sell privately at the local market to further supplement the family's income.

Local Bedfordshire village women and children of all ages could be seen ceaselessly at work, plaiting. Children would often carry a bundle of straw under their arm, plaiting as they walked to and from school. Their week ended at 4.30pm on Saturday, with the day off on Sunday – the day of rest and church.

There was no plait school on Monday mornings to enable the family to go to market (including the plait market). But schools opened again at 12.30 on Mondays and children were expected to make up the lost four hours during the rest of the week.

During the mid-1800s plaiters could earn reasonable money if they were skilful. For women and children, plaiting provided an alternative to becoming a servant. Their extra income also meant they had some money to spend and could buy nicer clothes. This independence was met with disapproval by higher society and soon plaiters were accused of being immoral and slovenly. Whilst it may have been true of some, it was not true of the majority.

However, the financial position changed from about 1860, when free trade meant that cheap imports of plait came from Italy initially, and by the 1890s, from China and Japan. Prices and work levels fell, reducing the extra income available to rural families like the Sharpe's. By the 1890s many straw-plaiters, according to *Pearson's Weekly*, were settling for starvation wages. Fortunately for the Sharpe family, by then they had other forms of income and were probably also being helped financially by Mary Anne, so would have been better off in later years.

The Sharpe Family:
'Precious Little Comfort'

Mary Anne unwound her woollen shawl and looked around the familiar room. Father's chair hugged the heavily blackened range for warmth. Its nubby arm caps were worn from years of tired fingers, its seat sagging and draped with a patchwork throw that spoke of a dozen items that mother had made – a sister's sprigged dress, a checked tablecloth, and father's old work shirts. Nearer the door stood a well-scrubbed pine table, surrounded by six mismatched wooden chairs. Against the side wall leant an old dresser, stacked with crockery and 'best' Willow pattern plates, cutlery, and basic kitchen tools.

A black clock ticked loudly on the mantel, flanked by her mother's pride and joy – two brass candlesticks, wedding presents from her parents. There also stood a pair of china dogs, dark eyes staring, that father won at the fair when they were first courting.

The stone floor was part covered by a handmade rag rug and on the walls, pictures Mary Anne and her sisters had cut from newspapers, together with three hand-stitched samplers. In one corner a brass oil lamp with an etched glass bowl cast an amber glow. It was simple but clean and warm and, best of all, it was home.

Her mother came out from the scullery wiping her hands on her apron, trailed by Mary Anne's youngest siblings – Minnie and Frank.

"Ah, there you are my love. Take them clodhoppers off and get the nippers to wash their hands will you, while I lay the table. Your Da' and Billy will be home soon, rarin' hungry as usual I'll be bound."

Mary Anne bent to unlace her boots whilst the children crowded round, eager to hear about her day.

* * *

So, we know of the work that the Sharpe women undertook, but what of the family's lifestyle? Mary Anne's father, a sawyer, and brother William, a journeyman carpenter, were considered a little more skilled than farm labourers, so they could perhaps have earned a few shillings a week each more than the standard ten shillings.

As a result, the Sharpe family is likely to have been better off than most, as both parents earned, as did four of Mary Anne's siblings by 1871 and seven of the nine, including Mary Anne by 1881. However, most rural communities lived in overcrowded, basic cottages and the Sharpe family is likely to have been the same. The cottage would be rented for around two shillings and sixpence a week. Coal was a shilling a hundredweight and a pint of paraffin for lighting the oil lamps had to come out of the weekly wages too. Careful housewives might be able to save a little for clothes, boots, amusements, and any illnesses that might require a doctor or shop-bought medicines, but this was uncommon, and most lived a precarious, 'hand-to-mouth' existence.

The cottage would typically comprise only two rooms upstairs, with the parents and youngest children sharing a room, the older girls in another and any older boys in the family sleeping downstairs in the kitchen. Beds were often so tightly packed that the siblings had to clamber over one bed to get to their own, or more likely they

*A typical rural cottage interior of the Victorian period.
Image courtesy of Mandy Burrows, primaryhomeworkhelp.co.uk.*

shared beds. Downstairs there would be the kitchen and maybe a parlour reserved for 'best', but more usually just a scullery.

The Sharpe family would probably not have running water, so drinking and washing water would be fetched in pails by the women from the village well, supplemented by rainwater stored in a tarred butt in the yard. The toilet would be an earth closet or 'long drop' open pit in a wooden shed in the yard or garden.

With heat and hot water being scarce, many villagers followed the country custom of 'doing up' the children for winter. They were sewn into their heavy clothes in October, always kept them on and were unstitched in the spring, which is where the saying 'cast ne'er a clout until May is out' comes from. Clearly, the clothes would be crawling in lice by then and the smell rank.

Some women refused to follow this practice and, in doing so, created a heavy burden of laundering – although clothes would still be washed far less than nowadays. In the backyard there would be a basic washhouse, where the mother and elder daughters would tackle the heavy weekly task of laundering bedding and clothes for the large family early on a Monday morning, before they went to the plait market.

More enlightened families would also bath once a week, usually on a Saturday night, in time for church the next day. This involved fetching and boiling gallons of hot water and filling a tin bath in front of the range. The husband would bathe first, followed by older boys, and then so on, down the line of boys and girls by age, with the youngest child and the wife having the water last. Although it would be topped up with fresh water, it would still be greasy and grim by the end.

Daily Meals

Most rural families in the area subsisted on a restricted budget and diet. An assistant commissioner underlined the monotony of the average rural labourer's diet in a report in 1869. When asked what she had for breakfast, a young girl said, *"Bread and butter."* When asked about supper, she answered: *"Bread and butter and cheese."*

Breakfast was usually tea and bread and butter, perhaps with homemade jam. Those going out to work or plait school would be sent off with a 'piece' – more bread and butter, the butter perhaps mixed with chopped, wild herbs to make it tasty. Alternatively, some households might manage to make a Bedfordshire 'clanger' for the older, working men. A clanger was an elongated suet dumpling, filled with vegetables (and possibly scraps of bacon). Sometimes the clanger was savoury at one end and had jam or fruit at the other.

There was usually only one hot meal a day (known as tea), in the evening, as the men would not be home during the day. Father would usually say a short grace before the meal, usually along the lines of *'For what we are about to receive'*. It was common to have bread or some sort of suet pudding to start, like a roly poly, to take the edge off the family's hunger. Meat was scarce and usually comprised bacon scraps, or sometimes a rabbit if the husband had been rabbiting. The small amount of meat was eked out among the family with lots of potatoes and vegetables, which were usually grown in the cottage garden or a village allotment. Puddings were rare. However, milk was cheap, and some women would make a milk or rice pudding, especially for the younger children, but often they went without.

With five people earning in 1871, it is likely that the Sharpe's had a better diet and more to spare than the lowest agricultural labourers, but probably still largely existed on the simple fare of suet puddings, boiled vegetables and diced bacon, and other meals of bread and butter (or lard) and cheese, or a sprinkling of sugar on bread for the children.

Gardens and allotments provided a range of vegetables, but families chiefly grew potatoes, beans, peas, and cabbage. The men of the family would work on the veg patch for an hour or two after their tea at night, when the light allowed it.

The garden might also feature a lean-to pigsty, housing the family pig, who would be fed from any leftovers or potatoes and 'mash', made specially to fatten the animal up for either selling or killing in the Autumn. Its manure would help grow vegetables and the pig would be much prized and cared for by the family. Children on their way home from school might gather thistles, dandelions, long grass, or snails to vary and supplement the pig's supper.

Once fattened, the pig would be killed by a travelling pork butcher, usually at night, and it was a noisy, bloody business but the resulting bacon, once cured, would hopefully see the family through a long winter. Otherwise, fresh meat was a luxury. The mother might get hold of sixpenny worth of 'pieces' (end scraps of the cheapest cuts of meat) to make a meat pudding on a Sunday, or for those better off, a small roast, which might be spit or pot roasted.

Female plaiters were often accused by outsiders of being poor housewives:

> *Utterly ignorant of such common things as keeping their houses clean, mending clothes or cooking their husbands' dinners.*

The truth was that with nine hour working days, plus further piecework in the evenings, these women had little time for housework and *"many families had precious little comfort."* It was only with the collapse of the straw plait trade, later in the 19th century, that the situation began to improve, as women and girls were forced to seek easier, and often better paid, work.

After a hard-working week, straw-plaiting families enjoyed time off from 4.30pm on Saturday to Monday at 12.30pm, when the plaiting schools reopened. On Saturday, if they had both the time or money, they might travel by horse drawn omnibus to Luton or Dunstable to view the bigger shops. On a Sunday, the girls dressed up in clean cotton shifts, leather boots and handmade straw bonnets to attend church, after which they had a heartier lunch. Then the family might play charades or cards before bed, in time for the working week to start again.

Mary Anne's Journey Begins

*M*ary gently shook her daughter awake and went downstairs to finish making breakfast. It was a late February morning in 1881 and the hoar frost jewelled the surrounding fields. Mary Anne stretched, taking in the bedroom lit by the soft glow from the kitchen range below. She looked over at her sisters, Emma, Minnie, and Lizzie, still asleep in their own bed. Her father had made them of simple boards resting on apple crates, topped by a straw-filled mattress, and worn but soft calico sheet and quilt.

By the door stood a rickety pine chair and a small chest, with a drawer each for their few possessions. An iron peg displayed her Sunday best straw bonnet, trimmed with a plum velvet ribbon and flower she had hand stitched herself after her day's work was done.

Mary Anne knew that today was an important start for her. Her new salary would be greater than that of her father's and she'd promised to send home any spare cash to supplement the family's income. Her eye rested on an embroidered sampler on the wall: "Work hard and success in life will surely follow."

With that motivation, Mary Anne got up quietly and, shivering, washed at the corner china basin. Coming downstairs dressed in her flowered cotton frock (new to her but cast-off from her elder sister), worn but best lace-up boots and carrying her black wool coat and straw bonnet, Mary Anne sat at the scrubbed table. Her mother set a bowl of porridge and mug of hot, sweet tea before her.

"Will the carrier be on time Ma?"

"I'm sure so. Don't fret Dear, you've got a long day ahead of you."

Mary Anne was breaking away and her mother and four sisters were proud (and a little envious) of her. She'd stayed at school the longest, learnt her letters the best and, helped by the scrimping and saving of her family, she was finally escaping the gruelling life of a straw plaiter.

After breakfast, Mary walked her daughter to the edge of the village, carrying a wicker basket with her simple lunch and a small trunk with her few clothes and possessions. They waited in silence until the carrier appeared out of the gloom. Mary kissed her daughter, knowing she wouldn't see her for nearly a year, until her two-week holiday. Smoothing the girl's unruly hair out of her eyes, she whispered: "Off you go now my Dear. Work hard, be good and make us proud."

Mary Anne climbed up into the cart and waved back at her mother. She sensed that her life would never be the same again.

* * *

When Mary Anne reached today's normal school age of five, in 1868, there was only limited free schooling available for children from low-income homes. In 1870, William Forster's Elementary Education Act came into force, making free state-funded education available to children between the ages of five and 13, although it exempted any child aged over ten who had reached the 'expected standard' (which varied according to the local school Board).

Mary Anne most likely attended the local straw plaiting 'school' from four or five onwards with her sisters, where the emphasis, as we have seen, was on learning the trade, with only the rudiments of literacy and numeracy being taught, if at all. She was aged seven when the Education Act came into effect in 1870, and it is possible that she was formally educated at a Board school for a further six years. The 1871 census listed her, aged eight, as a scholar but she may still have been at the plait school. Compulsory education for those aged between five and ten was not introduced until 1880 and, before this time, many poorer families were tempted to send their children to work to earn an extra income.

The local Board schools were better than the plait schools and aimed to teach every child to read and write, girls to sew and boys to do a little simple carpentry, and all to know the Lord's Prayer and Ten Commandments. Above all, working class children were taught to 'know their place'. The hymn *"All things bright and beautiful"* captures this sentiment: "The rich man in his castle, the poor man at his gate, God made them high or lowly, And ordered their estate."

Mary Anne may have stayed at school as late as 13 but with a large family on a low income and no compulsory education yet in force, she most likely left aged ten. That meant she would have had two to three pre-school years in the plait school, three to six years of formal education and had to face a further five to eight years in the straw plaiting trade, before moving to Annesley House as a junior nursery housemaid – we think – around 1881, aged 18.

However rudimentary her education, by the 1880s, Victorian employers expected their servants to have elementary literacy and numeracy. Perhaps Mary Anne received the full six years of Board school education, as later in life, she was said by family members to have been educated and good at her role as Lady of the house. This is likely to have been due, in part, to the efforts of the Chaworth-Musters family (particularly her mother-in-law, Lina) to supplement the minimal formal education she would have received when young.

We also do not know why Mary Anne, alone among all her sisters, decided to break away from straw plaiting, and seek more money and better opportunities elsewhere. It certainly shows a degree of intelligence, self-determination, and vision to break the mould. It is likely that Mary Anne or her mother saw an advert locally for the position at Annesley Hall, which was a significant distance of over 100 miles away.

Going into Service

Country house owners often used local employment registries in the 1870s/80s to recruit servants, for example, the free registry established in 1813 by the *London Society for the Encouragement of Faithful Female Servants*. It provided prospective employees with a list of available maids who had either been employed for at least two years in one place or had never been in service before. Again, we don't know if this was Mary Anne's first job in service, but it was likely that she had only done straw plaiting work before, like the rest of her sisters. Most adverts placed emphasis on the need for the girl to 'clean', 'strong' and 'hard-working'.

By the 1870s these registries were dividing their efforts equally between recruiting servants for their register and advertising more senior staff for hire. Around this time advertising in newspapers and, later, in magazines such as *The Lady* (1885 onwards) and *Country Life* (1897) became more popular for both employers and senior employees.

It was also in the 1880s that registries began having to advertise further afield, often more than 25 miles or more from the employer's base, to find staff, as country houses now had to compete with urbanised manufacturing and retail jobs. Fortunately, the increase in cheaper rail travel made it easier for servants to come from further afield.

Employers also had to work hard to promote the benefits of their position, usually focusing on the status and composition of the family (being from 'old money' helped), the lovely location of the main house and the number of other servants employed to help share the workload. Once the interview was successful, the final hurdle was presenting a satisfactory 'character' (reference). In Mary Anne's case, there may have been no previous formal employer, so she would have had to obtain a reference from the plait school owner or one of the local plaiting agents she dealt with, who could bear witness to her work ethic and quality.

The girls recruited as servants were mostly young (the average first job age was 14 or 15), and turnover was high. Girls would often stay less than a year and seemed to always imagine that the 'grass was greener' at another large house, or they wanted to try the new roles of shop or factory work. By entering domestic service, Mary Anne was going against a trend, as between 1881 and 1901, there was a 7% decrease in female servants aged between 15 to 20 years old.

Although wages were low, hours long, the work often hard and submissive obedience required, Mary Anne and her family would have undoubtedly felt the junior nursery housemaid role was an attractive alternative to the nine to twelve hard hours and drudgery of the straw plaiting life. Also, as a largely agricultural area with few large towns, there wouldn't have been many other options available to Mary Anne.

Maids earned between £10-£15 a year in 1891 (£984-£1,400 in today's money), compared with straw plaiters who earned around £8 a year (about £800 now). A maid's wages were not only better but included full bed and board, and for Mary Anne, the conditions of work would be more palatable.

It was also common for poor families to need their children to leave home for work, as with many children, there was not enough space for them all to remain at home. Lucy Lethbridge[8] reports of twelve-year-old Daisy being marched into service by her father:

---

8. Lucy Lethbridge, *Servants: A Downstairs View of Twentieth Century Britain*.

> *Well my lady, you're not gittin' your feet under my table: you git your feet under somebody else's table.*

This doesn't seem to be the case for Mary Anne, as her siblings are shown as being at home for longer in the census of the time. So, it is more likely that Mary Anne went into service as a positive choice of her own. Most girls had already been helping at home for many years and had experience of rearing younger children and doing housework and laundry. Like Mary Anne, they often started as 'tweenys', or between-maids, which was the lowest rung of the housemaid hierarchy and meant they were at the beck and call of most of the other household servants.

Employers sometimes made a small advance on the first year's wages to enable new servants to travel to their place of work and to buy fabric to make the two print dresses Mary Anne would have been told she needed, plus cotton to make her aprons and underwear. She may have also bought black serge (wool and mixed fibres) to make a smarter coat if she didn't have one, to enable her to attend church with the family and other servants. Her indoor work cap or bonnet would usually be provided by the mistress of the house, and as a straw plaiter, Mary Anne would provide her own outdoor bonnet. If there was no advance, her family would have had to scrimp and save to enable Mary Anne to travel with the clothes she needed, all of which would be carefully packed by her mother in a wicker basket or small tin or cardboard case.

We know from the census of April 1881, that 18-year-old Mary Anne was employed at Annesley Hall and listed as a junior house maid. It is possible she joined the household earlier – at any age from around 14 – but it is unlikely, as she would have been promoted to a higher role by the time of the census. As junior nursery housemaid she was responsible for all the maid duties relating to the nursery and expected to help the other nursery staff (senior maids, the under nurse, head nurse or Nanny, and possibly the governess too).

The family's children in the 1881 census are listed as Patrick's two sisters, Mary Catherine 18) and Catherine Emily, known as Kitty (17), and a visitor Geoffrey (aged seven). He was born at the family-owned Colwick Hall, so was likely to be a relative. There was also Patrick's brother Georgie (13), although he was not listed, as he was probably away at boarding school at the time.

Because there are several nursery staff listed in the 1881 census, it is likely that Mary Catherine and Kitty were still treated largely as children, and based in the nursery, although they would be on the cusp of 'coming out'. Coming out was reserved for young ladies who had reached an age of maturity, completed an education, and were ready to be introduced into society, and meant the girl was eligible to marry. By the 1880s, 18 was considered the age for 'coming out'.

Mary Anne was possibly only employed at Annesley Hall for two years, and we don't know if she was promoted in that time but if she was, the typical hierarchy was to rise from junior nursery housemaid (her role) to nursery housemaid, under nurse, head nurse and then maybe to Nanny if that's where her interest and skills lay. In terms of the hierarchy of the house, she would have been below the housekeeper, lady's maid, Nanny, nurse, and senior housemaids but senior to the kitchen, scullery, and laundry maids.

She would have been paid quarterly and her wages were likely to be about £13 pa (£1,244), rising to around £20 pa (£1,880) if she got promoted to under nurse. Male servants – even of largely equal rank – were paid around 50% more than women and their employers paid tax on them, as a luxury, whereas women servants were considered essential and were untaxed. Servant taxes were largely repealed in 1889 but did not disappear entirely until 1937.

It would have been a long journey the day Mary Anne left her home in Henlow to travel to Annesley, over 100 miles away. Often, the girl's case would be sent ahead by the local carrier to the railway station nearest their employer's residence and her mother would walk the girl the few miles to the nearest station in her 'best' clothes, accompanied perhaps by the youngest children if they weren't yet at plait school. Neighbours would come to their garden gates to see them off and wish them luck, calling out *"Mind you be a good gal now, an' does just as you be told!"* or, perhaps more comfortingly, *"You'll be back for your holidays before you know it!"*

The pair would set off hopefully and cheerfully, but observers recall often seeing the mother coming back several hours later, choked with emotion at having to send her young daughter away, knowing that she might not see her for upwards of a year. And we can only imagine what it would have felt like for Mary Anne, bound for an unfamiliar role, in a far-off place she'd never visited, among strangers.

Yet it was part of their growing up process and these young girls realised they had to make the best of it and could not fail at the job, for their parents could rarely afford to have them back home.

Mary Anne was not alone – in the early 1880s around one third of all girls between 15 and 20 years old were employed as domestic servants. The majority of these, like her, were country born and bred.

Mary Anne is likely to have started her journey with a walk or carrier (cart) ride to Southill station, four miles away. From there she would have taken a Midland Railway train[9] around 7.00am to Bedford, to change for Leicester, a journey which took two hours. At Leicester she would change trains to Nottingham, and then change again for the last leg, which took her to Annesley station, some four hours later.

At Annesley station she would either have a 40 minute, nearly two mile walk through the village to the Hall, or maybe her employers were kind enough to send a horse-drawn gig to collect her. Looking at the Midland railway train times of the day, Mary Anne probably would have arrived at Annesley Hall about 2.00pm on that cold February day.

---

9. Dave Harris, Coordinator, Midland Railway Study Centre.

'Polly': A Life in Service

*M*ary Anne stepped off the train and stood on the mainly silent village platform, looking about. Above the trees she could just see the top of a church spire and, some distance away, the iron tower of the pithead, raven-dark against the sky. She hadn't expected to be met by anyone from the Hall, but she had hoped for directions.

Head lowered, her dark watchful eyes peeking from under the brim of her straw bonnet, she walked slowly towards the station master, who was busy directing the removal of goods from his platform. Standing close, she put her basket and small trunk on the ground.

"Excuse me Sir, I'm looking for Annesley Hall?" The stationmaster turned, looked down and took in her fresh face, worn but clean boots and smiled.

"Yes, me Duck, tha' goes left out the station, left along Derby Road, left on Annesley Road and up Dog and Bear Lane, then bear right to the tradesman's entrance round the back. It's abaat a mile and a half. You can't miss it but be careful – it's proper muddy!"

Mary Anne nodded and bent to her bags. The stationmaster softened, "Leave your trunk with me Lass, I'll have it sent up later."

Thanking him, she picked up her basket and strode off to face her future.

Arriving at the rear door to Annesley Hall, she looked up, and up again. She took in the solid, unembellished stone, the walls ivy-covered and windows dark. She pulled gently on the iron bell handle and waited. Nothing. She pulled again, harder. An immense jangling sounded, reverberating down long, empty corridors. A few moments later she heard the scurrying of feet: the heavy door creaked open, and a flushed face appeared.

"Can I help?" the woman enquired.

"I'm Mary Anne, the new junior nursery housemaid. I was told to ask for the housekeeper."

"Oh yes, you were mentioned at breakfast. Come in and I'll take you to her room. Quick mind."

The maid set off at a tremendous pace into the gloom, Mary Anne trotting to keep up. The ceilings were high, the walls dun-coloured and the floor, bare dark stone. "What's your name?" asked Mary Anne.

"I'm Emma, one a' the scullery maids. Been 'ere four year or more now. You're not local, are you?"

Emma took in Mary Anne's sweeping gaze, and asked, "Is this your first time in service then me Duck?"

"Yes, I worked at home with my Ma and sisters."

"Don't worry, you'll pick it up quick. I'll take you to Mrs Wright."

Looking more serious, she turned to Mary Anne: "Now, remember to call her Mrs Wright first and then Ma'am, and give her a little bob when you meet her and when you leave. The uppers like that and it don't harm to start off on the right foot."

She shot off again and Mary Anne followed, now even more nervous.

* * *

Whether she arrived by cart or on foot, Mary Anne would have passed the gravel road that swept through a stone, arched gatehouse into the Hall's grounds. Annesley was an imposing sight – three storeys and multiple wings of solid Victoriana – it would have been much grander than anything Mary Anne had seen before, and this was to be her new home!

Once inside, we can imagine the servant's hall, kitchen, and various rooms branching off it were much like other grand Victorian country houses of the time, although perhaps brighter and warmer due to the plentiful coal to hand. The kitchen would have few windows, placed high, to prevent a view out and keep the servant's mind firmly on the job in hand. Walls would be painted in dun and cream colours; all designed not to show the dirt and be easily wiped down. A large cast iron, blackened kitchen range would dominate, with a well-scrubbed pine table sat in the middle of the room and a wooden dresser taking up one wall, set with burnished copper pans.

As a new maid, Mary Anne would report to the ancient housekeeper, Mrs Wright, and would probably have had a brief induction talk in her room. It's likely to have been cramped and crammed with furniture, typically including a small dresser, with blue and white china cups and saucers, a couple of easy chairs covered in worn chintz and a few side tables (all relics from upstairs). It would nevertheless be cosy and private.

As part of her induction, Mary Anne may have been introduced to the 'upper ten' – the senior servants, who apart from the housekeeper, included the butler William Batcock (30 years old) and Susannah Booker (45), the cook. Hierarchy was strictly adhered to just as much below stairs as above, and those three senior servants would have ruled the household and, in turn, be ruled by the Master and Mistress.

Maids reported to the housekeeper and were expected to address queries to her. Housekeepers could be formidable and superior in their attitude, and it was common for juniors, new to service, to mistake them at first for the Lady of the house, only to be corrected. Junior servants were usually expected to bob (a small curtsey) and lower their heads to the upper ten, addressing them as Sir and Ma'am. The same would apply to members of the family, but more so – usually a deeper bob was required, eyes lowered and stood with their back to the wall.

After the housekeeper, the next most senior female servant would be the lady's maid, who held a special position, due to her personal relationship with the lady of the house. She was often disliked by the other servants, as she usually came from a better-off family who had fallen on hard times, was better educated, and was considered to have certain 'airs and graces'. She was also suspected (often unfairly) of telling tales from below stairs to the mistress.

It is likely to be during this first meeting that Mary Anne was renamed by the housekeeper. This was possibly partly because owner John Chaworth-Muster's sister was called Mary Ann but also that there was another nurserymaid in the house of the same name: Mary Ann Hayes. Also, in Victorian times it was quite common to have a certain name associated with a particular job, for example, scullery maids were often called Mary, whether that was their actual name or not. So, not only had Mary Anne left home for the first time but she was also immediately stripped of her identity and had to get used to a new name – Polly.

During the induction meeting, the housekeeper would have outlined her key duties, working hours, mealtimes, and the names of those she reported to and worked with. She would have impressed upon Mary Anne that make-up was not allowed, and fraternisation with men heavily discouraged, even with the male servants she worked alongside. Mary Anne is likely then to have been given a tour of the servant's quarters, and maybe the nursery wing, where she would spend much of her time over the next two years.

Polly Gets the Tour

She would have seen the servant's hall on her way in, where the lower servants (her included) would gather and eat. She may have been shown the gloomy stillroom with its water-darkened flagstones, scullery sink, dank coconut matting and table. Here breakfast, tea and coffee trays would be laid, cakes and sweetmeats produced, wine bottled, and fruit preserved.

One of her duties as nursery housemaid would be to prepare meal trays and take them up to the nursery, so the kitchen and stillroom would become familiar to her. Annesley Hall may even have had a separate nursery pantry next to the stillroom, specifically reserved for assembling the nursery's trays of food. As many young girls from poor families weren't familiar with the extensive range of utensils or furniture they were expected to use or clean, household manuals were often in use, containing instructive pictures of the most common objects.

The upper ten servant's hall where the senior servants congregated and often ate separately, would contain better furniture, perhaps an oval mahogany table, some dark wood chairs, and the butler's armchair (woe betide any unsuspecting newcomer who sat in it). It would be a little more homely, typically with a worn but thick Brussels wool carpet, china dogs on the mantelpiece, and several dark oil paintings on the walls. All would be cast-offs from upstairs but, still, much prized by the upper ten.

Like the housekeeper, the Butler had his own room, although it was usually more modest. The Butler's pantry would contain a couple of Windsor chairs and a green baize table for shining up the plate. The upper ten servants would have had rooms in the main house, either in the basement or in the attic.

At this stage Mary Anne is likely only to have caught glimpses of 'upstairs' perhaps through green-baized covered doors. If so, what must she have made of the eclectic fabric and furnishings that Leonard Jacks described as giving the Hall its *"unmistakeably ancient look."*

After the talks and tour, Mary Anne would have been directed to her quarters. As a junior nursery housemaid, she would have lived above the stables, a few hundred yards from the main house. A stone arch divided the quarters, strictly segregating the rooms for male and female servants, each reached by a separate internal stone staircase.

Mary Anne would have shared a bedroom with one or two other junior maids, which after her crowded room at home, would have felt spacious. Maybe her trunk would have been delivered by now, so she would be able to unpack her scant belongings and start to settle in. We can imagine her taking in the room, dappled in wintry afternoon light. Two narrow single beds would fill much of the space, each with feather mattresses, covered with clean but darned cotton sheets and patchwork eiderdowns. A simple wooden chair stood by each bed, along with one small side table, with a candle in a brass holder.

A stout pine chest stood in the corner, on it a cracked china pitcher and basin, toothbrush holder and two tooth mugs. Beside it, two chamber pots, a metal pail, and possibly a small wardrobe, or at least a short hanging rail, part covered by a cotton curtain. On the wall opposite the beds might have hung a faded embroidered picture, with a typical saying: *'All hard work brings a profit, but mere talk leads only to poverty: Proverbs 14:23.'*

Heating would be optional. If lucky, they would have a small iron grate with a wooden coal box next to it and hung on the wall nearby, a copper pan for warming the beds with hot coals.

The room was likely to have smelt different from home yet be somehow familiar; comforting smells of old wood, carbolic soap, and beeswax polish, but mingled with disinfectant and mothballs. The window was small and barred, hung with faded sprigged curtains, and overlooking the stable yard, where she would be able to see the young grooms busy sweeping up muck and straw.

At the end of a tiring day of travel, we can imagine Mary Anne's apprehension in these unfamiliar surroundings. Would she be up to the job? Would she make friends? Could she stick at it? Not only that, but barely more than an hour in the house, and she already had a new name to remember. Her past life must have felt like a rapidly receding memory.

After unpacking her modest belongings, perhaps resting a little, and freshening up using the pitcher of water, Mary Anne would have made her way back to the main house. This involved walking across the cobbled stable yard, up the steep stone steps to the churchyard and along the back of the house, to enter the basement servants' quarters in time for her first house tea.

'Seen But Not Heard': Polly's Typical Day

*M*ary Anne woke at 6.30am, the frosty light filtering through her attic curtain. Her roommate and fellow nursery maid, Sarah, hadn't yet stirred, "She's a layabed!" Mary Anne thought. She washed quickly; face, hands, neck, and ears – that's what the uppers noticed.

Dressed, she ran down the stone stairs, across the yard and churchyard, to the kitchen in the main Hall. After her breakfast it would be non-stop all day, working to the sound of the children chattering and laughing in the background.

Accompanied by the quiet hissing of the kitchen range and ticking clock, she set about making the children's breakfast in the adjacent still room. Boiling water and milk, measuring out oats and stirring the porridge, she cut thin slices off a white loaf and buttered them thickly. She put a dish of jam on the clothed tray, choosing strawberry today, as she knew it was little Geoffrey's favourite. Her final task was to make a pot of tea and buttered toast with honey for Nanny. Tray loaded, she made the laborious three storey ascent to the nursery, wooden stairs creaking under her weight.

Opening the nursery door, she was hugged by the warmth and set the tray down on the central table. She smoothed the front of her starched white apron and straightened her cap. Mary Anne prided herself on being well turned out and cared what others thought of her. She walked into the day room and seven-year-old Geoffrey rushed at her, grabbing her hand, and tugging her along: "Polly, I've been waiting ages, come and play with me."

She knelt swiftly to the boy – smoothing his bed-warm hair and tucking in an errant shirt tail. He reminded her of Frank, her eight-year-old brother at home, who was unlikely to be missing her nearly as much as she missed him.

In her Bedfordshire burr, with its softly elongated vowels, she said: "Hold your horses Master Geoffrey, breakfast first and then perhaps you can show me your numberwork."

* * *

A popular saying of the time among agricultural labourers was 'those who would thrive, must rise by five'. Used to early starts, Mary Anne would likely rise by 6.30am latest, and after a quick wash in her room, would dress in her uniform of a simple cotton print dress, black leather ankle boots and wool stockings, white starched cotton apron and cap.

Uniforms were rarely supplied for the lower servants, apart from aprons or caps, and, if so, the cost was taken out of their wages. Servants also had to pay for their own boot and shoe mending. But employers would often give maids a bolt of cloth at Christmas to make up new work dresses for the year.

These dresses would be simple and plain, and maids were warned never to dress 'out of their station' nor to try to rival the ladies of the house. It was common for Victorian publications to carry cartoons ridiculing servant girls if they tried to ape the fashions of their betters. It was customary to instruct maids to wear straw bonnets rather than hats to Sunday church, in case they were mistaken for one of the family. However, like girls in any walk of life, the younger servant girls liked to spend money on ribbons and

A typical Victorian servants' hall at Ickworth House. Photo courtesy of Ariana Mullins, andhereweare.net.

feathers to trim and dress their own hats. As a former straw plaiter, Mary Anne was likely to have an intricate and well-dressed bonnet.

Morning Duties

After dressing, Mary Anne would make her way to the servant's hall for breakfast at 7.00am, which would be a hearty meal of cold roasted meat from yesterday's joint and bread, or porridge followed by ham and eggs. Breakfast for the family upstairs tended to be a similarly large meal and would have included ham, eggs, bacon, bread, and fish. After breakfast, Mary Anne's first job may have been to carry numerous cans of hot water upstairs to fill baths and basins for the children to wash, and to fill and trim the wicks on the many oil lamps that lit the nursery and schoolroom. A male servant would have lit fires in the nursery grates at around 7.00am to warm the rooms before everyone rose.

Whilst the children bathed, Mary Anne would make up their breakfast trays in the main kitchen and stillroom and take them up the back stairs for breakfast at 8.00am. Breakfast was likely to have been porridge with cream, and perhaps something like eggy bread.

In late Victorian England, cleanliness joined thrift and temperance as one of the key disciplines considered to contribute to virtue. Life expectancy for children had been so poor in earlier times and was still an issue, so extra care was taken, especially where young children were concerned. Nursery maids were taught to boil milk, water, and vegetables for at least ten minutes. Baths, basins, and other toilet articles needed special attention and housemaids had to use separate cloths, each marked and with its own peg for cleaning the nursery.

Mary Anne's nursery charges were a young child of seven, one of 13 (when not at boarding school) and two young adults of 16 and nearly 18, so the food served, and associated duties might have been slightly different, and the schedule less rigid. However, things would still be expected to run like clockwork, as this was considered to build character and conformity in both the servants and the children.

After breakfast, Mary Anne would wash the dishes in the nursery stillroom and take them down to the main kitchen. The family would also breakfast at 8.00am and the household, children and most servants would be expected to attend morning prayers at around 9.00am. Annesley Hall had its own ancient chapel a short walk from the main house with wooden pews down each side, so that servants and family members were strictly segregated.

After church, Mary Anne would return to the nursery for the hard work of the day. She would have cleaned the rooms, scrubbing them daily with boiled milk and water, made up beds, swept, and dusted – including under the furniture, sluiced out slops from the chamber pots (scalding them after with hot water), beaten rugs, cleaned and polished fire grates, wiped windows, and sills, and tidied up, collecting clothes to be hand-laundered.

Once a week each bedroom would have to be even more thoroughly 'turned out', with mattresses being turned and brushed, furniture moved and swept under, paintwork washed, and floors buffed and polished.

Without mechanical aids, the work was hard, and many of the cleaning 'products' used had to first be made by hand. Soda and chloride of lime (which took several days of preparation) was used for cleaning floorboards, beeswax, and turps for floors, blacking for boots and grates, and polish – all had to be made from scratch by the junior maids.

As rubber gloves were not used until the 1960s, the maids' hands became chapped and cracked. Many maids were so ashamed that they wore white gloves outside the house to cover their red, raw hands. This would have been familiar to Mary Anne, and perhaps she saw it as an improvement, as only her hands suffered, and not her mouth and lips, like when she had been a straw plaiter.

Lunch Time

The children would have been home tutored by their governess and would break at 11.00am for juice, fruit, and biscuits, before carrying on schooling until lunch. Luncheon for the family was likely to have been served at 2.00pm. Because of their age, Mary and Kitty may have taken lunch downstairs with their parents, which would have lessened the workload. But if not, nursery lunch would typically comprise a simple soup, fish, or chicken with boiled vegetables, followed by a milk pudding, such as rice or blancmange.

Lunch would be the main meal of the day for the servants, for which Mary Anne would have returned to the servant's hall at 1.00pm. Lucy Lethbridge[10] notes that the servants' meals would be

---

10. Lucy Lethbridge, *Servants: A Downstairs View of Twentieth Century Britain.*

"beyond the imagination of anything they had at home." She reports that when a new scullery maid saw the food laid out in the servant's hall, she:

> ... *'just stood and cried, wondering if mother and father had any food at home'. The maid's miner father was laid off long-term ill, and the family was living on bread and potatoes. On rare visits home, the maid had brought vegetables, butter and two pounds of scrag end of beef, and the mother wept, while her father fell to his knees and gave thanks to God.*

It would probably be similar for Mary Anne. Whilst her parents were better off than the poorest agricultural labourer families, the food on offer at Annesley Hall would still have seemed luxurious and plentiful beyond belief.

Among the servants, hierarchy was strictly observed at the table, with everyone seated according to their position – the butler at one end of the table, the housekeeper the other, with the senior servants sat closest to each, and the junior servants in between, the men down one side and the women the other. After saying grace, the butler would carve the inevitable roast joint.

Not only was the seating hierarchy strict but etiquette at servant's mealtimes was strictly observed. Tessa Boase[11] says that author, H G Wells, (whose mother was a housekeeper at Uppark in Sussex) was caustic in his observations about the servants' hall chatter, especially the *"absurd self-importance of the upper ten,"* who he felt provided a *"comic vignette but somewhat pathetic, aping their superiors but having nothing really to say."* He said they adhered to 15 bland remarks that got them through each mealtime: *"The days draw out nicely, the frost continues, the poor souls without coals must suffer etc."*

One such example of this etiquette and snobbery, is that after the main course, the butler would lead the upper ten (and any visiting valets and ladies' maids) to the housekeeper's room, each carrying their glass of water in one hand and their bread plate in another. This is where pudding would be served to them by a junior maid, the other servants eating theirs in the main servant's hall.

At 2.00pm, luncheon (usually much simpler than dinner) was served to the family. After her own lunch, Mary Anne would take up

---

11. Tessa Boase, *The Housekeeper's Tale.*

the lunch trays for the nursery, and afterwards wash the crockery and return it to the kitchen.

One of Mary Anne's major tasks each week would be laundry. Three changes of clothes a day were common for those living in country houses. The children would wear plain morning clothes for their time in the schoolroom, then might change for an afternoon outdoors or visiting and would change again to go downstairs for children's hour to be presented to their parents, around 6.00pm, or in Mary and Kitty's case, perhaps to join their parents for dinner.

Mary Anne's duties would include laundering the children's clothes by hand and doing any mending required. After hand washing, rinsing, mangling, and drying, clothes would be ironed, using heavy irons heated on the range, with frills starched and ribbons taken out, ironed separately, and rethreaded through petticoats, aprons, and nightcaps.

Afternoon Duties

Just before 4pm, Mary Anne would return to the kitchen to make up and bring up the nursery tea. The 'high ups', as the servants often referred to the upper ten, often took a nap from around 3pm-4pm and it would be Mary Anne's job to wake Nanny at 4pm with a pot of tea.

The children's tea comprised milk, thinly sliced bread and butter, delicate sandwiches with fish or meat paste fillings, homemade biscuits, and cake. Mary Anne would be on hand to serve, if needs be, smiling perhaps as Geoffrey immediately made a grab for the Victoria sponge. Nanny would gently reprimand him, *"Now, now, where's Mr Manners gone? Bread and buppy first, please, then cake."* Depending on the strictness of the Nanny, the meal might be a silent affair but as two of her charges were young adults, there is likely to have been more chatter.

After tea Mary Anne would store the cake and biscuits but be told to throw away the uneaten bread and sandwiches. This would always be hard for junior servants, knowing the hardships their parents and siblings were facing at home, but it was common practice in large houses of the day, continuing until the arrival of the Great War, when food shortages reduced the practice. Mary Anne would again wash the dishes, tidy up, stack the tray, and take the crockery back down to the kitchen.

The End of the Day Beckons

A simpler servant's tea would be served at 6.00pm, but even this was substantial, comprising cold cuts of leftover roast meats, pickles, bread, jam, and cake. This left time for the kitchen and 'above stairs' staff to prepare and serve the family dinner at around 7.30pm. After the family dinner, the upper ten often retired to either the butler's or housekeeper's room for the evening. This meant the junior servants could be livelier and spend the evening gossiping about the comings and goings of both the 'high-ups' and their employers. Servants were encouraged to be seen but not heard, so would frequently be in the company of the family and overhear their conversations, plans and opinions, all of which provided rich fodder for comment and analysis below stairs.

Returning to the nursery after tea, Mary Anne might do some final tidying, turn down the beds, warming them with a pan of hot coals. She would also have to carry up more cans of hot water and fill jugs, so that the young adults could wash before joining their parents – either for dinner or after dinner.

Mary Anne's working day would probably end around 7.30pm, when she was free to retire to the servant's hall to chat, play cards or dominoes, sew, knit, read, or write letters. Larger houses often had servants' libraries stocked with educational, improving reading matter. But high culture and books that were suitable for employers were discouraged, as it was felt that servants needed to know their status and station in life.

Servants were encouraged to write home once a week and their letters would be put in a wooden box in the main hall for collection with the other mail. Keeping in touch by letter was important, as junior servants were only given one or two weeks a year of holiday, and usually only after many months' employment. Mary Anne was probably at Annesley for two years as a servant, so may have had two such visits home, no doubt arriving with presents of food, cloth, and fripperies she had bought from her wages, plus many stories to tell.

Although precious, those visits home could be fraught. It would often be difficult for servants to fit back into family life again – they had been used to having to share a room perhaps with only one other, and had plentiful and varied food, with other staff to wait on them (e.g., to do their laundry and cook for them), so the relative privations of home could come as a shock.

In the evenings, the servant girls' other main preoccupation was to read *The Princess Novelettes*, a weekly magazine costing one penny (hence its nickname 'Penny Dreadful'). These were the Mills & Boon of the day, containing sensational stories of romance or mystery, often country girls meeting rich men and marrying well. They were written as an escape for young girls working hard, for low wages, but most servant girls knew that such things didn't happen in real life, or if they did, there wouldn't be a fairy-tale ending. Bedtime would not be late, usually by 10.00pm or 10.30pm, ready for the next day's early start.

A Chance Encounter

*T*aking off her apron and cap in her attic bedroom, Mary Anne donned her wool coat and straw bonnet. Checking herself in the mirror, she picked up her bag and umbrella, and set off. It was only her third afternoon off since she'd arrived at Annesley in February, and she'd not yet ventured further than a walk in the estate grounds. But today was a big adventure. She planned to explore Annesley village, visit the general store, and spend some of her first month's hard-won wages.

It was a bright afternoon in mid-March – the trees various shades of butterscotch and burnt toffee, the verges scattered with yellow primroses and a smell like pressed linen in the air. Mary Anne slipped on the step, and almost fell. She dropped her umbrella, cursed mildly, and grabbed the handrail.

"Whoops, careful young lady, you nearly came a cropper. Are you OK?"

Mary Anne felt a wide hand on her elbow and looked up. It was the heir to the estate, John P... a funny name, what was it? He stood over her, smiling broadly.

He was medium height and well built, with light brown wavy hair, a neat moustache and beard. Mary Anne had been told not to address the family directly and to speak only when spoken to. So hesitantly, she answered: "I'm fine Sir, thank you."

"You're new here, aren't you? Where do you work?" and she caught a faint hint of his hair oil as he bent to pick up her umbrella.

"Yes, I'm the new nursery housemaid Sir," she said, taking the proffered umbrella. He was smartly dressed in brown country tweeds, black riding boots and carrying a leather crop.

"Ah, that's why I've not seen you, tucked away up in the nursery. I hope my sisters and nephew are behaving well and eating all their greens?" He had a warm smile, the ruddy cheeks of an outdoors man and direct, dancing blue eyes. She thought that perhaps he was making fun of her.

"Yes Sir, they are very good children."

"Good! I'm John Patricius by the way, but everyone calls me Patrick. What's your name?"

"Mary Anne Sir, but there's another of that name, so they call me Polly."

"Well, I shall call you Mary Anne. It's a pretty name, so it'd be a shame not to use it. Anyway, I mustn't dawdle, I'm off hunting. Goodbye Mary Anne."

Patrick strode towards the stables, beating out a rallying cry on his boot with the crop. She was pretty enough he mused; slim, dark-eyed, and not too pert like some, nor too sullen. And he had enjoyed the mild discomfort that his gentle bantering seemed to cause.

Mary Anne stood for a moment, flustered. She could sense him glancing back at her. It was quiet, apart from rustling in the bushes, and the gentle snorting and stamping of hooves on cobbles.

With a quick glance at the stable door, she turned away, walking under the arch and up Dog and Bear Lane towards the village. The sunshine seemed brighter; birdsong audible above the breeze. She smelt fresh mown grass and its sharp scent reminded her of another – a mix of the bergamot and orange of his hair oil.

Absentmindedly touching the sleeve of her coat, she sensed a vague imprint of warmth from his grip. The stable yard had been unusually empty. Would he have spoken to her if others had been present, she wondered?

Just as quickly, she checked herself. He was her boss's son and not for her. She clasped her handbag, hearing the soft clink of hard-won shillings and decided to buy a small trinket to send her Ma for Mothering Sunday, as she never treated herself.

* * *

On 13th January 1881, Patrick came of age. As heir, his parents organised festivities to celebrate his birthday, including a supper for the estate employees and servants on one day, and a party for local public officials, including senior Colliery personnel the next. On both occasions, they served the commemorative beer that had been laid down when Patrick was born.

We think that Mary Anne Sharpe arrived at Annesley Hall in 1881. We know she was there in April that year, at the time of the census, but don't know if she was present at Patrick's 21st birthday celebrations in January. Either way, it wasn't long before she caught his attention, singled out from the six or seven other young women servants around at the time.

Similarly, Mary Anne theoretically had a choice of nearly a dozen eligible male servants, although maids were strictly segregated and were not allowed to have 'followers'. There were strict prohibitions on sexual relations between servants and one or other (usually the more junior female servant) would be dismissed if found out. Outside of the house, opportunities were also limited, as they didn't leave the house or grounds apart from once a week, on a curfewed afternoon off.

Servants' Rights

Domestic service was a precarious living in many ways. Once employed, young women would arrive with their 'boxes', containing their work clothes and undergarments, possibly a Bible and perhaps a few personal mementos. If a maid was dismissed, her box might well be retained – often to make up a deficit from any real or imagined thieving.

Employers were not obliged to provide any medical care or retirement pay for their servants, although some did. Various census and newspaper reports show the Chaworth-Musters provided both accommodation and retirement payments for long-serving senior staff.

Servants generally had very few legal rights, and the few laws that did exist favoured the employer. For example, the local magistrate had no right to interfere in a dispute between an employer and his servant. If an employer withheld a maid's wages or confiscated her belongings, she had very few options. She could sue her employer in a civil court, but this would have cost money and required contacts she would not have, plus taking this action would further ruin her chances of gaining another position.

Employers had the right to instantly dismiss a servant if they broke a legal order, the house rules (of which there could be many) or committed some other misdemeanour. Nor were employers legally bound to provide a character reference, which was essential for future employment in service. Without a box and a 'character', it was extremely difficult to find another position. If a girl was very lucky, her employer might look after her if she was somehow unfit to work, but if her family couldn't take her back and she had no savings of her own to fall back on, her situation was precarious.

If the girl became pregnant, the consequences were especially dire. With her reputation ruined, unable to get a character reference and find another servant's job, she would have to find menial, manual labour or worse still, be forced to enter the workhouse or resort to prostitution. It wasn't uncommon, especially in the larger towns and cities, for former maids, and some still in domestic employment, to offer themselves sexually, in return for trinkets and small gifts – these were known as 'dolly mops' in 19th century England.

In addition to dismissal by their employers, many young women in domestic service were severely punished in law for giving birth to illegitimate babies. In the late 1800s, it is estimated that around 6% of UK births were illegitimate. Very often, in sheer desperation, young girls tried to conceal their pregnancy to retain their job, and then disposed of their new-born babies in privies, ditches and on dung-heaps.

Patrick photographed in his early thirties

If found out, they were tried by all-male judges and jurors for abandonment or murder, if the child died. Although some were treated mercifully, others were hanged for their actions. As this became a growing problem, it is one of the reasons that the forerunner to the NSPCC was founded in London in 1884, to provide for illegitimate children.

With this historical context, it is remarkable that Mary Anne risked a relationship with Patrick, the heir to the estate. Such liaisons were not uncommon when pretty, unattached young servants lived close to young heirs, but they usually ended badly, with the girl being dismissed.

We don't know exactly how and when Mary Anne and Patrick met. It is likely to be soon after she arrived at

Annesley Hall in 1881, as by 1883, she was newly pregnant and living in Norway with him. Mary Anne would have spent most of her time in the servant's basement quarters or in the nursery on the third storey of the house.

It is possible that Patrick saw in the nursery, if he visited his siblings or spied her at the servant's party held in honour of his coming of age in January 1881. More likely though, they met as she crossed the yard, making her way from the servant's quarters above the stables to the main house. As a keen huntsman, like his father, Patrick spent much time in the stables visiting his horses and chatting with the grooms.

However, they met, it is easy to see the mutual attraction. Patrick took after his father and was of medium height and sturdily built, with thick light brown hair, piercing but twinkling blue eyes and a well-kept, dashing beard and moustache. This is evident from this photo of him (overleaf, above), thought to be in his late twenties. He is wearing the typical garb of the English Victorian country gentleman, a wool and tweed three-piece suit, with a folded wing tip collared shirt, a 'Four-in-Hand' wide necktie (the style of the 1870s and 1880s), gold Fob watch and chain, pocket handkerchief and a linen Homburg hat.

This photo of Mary Anne is thought to be taken in the mid-1880s, making her around 22 years old. She was of medium height and slender build (when young), with long dark, thick and wavy hair, and deep brown soulful eyes. She has a good nose and small lips.

The photo shows her demurely dressed in a plain white cotton blouse, with puffed sleeves, fastened at the throat with a simple broach. She is pretty, with a fresh-faced look.

In portrait photos of the period, most women either look at the camera or up and to one side. Mary Anne is looking down, so we can't see her eyes, and her lips are tensed. Maybe she felt uncomfortable with the unaccustomed attention of a portrait photo. It is noticeable that in none of her photos does she show her teeth.

We can imagine them meeting but it must have been difficult for them to form and maintain a romantic, sexual relationship. As heir to the manor and 'of age' at 21, Patrick would have a degree of freedom and money, but even so, he couldn't risk being seen fraternising with Mary Anne, for both their sakes. Their meetings were perhaps made easier because Patrick's father was largely absent from Annesley at the time – spending the spring/summer in Norway and winters in Aumont, France because of his ill-health. Patrick would have been the 'man of the house', so this probably gave him an added degree of freedom.

In the early days, the cluster of outbuildings and yards around the main house and the stable yards were ideal for gossip, with runs and warrens good for errands and brief flirtations. But as things got more serious and they started a sexual relationship, it is likely they would have had to meet on Mary Anne's one afternoon off each week and maybe made use of the wooded parts of the estate near the house. Also, less than a mile away and only a twelve-minute walk up Dog and Bear Lane stood the remains of the Norman motte and Bailey of Annesley Castle, surrounded by thick woods. Maybe this provided the seclusion they sought.

Mary Anne would have known of the dire consequences of being caught with Patrick, and worse, getting pregnant. Annesley Hall had witnessed this sad event before. In the 1600s a pregnant maid went missing under mysterious circumstances and the remains of a pregnant young woman were found under the stairs of the Hall, during renovations in the 1940s.

Society's morals change over time but in mid-Victorian Britain, unmarried sex was a serious issue, for the maid especially. Mary Anne's actions were therefore either reckless or based on a deep bond between the couple and perhaps Patrick made promises about their future together. Even so, Mary Anne must have harboured doubts about whether his actions would follow his words and, if she dared confide in a friend, for example her roommate, she would no doubt be told that she was risking everything with this liaison.

After a trip to the Mediterranean and a winter in France, searching for good health from diabetes-related illnesses, Patrick's father John decided on an extended trip to their Norwegian summer home at Lysne Lodge in Laerdal in 1883. In Lina's memoir, she mentions her, John and her daughters going to Lysne Lodge where they stayed *"and made no long expeditions"* but she makes no mention of Patrick accompanying them. This extended absence probably enabled the affair to start in earnest. So, risk it they did, and by September 1883, Mary Anne was pregnant with her first child by Patrick.

The Big News

John and Patrick strode the boundary of Top Field together, checking the fences, and stopping every so often to push a post deeper and tighten a wire.

"Have you heard from Pettit about his game?" John asked his son.

"Yes Pa. He says they're nearly reared. Two hundred or more birds."

"Good, we've got ten Guns, maybe more, so we'll take as many as he has for the shoot." They walked on in silence.

"Pa?"

"What lad?"

"Erm, I, well... I've got something to tell you that you mightn't like."

John turned to face his son and laughed. "Have you now. Well, let me guess. You've run through your allowance or maybe you've got that new mare of yours lame. Am I close?"

"No Pa. A bit worse than that I reckon."

"Worse! Well, spit it out Son. Best said, soonest mended."

Patrick looked down and scuffed the grass with his boot. "You know the nursery maid, Polly?"

"Slight lass, bonny, dark eyes?" Patrick nodded but said no more. John prompted him: "Well, what? Got designs on her have you?!"

"Designs of sorts, I guess. Me and Polly, we, we..." Patrick turned away sharply, throwing a stone at the gate, then continued: "We've been courting a while. I really like her Pa. Only... well she's in the family way."

His Father let out a low whistle. "I'll be darned. And is it yours?"

"Yes, Father! It is. She's not that sort of girl."

"Well, some might beg to differ lad. After all, she's lain with you." John dug his hands into his pockets, rocking back and forth, then spoke, hurriedly.

"Well, we can sort her out with some money, get her into a Magdalen home away from here and perhaps give her a reference, so she can get another job in a while. It'll work out, you'll see."

Patrick grabbed his father's sleeve: "Pa, stop now! That's not what I want. I mean to marry her."

"Marry?! Don't be soft lad. You can bed a maid, but you don't have to wed her!"

"I can and I will Pa. I won't give her up."

John looked at his 22-year-old son's anguished face and sighed: "Well, well. This is a world of trouble." His hand on Patrick's shoulder, he steered him towards the house.

"Come lad, don't upset yourself. We'll go and speak to your mother and see what she makes of it."

They walked back in silence, each lost in their thoughts.

* * *

Looking at the timings, it is most likely that on their return from Norway in the Autumn of 1883, Patrick's parents found out or were told of the affair and, possibly, the early pregnancy (Mary Anne would only have been a few weeks pregnant at this point). We don't know if his parents tried to break the couple up, but it is likely.

As we've seen, the family was among the landowning elite in the country, and Patrick's father John held a prominent position in county society. If Mary Anne had been of even proximate status to Patrick, maybe his parents would have arranged a hasty wedding, followed by several months travelling in Europe, and on their return, the pair could have proudly spoken of their 'honeymoon baby'. Such things did happen.

But Mary Anne was so far removed from Patrick in wealth and status that this wouldn't be possible. And we can only imagine the talk and reprobation of the upper ten servants, who might fear this behaviour reflected on them and their lack of supervision of junior servants, which could result in dire consequences for them.

Above all, there was the issue of moral appearances. Prior to the Victorian era, lovers, mistresses, and illegitimate children were common. But in the Victorian era, there was a lot more emphasis on maintaining family values in public, and DH Lawrence found his niche in skewering that Victorian hypocrisy. The morals of the day wouldn't allow for such inter-class marriage. As an example, JM Barrie, in his play *The Admirable Crichton*, intended to make the romance between

Lady Mary Loam and her butler, Crichton, end in marriage but decided against it on the grounds that *"the stalls [audience] wouldn't stand it."* The play debuted in 1902, so one can imagine how much stronger the feeling was in 1883, nearly 20 years earlier.

John and Lina may have feared the consequences of their heir marrying out of his class. It is highly likely that they would have explained this moral/societal stance to their young son and urged him to give Mary Anne up, perhaps promising to provide for her and the child if she 'went quietly'. We can't know, but whatever the tense family conversations, the whisperings, and sideways glances from staff, we do know that Patrick decided to stand by Mary Anne.

We also don't know if they became engaged at that point, although even if so, engagements were not necessarily the bind that people thought. In Victorian times both men and women broke off engagements frequently for various reasons, and they were entered into more lightly than before, as it was often a mechanism to sanction more privacy and intimacy between couples.

The Couple Move to Norway

Engaged or not, rather than insisting they marry, John and Lina decided to send the pair to Norway in late September. They must have made one of the last steamship sailings, before they ended for the season. The pair were unmarried and, if the pregnancy were known at the time, John and Lina probably hoped that the child would be born in seclusion. If the pregnancy had not yet been announced, they probably reasoned that, given time, the infatuation would wear thin and Patrick could be persuaded to give Mary Anne up at a future date and return to Annesley alone, with his reputation largely intact.

Maja Frønes, the Manager of the local Surnadal museum, confirms that Patrick and Mary Anne lived in his parents' house, Lysne Lodge, at Laerdal when they first arrived in 1883.

But Patrick acted swiftly, buying land in the winter of 1883. He refurbished (and possibly extended) a series of wooden houses in Årnes, in the province of Surnadal on the eastern side of Norway. This was around 350 km away from his parents' house in Laerdal, with a modern-day driving time of around five hours and a train journey of over seven hours.

By the time Patrick and Mary Anne's first child Margarita (Rita) was born on 16th June 1884, Patrick (24) and Mary Anne (21) were

Musters Husa in Årnestrøa. Photo courtesy of todalen.no

living in their new house in Årnes, and Rita's birth and that of three subsequent children – Elsie, Ruth, and Patricius (Pat) were registered there.

Choosing to build such a distance from Lysne Lodge perhaps signalled that Patrick valued his privacy and wanted to establish a separate life from that of his parents. Although the local society may have its own morals not dissimilar to those in England at the time, the family were unknown in Surnadal.

Patrick's house (photo above) was substantial; he clearly had money and didn't have to work to earn an income, and employed staff, so the family would have been accepted as legitimate. We know from letters of the time that the pair held themselves out as being married, with Mary Anne being referred to as Mrs Musters. Maya Frønes helpfully provided information on the family and their house in the area:

> The property they rebuilt/refurbished was called Årnestrøa/Trøinn and originally belonged to the farmers in Årnes who kept their cattle there. Årnestrøa is now owned by a family based in Trondheim and is used as a summerhouse. The local Surnadal museum houses a small collection of items from the family's time in Årnestrøa, including some furniture, and books related to their interests in birds and animals. The items show a glimpse of a lifestyle quite different from everyday life in rural Norway at that time.

Apart from keeping his distance from his parents' lodge, Patrick was probably attracted to the Surnadal area because of the well-known salmon fishing rivers there. According to a local history book written by H. Hyldbakk, Patrick lived at Årnestrøa permanently for five years (1883-1888) and, after that, he used the lodge in the summer for family holidays. He leased hunting rights in Årnes and in Nordmarka (a mountain area in Surnadal), and he fished for salmon in the rivers.

The Rural Iidyll

Looking at photos of the house and its surroundings, it seems very idyllic. We know that Patrick, like his father, was a keen huntsman who much preferred the countryside and outdoors to an urban, indoor life. Mary Anne, too, was a country girl with a preference for the simple life. Apart from the seclusion it afforded the couple, the simple lifestyle would have been to their liking.

It also gave the couple the chance to develop the skills they would require in later life. For Patrick, this was running an estate, and managing his money, whilst indulging his hobbies and interests. The house is quite large (although simple inside), with multiple bedrooms and receptions rooms. It would have given Mary Anne the chance to run a household of her own; manage a budget, control a small number of staff, deal with tradesmen and raise her growing family.

The family would have been comfortably well off. Patrick would have inherited an income from the family when he came of age, derived from their vast estates and royalties from the Annesley Colliery Company, of which his father was a director. Apart from managing his small estate, he would not have needed to work in Norway, so would have been free to indulge his pastimes, and spend time with Mary Anne and his young children.

Mary Anne would have been fully engaged running the household and it is likely that she largely raised her young children herself. Having had older and younger siblings, she would be used to having children around her and seen first-hand the way her mother raised them.

Also, having had two years as a nursery housemaid, she would have witnessed how the upper class raised their children and perhaps took on the role of 'Nanny' herself, employing the quaint phrases and sayings she would have heard in the nursery,[12] such as *"Don't care was made to care. Don't care lost a duck"*, *"No scraping your plate. We always leave something for Mr Manners"* and *"No squabbling... little birds in their nests agree."*

Given the size of the house and the growing family, Patrick and Mary Anne would have employed a small staff – most likely a cook, a maid, and an outdoor man to help on the estate. We know of two female servants in the household at the time but don't know their exact roles. One was Ane Nilsdatter Røv and the other was Johanna Torvik, who wrote to Mary Anne in Norwegian from Minnesota, USA, in January 1888.

In the letter (kindly translated by Maya Frønes), she says she is grateful for the way she had been treated in the Musters home, and that she'll never forget them. She adds that she has good memories of Mrs. Musters and her children, referring to Rytte (Rita) and Elsi, adding that Rita used to call her 'Dedi'. She says she would like to visit, but that it is too expensive and asks Mrs. Musters to send her greetings to Ingeborg (who may have been a fellow servant). She concludes the letter by saying she heard Mrs Musters had another baby and hopes she is well. This would have been Ruth, who was born in April 1887.

Because of their unmarried status and preferences, the couple may have kept themselves apart from the local society, so perhaps didn't have to entertain much, if at all. They may have only seen Patrick's family infrequently when the latter stayed in Lysne Lodge in the summer, as it was a day's journey (or more) away from Årnestrøa. And it would have been difficult for Mary Anne to keep in touch with her family in Bedfordshire other than by letter.

Patrick, Mary Anne, and the children learnt Norwegian and spoke it well, with their staff and the locals. Johanna Torvik wrote to Mary Anne, Elsie, and Ruth between 1888-1919 and all the letters are in Norwegian. We also know from other letters that their son Phil spoke Norwegian and that their youngest son Jim spoke Norwegian fluently, with a local accent, so it's likely that the whole family did.

From what we know from letters from the children later in life and family memoirs, their life from 1883 to 1888 in Norway was simple and relatively idyllic. Patrick was an amateur ornithologist

---

12. Noel Streatfeild, *Tea by the nursery fire: A children's nanny at the turn of the century.*

and naturalist. He put together one of the most important collections of stuffed birds and animals in the UK at the time.

Apart from British species, he preserved animals from Norway and from Iceland, Lapland, New Zealand, and Russia. He may well have been one of over 400 collectors employed by Lord Walter Rothschild, part of the banking dynasty. In 1892, Walter Rothschild created his own zoological museum at Tring Park, Hertfordshire, which on his death in 1937, he bequeathed to the Natural History Museum. Letters from Patrick in the NHM archive dated 1903, list him as a 'Tring correspondent'.

As PTA Musters records in his family memoir:

> *In Norway they had been bringing up their children in a paradise of mountain streams to be fished, bears to be hunted, and wildlife to be learned about – and respected. In later years when their sons wrote home from the trenches of the Great War... those letters contained mention of the butterflies to be seen, the partridge and pheasant to be hunted for the pot and the beauty of the countryside when they could get away from the shell-torn earth in which they had to fight.*

And before the Great War, letters from the boys at boarding school to their mother spoke enthusiastically about the various bird breeds spotted, fish caught, and hunting trips undertaken. It was clear that Patrick and Mary Anne's love of the outdoor life had been passed onto their children.

JOHN AND LINA'S LATTER YEARS

Whilst Patrick and Mary Anne settled into family life in Norway, Patrick's parents continued their society and county life at Annesley. In Lina's memoir she writes movingly of her husband's decline in health, aged only 42:

> *All that winter and spring [1879] he was wretchedly ill and depressed. Going to Norway did him good as usual but the winter of 1880/81 was as bad as ever and he hardly left his rooms or could bear to see anyone.*

Patrick may have inherited his father's solitary and depressive tendencies, as he too liked to spend a lot of time in Norway and, during the war years, his children's letters speak often about not worrying their father unduly and they ask Mary Anne to provide him with support and to cheer him up.

From 1880, John went to Norway each spring/summer and wintered in Aumont in eastern France, hunting with the Duc d'Aumale (a fabulously wealthy royalist, and descendant of King Louis-Philippe I of the French – the last French King prior to the revolution) and his hounds, shooting and beagling.

Lina would have spent a lot of time on her own (not unusual in Victorian upper-class marriages) and their five children (who by then ranged from aged nine to Patrick, aged 20) would have got used to a largely absent father. This maybe meant that Patrick matured quicker and felt (and indeed had) more freedom at Annesley than might otherwise have been the case.

Apart from visits to Norway and France, John was kept busy managing the estate, and handling colliery business. The colliery employed over 1,200 staff and was producing 250,000 tonnes of manufacturing and steam coal each year (for which John, as a director, received a decent royalty per ton), plus manufactured the bricks that built many of the houses and facilities in Annesley.

In 1882 John sold land on his Colwick estate for residential development. In 1883, he sold West Bridgford Hall, its grounds (but not its accompanying title), and 19 acres of land to Albert Heymann, a wealthy Nottingham banker and son of lace manufacturer, Lewis Heymann, who had rented the property for many years. In view of the timing of the sale, it is possible that John needed to raise capital to help Patrick and Mary Anne purchase the land and build their house in Årnestrøa, Norway.

Lina continued to undertake good works, and started a clothing club in the village school, which by 1885 had 200 members. Clothing clubs were a means of encouraging mothers to save a small amount each week, to clothe and shoe their families. Each women's savings and debits were recorded in a ledger and, often, the amount saved was boosted annually by donations from the local gentry, clergy, and charities.

Lina was also actively involved in the Annesley branch of the St John's Ambulance Association, which was praised for its work training members of the colliery to be on hand for emergencies at the pit. During this period, she also oversaw the building of nine pairs of cottages along the Derby Road for colliery workers and continued to entertain local society at summer balls, hunt dinners and open days.

A typical event was when she opened Annesley Hall and grounds to the public, for a small charge. The proceeds went towards a fund for alterations run by the Social Guild Institution in Nottingham, of which she was a member. The Guild managed properties rented to 360 tenants, with regular visits conducted by *"earnest ladies"*, who it was claimed, gradually *"improved the cleanliness and order"* of the families and their accommodation.

A local newspaper reporting on the open day at Annesley said a *"Large number attended this celebrated and historic spot on a fine day"* and went on to detail the Hall and its grounds:

> *The ivy-covered hall is seen with a pretty little pond in the centre of a splendid lawn.*
>
> *There are deer skins on the floor of the entrance hall, plus bear skins. A screen, covered with the amusing and comical squibs of fifty or sixty years ago, stood at one end of the room and curiosities met the eye in every quarter.*

> *One is a reptile bought by George Chaworth-Musters from the Nile in 1858.*
>
> *The dinner room is a lofty, light, handsome apartment, and attracted great attention. It holds paintings by Stubbs, one by Gainsborough and one by Sir Joshua Reynolds. There sits a large carved oak cabinet, evidently of great antiquity. The library with oak panelling from oak washed up in the flood of 1853 at Colwick, adjoining the river Trent. A small table, the top of which is made from the first piece of coal taken out of the Annesley pit. Specimens of rare china were very plentiful as are fine portraits... An old, flagged terrace leading to gardens, with walls most charming. The old church was open also.*

Once again, the description of the Hall reveals an informal, somewhat eccentric family home, but one displaying some wealth. Paintings by the 18th-century greats, Stubbs, Gainsborough, and Reynolds would still have been valuable at the time although nowhere near the circa £10 million, £5 million, and £10 million per painting respectively they fetch at today's auction prices.

The Sporting Life

It is not surprising the family had a Stubbs painting, due to their love of hunting and there are two related anecdotes. A predecessor, Jack Musters, commissioned the society portraitist to paint him on horseback. Jack had a humpback, which Stubbs (somewhat unkindly) painted in. Jack objected strongly and asked for the hump to be removed, whereupon Stubbs simply painted out the figure entirely and delivered a portrait solely of the horse.

Jack also commissioned six other pictures from Stubbs around the same time (1777-78). By far the most striking was a double portrait of John and his new wife Sophia, riding at Colwick Hall. Sophia was a society beauty of the day and was alleged to have had multiple affairs during the marriage, incensing Jack, who ordered Stubbs to remove her from the painting. Stubbs did so but took care to ensure his original work could be reinstated, and in 1936 when it underwent renovation, Sophia was once again restored to the painting.

Like their predecessors, both John and Lina had an all-consuming passion for horses. John was known as 'the hunting squire' to all at Annesley and there is a portrait of Lina riding, which shows a beautiful, intelligent, and determined face. Both John and Lina published descriptions of some of the better-known runs they had with hounds, one of which was 36 miles long and required three horses, as it was so long and energetic.

Making a name for herself in the hunting field and as an amateur historian, collector and publisher of hunting songs and anecdotes, Lina privately published a 200-page book in 1885, entitled *"Book of hunting songs and sport"*, dedicated to the 10th Earl Ferrers, a Staffordshire Peer and a Master of Fox Hounds. Her interest in local history meant that when it was suggested that a Nottinghamshire historical society was formed, Lina one of only two women interested and so became a founder member of the 81 members of the Thoroton Society in January 1887.

These interests continued throughout her life and in 1890, now widowed and having more time on her hands, she wrote and published *"A Cavalier Stronghold"*, a romance of civil war in the Vale of Belvoir, contributed a history on the Chaworth family to the Thoroton Society's *Transactions* journal, and in 1895, contributed an article on the role of the wife of a master of fox hounds to a book published by novelist, Lady Violet Greville, entitled *"Ladies in the field: sketches of sport."*

The Golden Jubilee

In June 1887 John and Lina played their part in the national Golden Jubilee celebrations of Queen Victoria's 50 years on the throne. The newspapers were full of news and photos surrounding the events in London. On 20th June, the Queen presided over a banquet attended by 50 European Kings and Princes and, the following day, took part in a procession through London to Westminster Abbey, escorted by the Colonial Indian cavalry. That same the evening, she held another banquet, receiving a procession of diplomats and Indian Princes, after which she was wheeled in her chair to watch fireworks in the palace garden. She also hosted a garden party in Hyde Park for around 30,000 children.

Many leading aristocrats and estate owners held their own parties on the day and evening of 20th June for local dignitaries, and John and Lina followed suit, as prominent Nottinghamshire landowners. But they did so in their own low-key way. The local newspaper reports that they held an afternoon tea, with sports, for their staff and tenants, serving *"buns and mineral waters for the children"* and presented attendees with medals that John had commissioned with Queen Victoria's head on one side and inscribed *"From John Chaworth-Musters"*, encircled with the words *"In memory of Queen Victoria's Jubilee 20 June 1887"* on the reverse.

John Passes Away

Amidst the celebrations, 1887 was to be a tragic year for Lina. Her father died early that year from "heart bronchitis" and her beloved husband John also died suddenly. John, Lina, and daughters Mary and Kitty visited Norway with Lina's brother in July, after the Jubilee celebrations. However, Lina (in her family memoir) makes no of them meeting up with Patrick, Mary Anne, and their children during this trip. The family returned to Annesley in August and shortly after, John set off for France, to spend the winter there for his health, as usual. Lina's memoir records the events that unfolded in moving detail:

> *He had seemed very well at the Jubilee dinner ...and gave medals to a great many servants and people on the estate... He went to Aumont in September and came back in October, when he was in remarkably good spirits.*

John spent the month back at home hunting and visiting most of his tenants. He set off again for France early on 24th October 1887. Lina reports:

> *He came to say goodbye to me in my room, saying 'take care of yourself, I shall be over in the Spring'.*

In Lina's opinion, John caught scarlet fever when passing through London on 25th October to be photographed for a publication (shown overleaf, with John looking much older than 50). Whatever the cause, only ten days after arriving in Aumont, France, John became ill with a cold and sore throat but was well enough to go hunting. John's lifelong friend Dr Forbes went to France and *"nursed him day and night from Monday to Thursday and was very unwell himself from the strain."*

Dr Forbes wrote to Lina to report that although John had got through the original fever, *"his old disease, diabetes, took such hold*

upon him that he had not the strength to stand against it."

Lina recounts an unusual premonition John had on his deathbed. He had been speaking about a local Annesley boy who had been seriously ill. Someone in the room asked John about him and he replied: *"He died at 7 o'clock."* Lina writes that *"no-one in the house knew but on inquiry it was found to be so."* John died on 17th November 1887 at 4.15pm, only two months short of his fiftieth birthday.

He was buried at Langar churchyard, a few miles south of Wiverton, part of the family's estate. Commentators of the time noted that John was: *"Deservedly popular...A thorough sportsman and an English gentleman."*

John's obituary and funeral was reported in full in many newspapers, not just the local ones, but also in London, Sheffield, Leicestershire and in magazines such as The Lady and Horse & Hound. The chief mourners, apart from his immediate family, are listed as Horace Packe (John's brother-in-law), Captain Sherbrooke (son-in-law), Henry Neville Sherbrooke (nephew), Captain Hamond (nephew) and several other non-family members. The papers report that attendees were *"chiefly hunting men and tenantry"*, including staff from their various houses.

The Mansfield Reporter gave much room to his obituary, (which contains such precise details on his decline and demise, that they must have got the information from Lina) as follows:

> *...He was very delicate in childhood and had uncertain health all his life. He frequently said he should not live to be fifty, and this presentiment was a true one... His constitution never recovered a very bad illness in the winter of 1880-81; he was then confined to the house for many months and was ordered by his doctors never to winter in England again.*

On 24th October he entertained friends to luncheon and planted a tree for the Queen's Jubilee in the park at Annesley, giving the labourers who assisted a sovereign between them. Next day he went to London, had a photo taken for a portrait collection and accompanied by his friend of many years, Dr Forbes of Eastwood, he went to France and accompanied him out stag hunting and to the races at Chantilly. Dr Forbes left on 1st November, when Mr Chaworth-Musters was apparently well.

On 6th, Mr Musters wrote he had a bad cold but was taking care of it, then that he would see a doctor, and on Wednesday the doctor pronounced it scarlatina. On Friday Mr Musters wrote home and said he was going well and Dr Forbes was not to come. On 13th he wrote, saying he was better and telegraphed on 13th that he was "much better". Dr Forbes went to France anyway and found him recovered from the fever but very weak.

Quantities of nourishing food were taken but disease of the heart of long standing prevented a lasting rally. Mr Musters was aware of his danger, and remained perfectly calm, conscious, and resigned to the last, sending messages to all at home. Death ensued from syncope of the heart [sudden unconsciousness due to heart arrhythmia] at 4.15pm on Thursday 17th, without pain.

None of his family had had scarlatina, so he wouldn't allow any of the family to be present. He passed away with his hand in that of Dr Forbes, his friend of 25 years' standing.

By his death the county loses a country gentleman it could ill-spare, and the poor a generous and bountiful benefactor. Probably no one in the county was so widely known as Mr Musters; his memory for faces was wonderful and many a face used to brighten when the Squire stopped with a cheery smile and a greeting.

His eldest son Mr John Patricius Musters is absent in Norway, where Mr Musters had a fishing box and which he and Mrs Musters only left in August.

John Chaworth-Musters was a captain in the South Notts Yeomanry Cavalry, which he left in 1875 after a service of 15 years.

> *A memoir of his hunting career is to appear soon. He amused himself from 1880 with the help of Mrs Musters in collecting a series of hunting songs and poems which have been published by him. One quoted of him:*
>
> *...His name will live – oh! May we all*
> *Acquit ourselves as well*
> *As this fine old English gentleman,*
> *One of a sporting line.*

John's decline following his severe illness in 1880/81 and his premonition that he would die young, would undoubtedly have meant that he placed great importance on seeing his heir set on the right course in life, with a partner as dedicated and supportive as Lina had been. Perhaps Patrick's announcement in 1883 that he had got a maid pregnant and wished to stay with her, would have caused his father great concern, which may not have helped his health.

John's Funeral – A County Mourns

John's obituary was followed by an extensive report of the funeral, which took place in beautiful weather, in Langar churchyard. The paper described the tombs of the Chaworth family from 1500s and noted that there had been no Chaworth burials there since the reign of Charles 1, when nearby Wiverton Manor was nearly destroyed by Parliamentary troops. It was John Muster's wish to be buried there. The report continues:

> *The family plan to place at the head of the grave as a headstone a piece of rock from the lovely valley in Norway where he went yearly. The Rector, Mr Wood, a personal friend of the Musters family, arranged the service but the service in the church was conducted by Rev C H Prance, the vicar of Annesley.*
>
> *There was an immense assemblage of over 1,000, and it would be quite impossible to give an idea of the genuine emotion displayed by them. It was a most striking sight...and showed us how much we had underestimated his great popularity. Hard bronzed men were sobbing like children, and in the midst of a genuine and almost un-English exhibition of grief, the Squire was*

> *laid to rest. Red coats of the hunt servants from Gedling, and Mr Rolleston, friend and prior Master of the South Notts hunt was present.*

The report lists the many family members present, excluding Patrick who was said to be unable to make the funeral in time from Norway.

> *At the head of the coffin lay a simple wreath of evergreens, attached to which was a card with the words 'Leaves from the Kennel Walk, Annesley', and another of hothouse cuttings with a card: 'From the gardens, Annesley, with much sympathy'. A superb bunch of violets was fastened near the front of the coffin. Shortly after 12.00 the coffin was lifted upon a light farm waggon, covered with Scotch fir boughs from the forest at Annesley which Mr Musters himself had planted.*
>
> *The vehicle was drawn by two Clydesdale horses, bred at Annesley and the long journey from Wiverton to Langar was accomplished slowly and without mishap, the country people along the road uncovering [their heads] as the coffin passed. Blinds were drawn in most of the village houses they passed through. The coffin was borne by twenty tenants, four from each of the estates of Annesley, Colwick, Wiverton, West Bridgford and Edwalton. It passed between a long line of tenantry in the churchyard and was placed on trestles near the nave.*

The style of funeral chosen for this wealthy man speaks volumes of the family and its humble values. Victorian funerals of the time typically involved elaborate hearses and carriages and many dignitaries. John's funeral seemed to be a much simpler affair, with focus on his family, staff and tenants, a farm wagon used instead of an elaborate hearse and the Scotch fir boughs perhaps a reminder of his beloved Norwegian forests. The family inscribed a memorial in Annesley old churchyard to John with the following, in commemoration of his great love of fishing and hunting:

> *Home is the sailor, home from the sea*
> *And the hunter is home from the hill.*

And in Langar churchyard, the family had a slate memorial fixed to the church wall, part of which reads:

Give alms of thy goods, & never turn thy face from any poor man, & then the lord will not turn away his face from thee.

After John's death, Lina wrote to his old tutor Dr Brereton, informing him of John's passing. Writing back of his sadness at the news, Dr Brereton said: *"My pupil had an affectionate nature, and very humble instincts."* From what we understand, both John and Lina were down-to-earth people and loving parents, traits they passed onto their son, Patrick, who displayed the same traits with his own family, friends, and staff.

Patrick missed his Father's funeral in December 1887, as he was living at Årnestrøa, in the east of Norway. This must have been of great regret for him, but it is likely that the weather would have made the journey impossible, as the steamship service would not be running past November.

In addition, knowing the funeral would be attended by the 'great and good' of Nottinghamshire, Patrick perhaps wouldn't have risked the inevitable questions about his five-year absence, continued unmarried status and three illegitimate children. In Lina's memoir she simply states that *"Patrick was in Norway and arrived too late for the funeral"*, making no mention of his reasons for being there, nor of his wife and family, nor that he didn't return to England to live for a further 19 months after his father's death.

'WE HAVE TO RETURN': PATRICK INHERITS

Rolling down his shirt sleeves, Patrick walked purposefully into the drawing room: "My Dear, it's no good putting this off, with Father long gone, we have to go back to England." Startled, Mary Anne looked up from her sewing.

He saw her mouth pinch, eyes downcast: "Can't you go without me, or give the job to Georgie? You know I can't face everyone."

"Mary Anne, if I could, I would, but I am the heir, and we must return." He waited, tensed, for her answer.

He no more wanted to leave this idyll than she did. He had fought against tradition his entire life – leaving Eton early, flunking out of Oxford, preferring estate business to a role in the city – and most crucially, choosing a mate from a lower social rank and fathering four illegitimate children. But he was torn. Loyal to his ancestry, his family, the house, land, and servants – he knew where his duty lay.

Mary Anne pondered the daunting new role she faced. Sensing this, Patrick persisted, more gently: "Dearest, why worry how others will judge us? I don't give a damn for anyone's views on how we live our life! But we must face this together, can't you see?"

She understood her husband's divided loyalties. And whilst she had no choice, she too, came from stock where hard work, and 'sticking at it' were paramount. So, on that warm June day, it was decided: they would leave Norway for Nottinghamshire straight away.

* * *

On the November day of his father's death, Patrick's carefree life changed forever. He was a loyal family man, and a man of duty, so knew he had to return to England and take over the running of the family estates. PTA Musters records that: *"Patrick realised that he and Mary Anne would have to give up their idyllic existence and return to run the Annesley estate,"* and that they *"reluctantly"* returned to UK.

Lina's memoir recounts that immediately following John's death, Patrick had to *"spend some months in England as a great deal of business devolved on him."* Again, she makes no mention of Mary Anne and his children accompanying him, so it may be that Patrick returned on his own.

Attending to Finances

Patrick would soon realise that there was cause for concern over the family's finances. There had been an agricultural depression since the mid-1870s (which is estimated to have lasted until 1896), with income from farm rents decreasing, affecting the Chaworth-Musters' estates. There were also recent signs that John had tried to rein in expenditure. In March 1887, he had surprised the committee of the Royal Agricultural Society who were trying to raise a fund. They reported that John wrote saying that:

> *Owing to the badness of the times as regarded agriculture, both for landowners and tenant farmers, he regretted that he could not subscribe towards the fund required.*

The Society's report went on to state that:

> *When they looked at Mr Chaworth-Musters' estate in West Bridgford and saw how the land there had increased in value, he [the Chairman] felt more than surprised at the letter.*

However, John was not alone in giving this excuse. The Duke of Rutland had also written from Belvoir Castle declining to subscribe for the same reason.

John and Lina's expenses on their improvements to the house and grounds, their staffing, estate management, hunting, their home in Norway and travels to it and to France would have taken its toll on their finances. Patrick received a letter concerning his father's finances, written from the Continental Hotel, Tangier on 17th December 1887, possibly from Nicholas Charlton, one of his father's executors (the signature is illegible, but it appears to be initialled

NC). Nicholas was from a wealthy landowning and mining family whose seat was Chilwell Hall, Nottinghamshire. It read:

> *I was most shocked and surprised to hear of your father's death. He was as well when I saw him last, just before leaving England [Nicholas had probably been invited to the last luncheon John held, before leaving for France]. It will be a long time before there is so good a sportsman again...*
>
> *You will I am sure take care of your mother and sister(s) who have not been accustomed to want for anything, and for goodness sake, at once cut down the expenses of the estate, every day makes a difference. I know there are heavy charges on the property but with an estate situated like the one you have succeeded to, you will be able to do a great deal towards clearing it, by selling near Nottingham. I can't say more until I receive a general summary of the Will.*

This letter clearly shows that the family were used to spending (*"not been accustomed to want for anything"*) and that finances were not what they once had been. Lina records that Patrick had to sell off the best pictures from various properties (presumably the Stubbs, Gainsborough, and Reynolds oils amongst them) to *"pay £10,000 that John had given his brother and sister nearly thirty years before"*. This might account for the *"heavy charges on the property"* mentioned by his executor, as in 1845 John had to raise around £1 million (in today's money) eight years after his father's death. Since then, spending had been high on property renovations, extensions, and general living expenses.

So, amidst the sadness of his father's passing and the uncertainty surrounding his own (somewhat unconventional) family circumstances, 27-year-old Patrick had to act decisively and effectively. Almost certainly spurred on by the letter from Nicholas Charlton, in 1887 Patrick decided to sell Edwalton Manor and its seven tied farms to Sir Thomas Shipstone, son of the founder of Shipstones, a major Nottinghamshire brewery.

Until the 1880s, Edwalton village's population was around 130, with only 27 houses. However, in 1880, Edwalton Station had been opened on the Nottingham-London Midland railway line, making the four miles distance from the city centre very commutable.

Spotting this opportunity, John Chaworth-Musters had already begun selling Edwalton land for building plots and within ten years, the population had doubled, as Nottingham businessmen and their servants moved in.

Nicholas Charlton was right to say that land of that type near Nottingham was fetching a good price, so Patrick must have felt that selling off the manor and the remainder of its estate was a shrewd move. However, PTA Musters notes that, in doing so, Patrick missed a financial opportunity:

> *Perhaps their reluctance to return from Norway, coupled with the stress and upheaval and stress of taking on the estate, caused Patrick to ignore the results of the exploratory bore holes made at Edwalton [for coal]. Whatever the reason, the chance of enrichment passed them by at this time and plots were sold off for building.*

It is worth noting that these boreholes didn't lead to any mining in the immediate area. A brick works was built to supply the local housebuilding but, apart from that, all the development in Edwalton was purely residential housing, so perhaps Patrick did the right thing after all.

As his mother records, Patrick spent a few months in England attending to business in 1888, before returning to Norway. We don't know whether she tried to persuade him to come back alone but it is unlikely. Lina was a loving mother and grandmother to Patrick's three children (who she would most likely have met in Norway) and wouldn't wish to see them made fatherless. She records in her memoir that she moved to Wiverton Hall (the traditional home of family widows) in February 1888. This is corroborated by letters sent to her at that time to Annesley Park, which had the address crossed through and the post forwarded to Wiverton Hall instead.

The Couple Marry

Patrick travelled to England with Mary Anne by train and boat in March 1888, four months after his father's death (and as soon as the steamship service restarted). The five-day journey must have been long and relatively uncomfortable, as Mary Anne was by then six months pregnant with their fourth child. The pair married quietly at St Pancras Register Office in Middlesex on 13th March 1888.

CERTIFIED COPY OF AN ENTRY OF MARRIAGE GIVEN AT THE GENERAL REGISTER OFFICE

Application Number 11374074/2

[Marriage certificate: 1888. Marriage solemnized at the Register Office in the District of Pancras in the County of Middlesex. No. 91. When Married: Thirteenth March 1888. Names: John Patricius Chaworth-Musters, age 28, Bachelor, Land Owner, Great Northern Hotel Pancras, father John Chaworth Musters (deceased), Gentleman; Mary Ann Tharpe, age 25, Spinster, Clifton Biggleswade Bedford, father George Tharpe, Gentleman. Married in the Register Office by Licence before Martineau F. Lance, Registrar, A. J. Davis, Supt. Registrar. Witnesses: Harriet Lance, Annie Showell.]

A copy of the marriage certificate (shown above) appears to confirm that no family members were present at the couple's wedding. The Registrar is listed as Martineau Frederick Lance and the witnesses are his wife, Harriet Lance, and the Superintendent Registrar, Annie Showell. Moreover, the wedding was not reported in the local Nottinghamshire press, unlike any of the other family weddings before or after. More significantly, nor was it mentioned in Lina's family memoir.

The significance of their marriage shouldn't be underestimated. Victorian family values were well known and strictly adhered to, especially by those in positions of power and status in society. They are reflected in a popular play, *Caste* by T W Robertson, which opened in London 20 years before. Discussing marriage across classes, two characters state:

> *All those marriages of people with common people are all very well in novels, because the real people don't exist. But in real life, it's absolute bosh. It's worse – it's utter social and personal annihilation and damnation.*
>
> *No gentleman can be ashamed of the woman he loves. No matter what her original station, once his wife, he raises her to his rank.*
>
> *Yes, he raises her – her; but her connections, her relatives. Ow' about them?*

So, Patrick may have been perceived by family and friends as risking 'social and personal damnation' but marry he did. PTA Musters commented:

102

> *As for Patrick, if he felt he wished to marry his Mary Ann [sic], then he was a greater gentleman for it – and she a greater lady.*

Perhaps, for a young woman of 25, Mary Anne would have been disappointed that she didn't get a grand church wedding, with her own large family in attendance. But overall, in view of her precarious position, both financially and in terms of reputation, she is likely to have felt huge relief. At last, their six-year union was official, legally binding and it showed those that knew of their circumstances that Patrick had done the right thing by her and their children.

Patrick had been busy before his wedding. Apart from arranging the marriage licence, he had applied for a Royal Licence to change the family name and arms by deed poll to the hyphenated Chaworth-Musters, which was granted on 6th March 1888, a week before his marriage. Although Patrick and his father before him had used the Chaworth-Musters name for some time, he may have had several reasons for making it official.

Primarily, it is likely that in doing so, Patrick felt it would preserve the ancient name of Chaworth within the family. Secondly, County and Rural District Councils were first created in 1888. Before then, local squires like John and now Patrick, had ruled their land autocratically. Following the creation of local authorities, they would rule unconstitutionally but with passive consent of the locals.

Taking the arms and name of Chaworth-Musters officially could, Patrick perhaps felt, help him maintain his position and status in the county. And finally, their fourth (as yet, unborn) child may have been their first son (and therefore heir), and thus he would be born a Chaworth-Musters. On marriage, he and Mary Anne became the Chaworth-Musters and Patrick lobbied, successfully, for their three previous children to be recognised as heirs to the family name.

We don't exactly know how long they stayed in the UK after marrying but probably not long, in view of Mary Anne's advanced pregnancy. The marriage certificate gives Mary Anne's place of residence at the time of marriage as Clifton, Bedfordshire. This was the home of her parents and probably given for propriety's sake, to hide the fact that the couple were living together whilst unmarried. Interestingly, Patrick's residence is given as the nearby Great Northern Hotel in St Pancras (the grand hotel built by the railway company of the same name), so it is unlikely at this point that he had returned to Annesley.

The couple may have lived at Annesley Hall for the two or more months they were in England, and visited his mother at Wiverton Hall but possibly not, as awkward questions may well have been asked by staff about their recent marriage, existing children and Mary-Anne's advanced pregnancy. It is notable that Lina's memoir makes no mention of a visit from the couple or any children at that time, just that Patrick had to spend some months in England, which he may have done whilst being based largely in London with his family.

A New Home in Norway

Whatever the circumstances, we do know that following their marriage, the couple returned to Norway in time for the birth of their first son and heir, Patricius George (Pat), on 14th June 1888, in Årnes, Norway. Shortly after the birth, the family gave up the property in Årnes. Local historians record them living there from 1883 to 1888. By October 1888, they had moved nearly 500km northwest to Vaulen in Surnadal, near the coast of Norway. Patrick probably figured that now they were soon to be living in England permanently, it made sense to have a base closer to the coast and therefore easier to get to and from England for family trips.

However, there is no record of the family buying the property in Surnadal until eight years later, in 1896. This is probably for two reasons. Patrick may have been unwilling to invest in a permanent base abroad, as he hadn't yet taken on the full running of the estate and would not know how much time it would consume. More likely however, was that he was sufficiently concerned about the state of the family's finances. He may have used the proceeds of the sale of the Årnes property to help the short-term cash flow and decided rental at Vaulen was a better option at this point.

Shopping in Paris

Knowing that they would be returning to England soon to take up their role as Squire and Lady of the manor, Patrick suggested a trip to the Paris Exposition Universelle in 1889. Perhaps his aim was to soften the blow for Mary Anne of leaving Norway and thinking that she might like to add her own touch to the interior of Annesley Hall. The couple were back in England by July, so they probably visited the exhibition in late June, on their way home to England, and with Mary Anne, once again, being around five months' pregnant at the time.

The difference between a small village in rural Norway and the city of Paris would have been overwhelming. The crowded streets, fancy carriages, stunning architecture, and massive numbers of well-dressed, cosmopolitan people going about their busy lives, would have amazed them both, but Mary Anne especially.

The Paris Exposition was a showcase for scientific and technological advances, held from May to the end of October 1889, and attracting over 32 million visitors. 1889 was the 100th anniversary of the storming of the Bastille and the Expo included a reconstruction of the Bastille and its surrounding neighbourhood.

However, the main attraction was the Eiffel Tower, which served as the entrance arch to the grounds and from where, on its second platform, visitors could pay to see panoramic views of the city. The Palace of Machines – a vast nave of glass and iron – housed innovations such as atmospheric hammers, voting machines, cigarette makers, Tissot's clock-making workshop, as well as phonographs and telephones. It also debuted the first car ever to be shown in Paris, by manufacturer Gottlieb Daimler.

Other major attractions included the 'Negro village' where 400 people of colour were displayed to the mainly white visitors and Buffalo Bill recruited American sharpshooter Annie Oakley to re-join his Wild West Show, which performed to packed audiences. It is likely that Patrick and Mary Anne visited the most popular exhibits and attractions, and we do know they visited the Galerie du Meuble, as family records show they purchased furniture for their drawing room at home.

Given Patrick's interests, it is probable that he also persuaded Mary Anne to spend time in the Gallery of Hunting, Fishing and Horticulture. After village life in Bedfordshire, a few years in the small village of Annesley and five years in the remote idyll of Norway, Paris and its Exposition would have been eye-opening for Mary Anne. As country people at heart, the pair were perhaps glad to return to the slower pace of life at Annesley, albeit now proud possessors of the latest style in drawing room furniture!

'Learning the Ropes' at Annesley

*M*ary Anne heard the jangle of keys in the hall, a heavy tread – the determined step of someone going into battle – and shifted in her seat. It was time to give her daily orders to Mrs Hunt, the housekeeper – a formidable woman who both knew, and often spoke, her mind.

Mary Anne was the lady of the house and should expect the staff to treat her with deference, respect even. But word had got to her, despite Patrick's best efforts to shield her from the gossip, that some of the servants resented her new position. She came to dread each day in charge of the household and felt them watching her, hoping she would fail and prove them right.

With the phrase, 'the higher they climb, the further they fall' running through her mind, she clutched the chair arm. There was a firm rap on the door, and it swung open. Taking a deep breath, she greeted Mrs Hunt and so began her public day.

* * *

The family finally arrived back in England in July 1889 to take up permanent residence at Annesley Hall. Lina's memoir records only the baldest of details of this major event: *"Pat brought his wife and children from Norway and settled at Annesley."* Even the phrasing might be telling; it could have been warmer. Lina records Mary Anne's maiden name, states that she is three years younger than Patrick and that they had three children in Norway and three in England *"up to the present time"* (written in 1893). She gives no background on Mary Anne's origins, how they met and doesn't mention their marriage, whereas she goes into detail about the weddings of other family members.

We can only imagine the trepidation that Patrick but, especially Mary Anne, must have felt about returning to England. The locals may have heard whispers of the couple's recent uncelebrated marriage in a London registry office or at least questioned the reason for the heir's continued absence, 19 months after his father's death.

Mary Anne faces up to the servants

At least Patrick knew what awaited him in terms of his role. He had spent his young life walking in his father's footsteps, living at Annesley Hall and learning first-hand how to run the estate. Whereas not only did Mary Anne have to face a massive change of lifestyle and a daunting, unfamiliar role, but she is likely to have feared the reception she would receive from the servants at Annesley. The young female servants may well have been happy for Mary Anne. After all, she had achieved the status and wealth they perhaps dreamed of and read about in their 'Penny Dreadfuls'.

However, the 'upper ten' would almost certainly *not* be as welcoming. Mary Anne had left on a junior rung of the domestic ladder, only to return as the Squire's wife and mistress of them all. The well-established chain of domestic hierarchy was known to have encouraged rivalries and jealousies among servants. To help avoid this, talk of wages and bonuses was discouraged between servants. This new situation represented that very hierarchy overturned. Mary Anne would see how it might go. Being unable to express their disapproval, the upper ten might do so covertly, perhaps by failing to respond quickly to her instructions, and seeking to catch her out at every turn.

Mary Anne's discomfort at her new role might well have been increased by the fact that servants in large houses rarely, if ever, knocked before entering a room. Not only was it considered 'poor form' on the part of the employer but, more importantly, it was accepted that servants were of a level that nothing had to be hidden from them. She would therefore have to get used to the fact that the servants (her former colleagues and bosses) may have overheard much of what she said in the early days, just when she was at her most insecure.

Most people have a level of insecurity about themselves and how they measure up. Lack of self-worth can make you avoid risk and shun society, or it can spur you to take on the world and try to control it with an iron will, to prove others wrong. There are signs that Mary Anne wrestled with both sides of her nature daily.

Sensing her discomfort, we know that Lina looked out for her new daughter-in-law. PTA Musters comments that both Patrick and his mother:

Took trouble to give Polly [Mary Anne] an education to get her through life more easily and she, being a highly intelligent person, made good use of it.

Lina was known as a kind and down-to-earth person and is likely to have helped instruct Mary Anne in the many complexities of running a large household, including hiring, and managing staff, approving menus, setting budgets, controlling expenditure, entertaining guests, and overseeing the care and education of her children.

Mary Anne would have been aware of the enormity of the role. Handbooks, advice manuals and religious literature of the period exhorted women to maintain a well-ordered household, to be a

Photo of the staff at Annesley, c. 1910. The governess is seated in the centre in black, with the cook and housekeeper to her left. Vernon, the butler can just be seen at the back, his wing collar shirt and tie denoting his status. Photo courtesy of picturethepast.org.

helpmeet to their husbands and to minister assiduously to the needs of their family. It was also expected that the wife would shape the spiritual and moral authority of the family and, to a degree, its staff.

Annesley Hall employed about 30 house and estate servants in 1881, and it may well have been a similar number when Mary Anne first took over the running of the house in 1889. When a new lady of the house arrived, it was the tradition for the housekeeper to hand over a duplicate set of keys to the pantry, still room, silver room, cellar and so on, so that Mary Anne could check on the household's consumption and manage budgets. That large bunch of keys would be a daunting sight for Mary Anne. Many servants reported fearing the jangle of keys, expecting them to herald either the formidable housekeeper or possibly equally formidable lady of the house.

Lady of the Manor's Tasks

One element of Mary Anne's role would be overseeing staff management. New servants had to be shortlisted, interviewed, appointed, inducted, and managed day-to-day. The housekeeper would largely be responsible for this, except for hiring or firing the lady's maid and the nurse or nanny, which fell to the lady of the house. Agencies would be consulted, interviews set up and references required. Servants with allegiance to the Church of England were much preferred (we know the Chaworth-Musters were protestant) and they were expected to attend brief daily prayers led by the master of the house or the Butler, as well as the local church service each Sunday with the family.

Mary Anne would have to write out daily orders, choose menus, handle accounts, supervise the smooth running of the household in matters such as spring-cleaning, replacing linen, and stores etc. She was usually expected to check on provisioning; both the quantity and quality of food and beverages bought and used.

Stores were kept locked away and usually distributed once a week by the mistress or with her explicit permission. The lady of the house was expected to notice and query any excessive use of provisions, which would need to be accounted for by the cook or housekeeper. Often, any lack of confident leadership from the lady of the house would be exploited and could often lead to petty internal squabbles between senior servants – usually the butler, cook and housekeeper.

These duties meant that Mary Anne needed to quickly build a close and trusting relationship with the housekeeper and other key members of the upper ten. She may have been able to do this, in part by firing and hiring new staff – so she didn't have the embarrassment of her former role haunting her.

Managing the household budget would have been the most daunting part of Mary Anne's role and could be a source of tension between husbands and wives. During the period 1871-1901 female servants' wages rose by about 30%, partly due to competition from the manufacturing and retail sectors, and partly because The Education Act meant children stayed in school for longer. As a result, they entered service at a later age, and were paid higher wages.

We do know that finances were a concern for the family in 1888, as Patrick had to sell land and properties. To give an idea of household costs, the Harcourts in Oxfordshire (a similar landed family), had around 20 servants between 1883-90 and spent an average of £950 pa on servants' wages, board wages (cash in lieu of board/food), liveries and servants' travel. This excludes the significant cost of feeding any servants not receiving board wages, which for the live-in household staff, would be the majority. In today's money, this amounts to over £95,000 pa, excluding food, cleaning, furnishing, and heating costs.

At this point, Patrick and Mary Anne had around 20 indoor and outdoor servants, so their annual salary bill would be of much the same order. They may well also have taken several staff with them on their annual trips to Norway, thus increasing their travel bill.

It was quite common for wives to run into debt through the mismanagement of household accounts, with some resorting to selling their own jewellery to keep this fact from their husbands. Other ladies of the house kept a tight rein on budgets, insisting that all expenditures were approved by them prior to being incurred. Bills were queried and the debts run up with local tradesmen were monitored closely. Mary Anne would have to update tradesmen's accounts weekly by hand in a leather ledger. It is likely that coming from her humble background, combined with her and Patrick's early start of a simple married life, meant that Mary Anne was a careful and economical housewife.

Apart from keeping an eye on budgets, the lady of the house was expected to take a degree of responsibility for the moral wellbeing of her staff and had to be vigilant against pilfering, idleness, sexual impropriety, and staff entertaining visitors in their quarters. It was felt that standards needed to be maintained to reflect the social standing of the household. This, not surprisingly, put great pressure on the wife. Even when travelling and away, she had to write home and try to maintain order in the family home. Women new to this role often became anxious and ground down. The second Duchess of Marlborough, mistress of Blenheim Palace said, *"I married a house not a man."*[13] Although Blenheim was a much grander affair than Annesley Hall, we know from letters exchanged between Mary Anne and her married daughters, that she found managing the household and maintaining social appearances somewhat of a chore and a worry.

Raising a Family

Within a short time of their arrival at Annesley it would be painfully clear to Mary Anne that life with her family would change from the idyllic years spent in Norway. She and Patrick had four young children and more soon to follow, so one of her immediate concerns would be to recruit a nanny and suitable nursery staff.

Child rearing in landed Victorian families meant that children were handed over to a nanny at an early age, as mothers with active social lives and little experience didn't want to become overly involved. Mary Anne may have differed, at least early on, as she had close involvement in raising her first four children, but it is likely that the other pressures of her role meant that she would soon have to let her children be raised by others.

Some nannies were known to be unreasonably strict – even cruel – to their young charges, smacking them for little reason. If Mary Anne had witnessed this in her days as a nursery housemaid, it would have made it more likely that she took special interest in recruiting nursey staff with good references and might have appeared regularly in the nursery, unannounced, to check on the nanny's behaviour towards her children.

It was typical in Victorian landed gentry households for the children to spend little time with their parents, just brief visits downstairs at teatime, or on walks or family visits. Happily, most children loved their nanny, who brought stability and affection into

---

13. Pamela Horn, *Country House Society*.

their lives. The children's characteristic memories of their nannies are that they smelt of castor oil and cabbage and were often given to runic sayings. Nursery staff reported being sad when parted from the children in their care and the nanny often continued to be employed when their charges grew up and left home, continuing their interest in their lives, and later, those of the children's own families.

Children spent much of their time with servants – especially the nursery staff but also gardeners and gamekeepers. Anthony Packe, a Norfolk relative of the Chaworth-Musters, recalls the relationship he had as a child and young man with the butler, groom, and head gardener at Annesley Hall in the 1900s:

> *All were our friends and we used to have tea with them frequently in their own houses. Billy Beecroft [the Butler] was a special friend. He was a good cricketer and gave me my first bat – quality and spliced from one of his own...We used to go with Bill Tidy, the gamekeeper, to set traps and shoot rabbits on parts of the farm.*

It's likely that Patrick and Mary Anne ran a more relaxed, informal household, as that was their own experience, and their children display great affection for their parents in letters. The children shared many interests with the couple, including a love of nature, birdwatching, wildlife, and outdoors sports. Nonetheless, their parents followed tradition in that the boys were all sent away to Rugby School as boarders when quite young, whilst the girls were home tutored.

Holidays in Norway

Typically, during the school holidays, Victorians would send the nanny and nursery maid on holiday with the children (who often stayed with relatives for extended periods), whilst their parents stayed at home. However, this was not the case for Patrick and Mary Anne, as there are records of ongoing family trips to their house in Norway in the summer and to Patrick's brother George's house near the Norfolk coast from 1900 onwards. So, summer would be a busy time for Mary Anne, involving much decamping of luggage, sports equipment, pets – and maybe key servants – via carriages, train, and ship to either Norway or Norfolk.

*Salmon fishing on The Lågen river c. 1890.
Photo courtesy, Morten Harangen.*

The family would visit Surnadal for a month or more in the summer: a journey that was not to be taken lightly, as it involved a long steamship crossing. The steamships ran from the end of March to the end of September, limiting them to visits within that six-month period. The family would take a train from Annesley station to Nottingham and then onwards to Newcastle for the Bergen Steamship Company (BDS) sailings, which started in 1888.

There are occasional references in family letters to sailings from Hull to Bergen, but it is likely that this route was less used, as it was the main choice of the mass emigration of Norwegians to the USA, via the UK. These routes (monopolised by the Wilson Line) had an extremely poor reputation for the quality of accommodation, hygiene, and food on board, so the family is more likely to have chosen the Bergen Line.

The BDS company laid on a horse-drawn bus at Newcastle train station to transfer passengers to the port, although the large (and wealthy) Chaworth-Musters party may well have hired private carriages. The sailings were usually overnight, boarding at 9pm and arriving in Bergen in the early morning, two days later.

The family would then take a train (or several trains) to Surnadal (over 600 km away), a journey which would take around 14 hours nowadays, and longer in the 1890s. In total, this would be a significant journey, taking around four days, each way. In later years, Patrick and Mary Anne would be undertaking this with up to twelve family members, key staff (nanny and possibly the governess) and luggage for four to six weeks: a truly logistical feat for Mary Anne to organise!

Victorian married couples were often apart frequently and for extended periods. Both usually spent time visiting friends and relatives and travelled for business and holidays – abroad as well as in the UK. Husbands and wives did not expect one another – unlike today – to be the sole source of companionship or even intimacy. This was certainly the case with John and Lina, who spent many months apart each year in later years, but things may have been different for Patrick and Mary Anne. Initially, the circumstances of their first few years as a couple living abroad in a small household may have established a pattern whereby, they didn't seek to spend too much time apart.

History Repeating Itself?

The summer of 1889 was noted for disruption in Norway for the family. Not only did Patrick and Mary Anne finally make the permanent return to England but there was a potential scandal to deal with. There had been rumours (not necessarily at the time) of there being another family in Norway of Chaworth-Musters parentage. A video documentary about Vaulen produced in 2008 by amateur social historian, Eistein Bæverfjord, stated that Patrick fathered an illegitimate daughter whose mother worked in the family lodge.

As a family member told me, it could have been "a case of history repeating itself." Other family members felt this was not the case and I was told not to mention it if I met a great granddaughter of Patrick and Mary Anne. I have discovered (with the help of Maja Frønes) that the rumour of Patrick's second family was fortunately not true.

There was, however, a Chaworth-Musters illegitimate child. A girl called Brit Georgsdatter Røv was born on 8th August 1889 (and died on 30th August 1942). Her mother, Ane Nilsdatter Røv, was a servant in Patrick and Mary Anne's Vaulen household. However, Brit's father was not Patrick. A key clue is that the custom in Norway is for a girl's middle name to be that of the father, hence Georgsdatter, meaning literally, daughter of George.

Brit's grandson Jon Olav Ørsal, and his sister Dordi Ørsal Oterholm, confirmed this:

> *It is not likely that Patrick was the father of our grandmother Brit. The church book where the baptism of Brit is registered says that George Musters is the father... My aunt told me that she had visited the Musters. We have not had any contact with them after this, except my cousin met [a Chaworth-Musters family member] when they visited Vaulen some years ago.*

Lancelot George (Georgie) was Patrick's then unmarried younger brother. He regularly stayed in Norway with the family over the summer, hunting and fishing with his brother. Brit was born in August 1889, which meant that she was conceived in November/December 1888, when Patrick and Mary Anne were still living in Norway, having only recently moved from Arnes to the Vaulen house in Surnadal.

Brit was born in 1889, so George would have been 21 years' old when he fathered her. However, the outcome wasn't the same as for his brother Patrick's relationship and George didn't stand by Ane. He may have supported the mother and child financially, although there seems to have been little contact over the years, so possibly not. It is likely that Patrick would have made an initial financial provision for Ane, who would probably have left their employment. Perhaps Mary Anne encouraged the financial help, as she could so easily have found herself in the same life-changing position only six years before.

The family departed for England in June/July 1889 – earlier that year than normal, considering the steamships ran until the end of September. It's likely that this was deliberately timed to miss the birth of the child in August and thus avoid any potential embarrassment surrounding George's failure to stand by Brit's mother. Happily, Ane later went on to marry a local carpenter, Lars

Marjorie (Mabel) with Dick, their first child c. 1896

Pedersen, who raised the child as his own and the couple had ten more children.

Whatever the 'behind the scenes' machinations, George returned to the UK with Patrick and Mary Anne, and worked for Patrick as land agent on the Annesley estate. In due course, he met Mabel Watson, who was employed by Patrick as a governess for their four girls. She was called Marjorie in the house, as they already had a Mabel on the staff. Mabel was a teacher, as well as (according to PTA Musters) a *"confidante and much-loved friend"* to the girls.

She had been to art school in Nottingham and maybe helped Mary Anne in this respect, as Richard Toller, a modern-day descendant, reported that Mary Anne was considered artistic.

This time, it *was* a case of history repeating itself, as George fell in love (aged 25) with servant Mabel and married her on 3rd October 1893, living in Park Lodge on the estate. Marjorie (as she became known) was said to be: *"A wonderful character and everyone adored her."* They had two sons, Richard (Dick) and Roger, and one daughter (Joan) and moved to Norfolk around 1900, where Patrick and Mary Anne visited often in the summer.

George and Marjorie's home, Park Lodge

Roger, pictured leaning on the propeller of his plane

Both sons were pilots in the Royal Flying Corp (later the RAF). The youngest, Roger, was killed in 1917 in World War One (aged only 18) whilst the eldest, Richard, died in 1941 in World War Two, aged 46.

'Great and Good': The Couple Blossom

A hot, still summer Saturday and the lawns of Annesley look as if they've been invaded by exotic birds. Wide hats, plumed feathers bobbing, twirling parasols and full, frilled skirts throng the lawns. It is the annual garden party fund-raiser for the local Conservative party at Annesley, hosted by Patrick and Mary Anne with the 'great and good' of Nottinghamshire society in attendance.

The couple circulate separately, Patrick welcoming guests with his usual twinkling eyes and hearty bonhomie. Mary Anne mingles with a daughter in tow, receiving the plaudits from the ladies on the abundant flower beds, the delicious refreshments and her simple but elegant costume with a gentle nod of her plumed head.

* * *

Whilst Mary Anne's early years spent learning to become lady of the manor were undoubtedly stressful for her, she perhaps got more used to her role and only became anxious over very major events, such as their annual garden party or her daughters' weddings. Certainly, PTA Musters confirms her 'Grande Dame' status:

> *Close relatives back in England who were aware of the situation were interested to see how she, the one-time nursery housemaid, would cope with it all. To their surprise she did so extremely well, as far as we know, never once putting a foot wrong.*

Managing a Growing Staff

Much of Mary Anne's time would continue to be taken up with supervising the smooth running of the household and its staff.

The family was noted for its loyalty to long-standing staff, including a lady's maid; the housekeeper, Mrs Wright; and Alex Young, the farm bailiff.

In January 1899, Patrick and Mary Anne held a retirement party at Annesley Hall for Mr Young, to mark 44 years in service. They had previously given him a silver tea service to mark his fortieth-year anniversary and this time, Lina presented him with a portrait and a cheque for £60 (a retirement payment of around £6,000 in today's money) and Patrick made a speech thanking him for his loyal service to the family. One wonders why Lina made the presentation and not Mary Anne, who by now had been the lady of the house for ten years. Maybe this was due to Lina's seniority and the fact she had known Alex for longer. But possibly, Mary Anne may have preferred not to take centre stage, feeling uncomfortable at presenting to a man who would have been much her senior when she joined the staff in 1881.

The couple's family was growing fast, as revealed by the national census that took place at Annesley Hall in April 1891. By then the household comprised Patrick (31), Mary Anne (28), six children (aged from six years to five months), Patrick's mother Lina (49, who lived at Wiverton but may have been visiting that day or staying with them temporarily), his sister Catherine Emily (Kitty, 26), brother George (23, listed as land agent), and a military officer cousin on Lina's side, Penn Curzon Sherbrook (19). Penn may have been visiting or may have already lived there, as he married his older cousin Kitty two years later in 1893.

There is no mention of Lina's eldest daughter, Mary Catherine, so perhaps she was elsewhere at the time of the census. She never married and lived to the age of 82. Mary helped teach her younger cousins at Annesley, was vegetarian and considered to be somewhat eccentric. Nor is there any mention of Mabel Watson, who was employed as a Governess, who George would marry only two years later, but maybe she hadn't yet joined the household.

The household of twelve was served by eleven indoor servants (all women) and nine outdoor staff living in tied cottages, including retirees, Mrs Wright, and Alex Young. There are several interesting points to note about the composition of the household. Firstly, Patrick is employing roughly a third fewer servants than his parents did in 1881, for what was then a smaller household of only six people. This is a sign of the times (it was getting harder to recruit servants), but may also have been out of necessity, due to the financial constraints Patrick found himself under since 1887, when his father passed away.

Only two years after Mary Anne's arrival as lady of the house, the census also shows that all the servants (bar one) were different from those of 1881, when she joined the household. There are three new senior servants: Margaret Hunt (58), Eliza Andrews (53) and Annie Wilson (34) and it is likely given their ages, that they are the housekeeper, cook and nanny, although the census doesn't list their exact roles. This change of roster may be accounted for by natural turnover among the junior servants, but it is likely that the changes of the 'upper ten' were made by Mary Anne – perhaps a case of a 'new broom' sweeping away those connected with her past. The latter option is certainly appealing, from her point of view.

Mary Anne's Parents

The 1891 census also reveals a change in circumstances for Mary Anne's parents. George and Mary had moved to a nearby Bedfordshire village and were living at 6 Jubilee Terrace, Biggleswade – a modest but pleasant looking – two (possibly three) bedroom terraced Victorian house, with only two of their eight children. Minnie (aged 25) is listed as a dressmaker and son, Frank (aged 18) is a journeyman carpenter.

The main difference is that George is no longer working as a sawyer, nor his wife as a straw plaiter and, instead, he is now listed as 'living on own means'. He was aged 59, so may have retired but it is more likely that Patrick was making some provision for Mary Anne's family, which would spare them from an ongoing life of hard work for meagre return. Thinking back to 1883, only eight years earlier, when Mary Anne announced her unwed pregnancy, her parents must have felt huge relief that everything had turned out so well.

We don't know how diligently Mary Anne kept in touch with her own family, but it is unlikely that they would have come to stay at Annesley, as both sides would be keenly aware of the social divide that existed and might be uncomfortable. There is no mention of her relatives in any of the hundreds of surviving letters from her children. Instead, Mary Anne probably made one or two short trips each year by train (about 4 hours each way) from Annesley to Bedfordshire to visit her family, maybe taking one or two of her elder daughters with her.

An Expanding Family

Apart from managing the staff, Mary Anne would also be busy with her growing family. By the late 1880s, she had five children, each borne twelve to 18 months' apart. Patrick and Mary Anne's fifth child (and fourth daughter) was born in October 1889, three months after they arrived home at Annesley. She was named Catherine Lina but known as Lina, in honour of Patrick's mother, probably to thank her for her kind acceptance and support of their situation. On 14th October 1889, the couple had all five children baptised at Annesley church by the vicar, Reverend C Prance.

On 27th November 1890, their sixth child and second son, John Neville (known as Jack) was born at Annesley, followed 17 months later by their seventh child, Anthony (Tony), born on 3rd April 1892. Unusually, there was a three-year gap before Mary Anne gave birth to her eighth child and fourth son, Philip (Phil), on 9th April 1895.

A year later (returning to her former 'schedule'), she gave birth to her ninth child (and fifth son), Robert (Bob) on 24th July 1896. Two years later and Douglas, her tenth child (and sixth son), arrived on 2nd June 1898. Their eleventh child, and seventh son, James Lawrence (Jim), was born on 1st July 1901. Mary Anne was by now 38 and had been bearing children for 17 long years. Whether by design or not, this was to be her last child.

Good Works and Socialising

Apart from running the household, and attending to family, Mary Anne would be kept busy with church activities and good works. Landed families typically looked after their staff in a paternal manner and expected staunch loyalty in return. It was traditional to give Christmas gifts of logs, coals, hams, clothing and soup to outdoor servants and the estate poor, often accompanied by a visit from the 'lady of the manor'. Because of her background, Mary Anne may have well felt more comfortable with these visits to the cosy firesides of modest country cottages than those duties involving the local 'great and good'.

Mary Anne may have taken on the running of the Annesley clothing club from Lina, although possibly not, as we know Lina was a 'powerhouse' who liked to keep busy and didn't die until 1912. And with so many children and a large household to run, Mary Anne would have been very busy.

Similarly, Lina may have remained as the administrator of the family's charitable trust, founded in 1832 in Mary Ann Chaworth's name. This was an annuity that provided monthly sums to five or six 'deserving poor' in Annesley, with any remaining funds helping pay for those who were sick to be treated in hospital. We do know that Mary Anne was involved in the Thoroton Society, the local history group that Lina co-founded. She may also have been part of the local Women's Institute; local dignitaries' wives were often made President because of the likely patronage that would follow.

We know from newspaper reports of the time that she also ran charity bazaars in aid of the church and held fund-raising events for local political parties, supporting Patrick, who actively worked to promote a local Tory MP. Whatever Mary Anne's chosen good works, she would certainly be expected to know everyone in the village and to patronise the local shops.

A particular trial would have been continuing Lina's tradition of hosting formal dinner parties for local dignitaries. A typical dinner party menu in the 1880s could involve two soups, two fish dishes, followed by four entrees, including oysters and caviar. Next came the meat course – a huge roast of beef or mutton, plus a turkey. Halfway down the long table might sit a large dish with a variety of cold sliced meats – ducks, a ham or tongue or a beefsteak pie. The hostess' aim was that all guests' preferences was catered for.

Following this, sweet would be served, which often comprised a tower of spun sugar and pastry, filled with preserves. There could be two side dishes made in elaborate moulds, one a milk pudding, the other a vanilla or pink cream, or a wine jelly. Wines would be served throughout the meal, including dessert wines and punch. This lavish scale of entertaining continued until after Queen Victoria's death in 1901, when the trend for all things anti-Victorian meant dinner party menus were simpler and by 1910 or so, were much reduced in scale.

High society life would also include attending or giving balls. I didn't uncover any newspaper reports of balls given at Annesley once Patrick and Mary Anne were in charge, so it may be that the couple confined themselves to attending the few major events they felt was necessary in their position. As an example, on Saturday 19th November 1898, Mary Anne and her daughter attended the Welbeck County Ball, at Welbeck Abbey, home to the Duke of Portland. We don't know which daughter, but it was probably her eldest, Rita, who would have been 14 at the time.

Patrick is not listed as a guest, so her daughter probably stood in for him. The pair were among 1,100 guests who attended, including HRH The Duke and Duchess of Connaught (Prince Arthur, the Duke, was Queen Victoria's third son). This would have been a very grand affair. Leonard Jacks, in his 1881 portrait of the great houses in Nottinghamshire, reported Welbeck Abbey's likely ballroom thus:

> *The floor of this magnificent art gallery is of polished oak, and the inner portion of the roof, which is in the style of Westminster Hall, is painted to represent a glorious sky...The tall doors are wholly, and the walls partly, covered with looking-glass, which gives effect to what would make one of the finest banqueting halls in the kingdom. Four cut-glass chandeliers... are suspended in a line from the roof; from the hammer beams are twenty-eight smaller cut-glass chandeliers, and on the walls are fastened sixty-four cut-glass brackets or side lights. There are in all 2,000 gas lights in this grand apartment.*

Mary Anne, aged only 35 and originally from the other end of the social spectrum, must have had to contain her wonder at the spectacle, and perhaps find the social 'chit chat' required, with its emphasis on 'old money' and family connections, somewhat daunting.

There are records of the couple attending more family social events, than grand ones, which would have been less of a trial for her. As an example, on 19th September 1899, Patrick, Mary Anne, mother-in-law Lina, and brother George attended the wedding of Lieutenant Henry Graham Sherbrooke (relatives on Lina's side) to Florence Franklin, at Oxton – the Sherbrooke family seat. Wedding reports of society notables in newspapers of the day generally listed all the guests, together with the presents they gave the couple. In this instance, the paper lists Lina as giving a carbuncle ring (a red gemstone, probably ruby, considered the stone of love), whilst Patrick and Mary Anne gifted a miniature table.

On 14th June 1893, Patrick's sister Kitty married Penn Sherbrooke (her younger cousin) at Annesley. It is likely that Lina would have taken on the task of organising her daughter's wedding, but Mary Anne would also have been involved in the organisation for such a large event, described by the papers as *"one of the most fashionable weddings of the season."* The newspaper report went on to say that the Chaworth-Musters were *"well known, esteemed and highly respected by the inhabitants of the numerous villages."* Rita (nine), Elsie (eight) and Ruth (six) were bridesmaids, dressed in pink silk with wreaths of pink roses in their hair. As Kitty's father John was dead, she was given away by the heir – her brother, Patrick.

Patrick Runs the Business

Apart from socialising, Patrick would have been kept busy with the business of running the various family estates, and his directorship of the Annesley Colliery Company would have involved him in regular Board meetings. Patrick also continued to improve Annesley, having designs drawn up and an icehouse constructed and added an ornamental lake in the park.

However, Patrick was also aware of the family's financial precariousness and took steps to secure their future. In June 1889, he sold the Lordship of West Bridgford and the remaining estate lands to Colonel Horatio Davies. Alderman Davies became Lord Mayor of London in 1898 and lived in Kent, having made his money in land and commercial development in the City of London. It is worth noting that the Chaworth-Musters family hadn't used the Lordship title since inheriting it in 1827 and, once sold, they had no titles in the family. This perhaps speaks to the fact that they were down-to-earth people, with no wish to 'Lord it up' – either literally or metaphorically.

In 1890 Patrick strengthened the family finances further by selling his father's fishing lodge, Lysne Lodge in Sognefjord, Laerdal to a friend, Edwin Berkeley Portman, son of 1st Viscount Portman and a barrister and Liberal MP. The family no longer needed it, as widow Lina was becoming elderly, and the younger family had their own home in Surnadal. The Portman family kept the lodge largely as it was when purchased. PTA Musters states that a visitor, Mr Wade, described it in 1948 as like stepping into the 1890s:

> *There was even a complete set of silver with not a spoon or fork missing – all bearing the Musters crest. Rod Milward (Elsie's youngest son) confirms that in 1966 there were still pictures of Nottingham castle on the walls, and in the attic were children's cricket bats and*

tennis rackets which had remained there throughout the German occupation in World War Two.

In 1894, the family was listed in *County families of the United Kingdom; or Royal manual of the titled and untitled aristocracy of England, Wales, Scotland, and Ireland."* (known as Walford's County Families), showing that it was still clearly ranked as a leading family. However, their assets were fast dwindling. In 1896, Patrick sold Colwick Hall and its remaining estate to the Nottingham Racehorse Company.

PTA Musters said the sale was *"for reasons of sensible economy"* and Lina's memoir recorded that *"It was found impossible for him [Patrick] to keep Colwick and West Bridgford, so it was sold."* It is also possible that Patrick was advised to plan for the predicted increase in Death Duties tax, which arrived in 1894.

Armed with the proceeds of this sale, in 1896 Patrick bought their rented property at Vaulen, Norway – an old farm in the mountains in Surnadal. The farm had been occupied until 1717, after which it was used as a temporary pasture. The Muster House (as it is now known) sits on the east edge of the farm. According to the local history books, the formal owner was Mary Anne. It was quite unusual for women to own land or property at this time, even though the arrival of the Married Women's Property Act in the UK in 1883, enabled them to do so.

There are probably several reasons Patrick did this. In 1894 Liberal Chancellor, Sir William Harcourt increased the tax on land-based assets, so Patrick may well have purchased Vaulen in Mary Anne's name to lessen the death duties payable on his death. He may also have been trying to protect her. She had no family money of her own, so the house would give her an asset on his death. Another likely reason is more personal; her owning a property in Norway was symbolic of the start of their life together.

The family was listed in *The Kelly's Directory* of 1895, showing that Patrick was now a Justice of the Peace (JP). He also served as a magistrate and acted as a patron of the local church. The landed gentry very often took on such unpaid roles – both to give back to the community and to confirm authority, though their dominance was not what it was pre-1888, when local authorities were established.

Patrick also stood as a Parish Councillor in March 1896. His JP role probably arose as he had been a member of the Nottinghamshire

Standing Committee for some time, regularly attending meetings to discuss issues such as police pay and pensions. As a JP, he would have conducted arraignments in all local criminal cases and tried misdemeanours and minor offences in relation to local ordinances and bylaws.

Socially, although Patrick was a member of the (Conservative-affiliated) Carlton Club in London, and the County Club in Nottingham, he rarely visited them. His social life revolved around local hunting and country pursuits, with annual trips to Norway and Norfolk.

The Edwardian Family at Its Height

Queen Victoria's death on 22nd January 1901, heralded a turning point in social history, culture, and morals of the time. As significant local dignitaries, Patrick and Mary Anne would have observed the national mourning (including the wearing of black) that followed.

Her death ushered in the Edwardian era, with her eldest son, Prince Albert Edward becoming King Edward VII. Set against a backdrop of unrest in Africa, and the continuing Boer War, the era heralded great technological and social change. In 1901 alone, the first electric trams were introduced in major cities; the first permanent cinema opened in London; Alexandra Palace ('The People's Palace') was made free to the public for entertainment purposes; and the minimum working age for children was raised to ten years, with improved working conditions.

The Vaulen House Expands

In keeping with these changes, in 1901, Patrick built a new house on the Vaulen farmstead (photo overleaf) and installed a telephone, which was unusual for the locale. The house had about six bedrooms and though sizeable for the area, was still modest for such a large and wealthy family. Photos of the time show a simple wooden interior, stuffed with hunting trophies, furs and bird specimens. Surnadal is known for its great diversity in flora and fauna, and this was a major part of Patrick's motivation for spending time there. He was an educated ornithologist and a keen collector of birds' eggs and stuffed animals, a love that he passed, in particular, onto his youngest child, James (Jim).

Jim lived at Vaulen for many years from the 1920s onwards and inherited the house on Mary Anne's death in 1930. Vaulen has been owned by the municipality of Surnadal since 1978, and it is now possible to rent the house, which was modernised in 2002.

*The Vaulen house, restored in 2002-2004.
Photo courtesy of Astrid Meland.*

Jim Chaworth-Musters (on left of photo) outside Vaulen in the 1930s

Annesley Grows Too

Left to right; Ruth, Rita, Elsie and Lina in 1900

The 1901 census shows that the Annesley Hall household had once again grown to employ similar numbers as in the 1880s. It lists Patrick (41) and Mary Anne (38), together with seven of their ten children (three of the boys would have been away at boarding school). They now employed eleven live-in house servants, including a governess, and a further 20 house and estate servants: William Pettit (a retired gamekeeper), the housekeeper, butler, bailiff, five gardeners, a hall boy, a joiner, game keepers and grooms, all lived in estate cottages.

Patrick's brother George still lived in Park Lodge, acting as the estate's land agent. His wife Mabel was no longer the children's governess, and now had two children of her own. Shortly after this, George and Mabel moved near to the Norfolk coast, living in the six bedroomed Old Vicarage in Field Dalling, and their daughter Joan was born in 1907.

The Old Vicarage became open house in the First World War to many of the Nottinghamshire troops stationed nearby, who would ride over on Sundays for tea or supper. Patrick and Mary Anne, (and

Marsh House, Wells-next-the-Sea

Patrick's siblings Mary and Kitty) often visited George and Mabel in the summer. Nearly all of them had a passion for sailing and the men were attracted by wild fowl shooting and sea fishing.

Despite the house's six bedrooms, Patrick's sizeable family meant he had to rent Marsh House at Wells-next-the-sea (pictured above), about seven miles away from George. This eight-bedroom Georgian house, thought to have been run as a girl's school at the time, had an acre of grounds, a coach house, stables, paddock, and tennis court and became home to 20 or more Chaworth-Musters in the summer, who travelled from Nottingham to Wells by train.

The 1901 census also shows that Mary Anne's parents, George and Mary had again moved, and were living in Potton Road, Biggleswade in Bedfordshire. Both aged 69, they lived with their grand-daughter Agnes (whose mother may not have been at home at the time of the census). They are once again listed as 'living on own means', so were probably supported financially by Patrick. Sadly, for Mary Anne, her father George died later in 1901 – we don't know of what cause, but it is likely that Mary Anne made the trip home by train to attend the funeral.

To mark the event of their completed family (the final child having been born in 1901), Patrick commissioned a photograph of

Left to-right: Lina, Bob, Ruth, Jack, Rita, Patrick, Douglas, Mary Anne with Jim, Pat, Eliza, Tony, and Phil in 1902. Photo courtesy of Nordmøre Museum, Norway.

his brood. The photo, shot on a bright, chilly May day in 1902, was taken in front of the icehouse that Patrick had built, below the terraced garden, and is the only one that exists on public record of the whole family together.

Patrick stands at the back of the group, centre stage, hands thrust into the pockets of his tweed suit trousers, sporting a gold watch chain and Homburg hat – looking every inch the Edwardian country gent. Aged 42, he is still handsome, with twinkling eyes, though his beard is lighter, and he is clearly stockier than in his photo taken about 15 years' previously. He is flanked in front by his eldest daughter Rita (18) and wife Mary Anne (39).

Patrick 1902

Mary Anne cuts a slight figure – mostly hidden by baby Jim – with her sons and seated eldest daughters towering over her. She looks a little older, but still has dark brown wavy hair, tied back and is wearing small earrings. Her dark brown eyes seem watchful and her face solemn, lips tensed, with no hint of a smile. Overall, she seems somewhat careworn and resigned.

She is dressed conservatively in a plain, dark wool coat, with what looks like a massive fox fur stole (perhaps not surprising given Patrick's love of hunting). Her daughter, Rita, alone among the women, wears a fancy hat of the period. Mary Anne, in contrast, wears a simple straw boater, as do her other three daughters. The choice of hat is perhaps a reminder of her family's roots as straw plaiters. With her simple outfit and shy demeanour, she has the air more of the children's nanny or governess (which is what her original role may have led to), rather than the lady of the manor, which she had been for twelve years.

The three elder boys all wear their Rugby School caps. Mary Anne's youngest child, 10-month-old Jim, sits swaddled on her lap in a white bonnet and dress coat, with the family dog at her feet. The couple's children (ranging in age from ten months to 18) mostly look rather bored or cross, but that might be expected, as no doubt the photo took time to set up.

Another reason Patrick may have commissioned the photo – apart from marking the completion of their family – is that it also represents a high point in the couple's social standing. Patrick had served as a magistrate for Nottinghamshire for some time, but in 1902 he was appointed both as Deputy Lieutenant of Nottinghamshire, and High Sheriff. The former is a Crown appointment, representing the Lord Lieutenant in his or her absence, including at local ceremonies and official events.

The role of High Sherriff is largely ceremonial, and Patrick would have attended any Royal visits to the county, acting as the returning officer for parliamentary elections in the county, and announcing the accession of a new sovereign. Patrick considered these appointments as an honour, and he took his duties seriously.

Mixing with Royalty

The new roles were timely because, as a judicial appointee of the sovereign, it meant that Patrick and Mary Anne were invited to attend the Coronation of King Edward VII and Queen Alexandra on 26th June 1902, at Westminster Abbey.

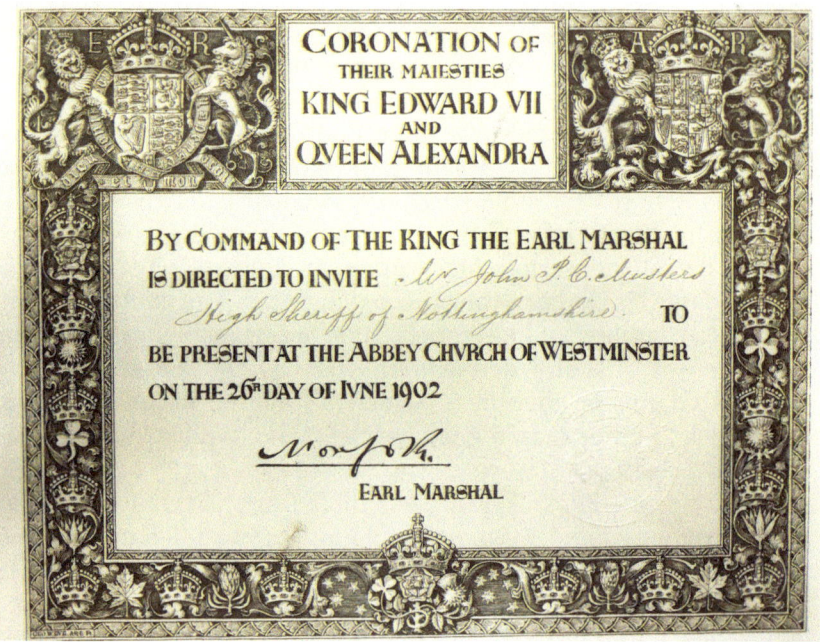

The family collection in Nottingham University's archives still contains the two large invitations, printed in black on stiff white card with handwritten names, *'Mr John P C Musters, High Sherriff of Nottinghamshire'* and Mary Anne's invitation, addressed to *'Mrs Patrick Musters'*.

Unhappily, Edward VII developed appendicitis two days before the event and was operated on, so the coronation was delayed until 9th August 1902. Over 30,000 men marched or lined the route, representing the British services and colonial, Dominion, and Indian forces. Patrick and Mary Anne would have found themselves among 8,000 guests at Westminster Abbey, including the prime ministers of the British Dominions, 31 rulers of the Indian princely states, and various Sultans.

Even on the day, the coronation didn't run entirely smoothly. The service was conducted by the elderly and infirm Archbishop of Canterbury, Frederick Temple, who died only a few months later. He had to be supported throughout the service and, unable to rise after kneeling, he was helped up by the King and several bishops. He placed the crown back-to-front on the King's head, and when a concerned colleague discreetly enquired after his well-being, he was told to *"go away!"* in a loud voice that was heard by the congregation.

The Speaker of the House of Commons.

Apart from these slight hiccups, the Coronation would have represented British pageantry at its best. High sheriffs customarily wear velvet Court Dress on formal occasions, and it is likely that Patrick did the same. He would have purchased his suit from one of several court tailors in London and the outfit followed a strict style: a velvet frockcoat with seven buttons, fastened edge-to-edge on the chest by a hook and eye.

In addition, Patrick would have worn a black silk flash or wig-bag, and lace frill and ruffles, along with a white satin or black silk waistcoat, velvet breeches, silk stockings, black patent leather shoes with steel buckles, a black silk or beaver hat, steel hilt sword and black scabbard, with white gloves. It would be a trial for him no doubt, being so far removed from the country tweeds he favoured.

Ladies were expected to wear smart fashions of the day, with a few deviations. Most noticeably, court dresses (regardless of style) were expected to have a sizeable train (usually separate from the dress) of a minimum of three metres long. The dress itself was expected to be long and somewhat low-cut.

The prescribed headwear was also distinctive: ostrich feathers (usually three) worn 'mounted as a Prince of Wales plume'. In addition, women wore a short veil, and/or lace lappets. This photo of Viscountess Hayashi, wife of Japan's minister to the UK, in 1902, is typical of the standard expected.

Sadly, there are no photos in the family collection of Patrick and Mary Anne in their coronation attire, but they must have looked splendid. As a couple with an informal, relatively simple lifestyle, the costumes and event itself must have seemed very grand. Picture the contrast between Mary Anne's conservative and simple outfit chosen for the family portrait only months before and the required court wear. Once again, she must have marvelled at her rise from junior nursery housemaid to mixing with UK and international Royalty in only 20 years. No doubt her family would have been immensely proud, even if she felt somewhat out of place.

Apart from attending the coronation, Patrick and Mary Anne – like many country house owners – probably held their own coronation celebrations, with parties for their servants and tenants. Typically, this involved an ox roasted whole, and a family supper party with friends in a marquee on the lawns, with fireworks afterwards.

Entertaining at Home

With Patrick's high-profile roles, his and Mary Anne's life may have involved several social duties, entertaining fellow dignitaries and the 'great and good' of Nottinghamshire. A large dinner party could easily comprise over 20 guests, and for these and their garden parties, extra staff may have been employed at Annesley to help, both behind the scenes and 'front of house'.

Although on a less lavish scale than in the 1880s, country house owners in the Edwardian era would be expected to host big dinner parties three or four times each year, and/or an annual ball. Apart from copious amounts of food and alcohol, good conversation was the staple for such evenings, occasionally rounded off by cards or billiards. Well-informed guests with wit and a good line in anecdotes were in great demand. From all accounts, Patrick was much liked and had a range of interests, so was likely to have been a good host.

The era was especially noted for house parties, involving shooting and hunting weekends that typically lasted three days. The hosts and staff had to provide elaborate meals (three each day, plus afternoon tea), clean linen, constantly replenished coal fires, and extra laundry, not just for the guests, but also any of the staff (a lady's maid or valet each), they brought with them.

It was like running a hotel and visitors would judge hosts and compare notes later. Although keen on hunting, there are no mentions of weekend parties in letters to and from their children, so it may well be that the couple did the bare minimum, preferring a simpler, home-based life, mixing mainly with their large family and those of Patrick's siblings.

The family archives record a flurry of correspondence between family members in 1909, notably between the Hamond's (Patrick's cousins in Norfolk), Patrick and Lina. All mention the *"scandalous book"* just published by Richard Edgcumbe, entitled *"Byron: The Last Phase"*. In it, the author claims that Byron had an affair with Mary Chaworth in 1808, when she was married, which resulted in a daughter, Madora Leigh, who was raised by Mary's mother as her own child.

There is no concrete evidence to support this, with the author drawing on Byron's writings to infer the facts. The family also claimed there was no registration of the child's birth. In a moving letter, almost illegibly handwritten by the nearly blind Lina (aged 67), she says: *"I have shingles in my eyes and can't see very well"* and she complained about the book. Family members discussed combining efforts and taking legal action against the author but didn't pursue the action.

Letter writing is a notable feature of the Chaworth-Musters family. As the couple's children grew and left home to go to boarding school or set up family homes of their own, they corresponded frequently. Letters were often long and detailed, linking relatives over great distances and containing minutiae of daily life, local news, and gossip.

It was often thought that letter writing was the province of women in the main but in Victorian and Edwardian times, fathers, brothers, and sons wrote profusely too. This was certainly the case with the Chaworth-Musters, as the extensive collection of letters from their children testifies, especially during the First World War. It is clear from the letters that both parents expressed great emotion towards their children and were not as aloof as parents of the time were thought to be.

Some insight into family life emerges from letters written to Mary Anne in spring 1910 by her second daughter Elsie (then 25), who was holidaying with her sister Ruth (23) in France. Mary Anne had clearly been ill, as Elsie writes: *"I do hope you are feeling alright again and are allowed to get up and do what you like."* Perhaps to amuse her bedridden mother, she relays a few stories: *"Ruth has been golfing a good deal with different young ladies. She gets rather bored with me as I don't go off golfing. I'm learning French."*

And, later in the trip she says: *"I went to church twice a day, every day, as Aunt Maisie did but I must say it was a relief when it was over!"* Elsie was probably referring to Aunt Mary, Patrick's eccentric spinster sister, who acted as chaperone on the trip.

On the same trip she writes of meeting King Edward VII, who visited a local golf course:

> *He stayed two and a half hours, played golf and croquet. There were not very many people, so he was treated like an ordinary person, except to being bobbed to as he went away. I kissed his little dog Caesar when no one was looking. He had 'Caesar – I belong to the King' written on a little medallion on his collar.*

Patrick's Mother Dies

In 1912, both Patrick and Mary Anne would have felt great sadness when his mother Lina died on 1st February, aged 70. A short announcement was published in The Times:

> *Mrs Chaworth-Musters, who had been in indifferent health for many weeks, died yesterday at Wiverton Hall, Notts.*

The epitaph on her memorial reads: *"She was a friend to many and always a friend when most wanted."* This touching phrase perhaps indicates how fond both Patrick and Mary Anne were of her, as we are told that Lina did her best to help Mary Anne grow into the role of 'Grande Dame'. The newspaper report continued:

> *Her remains were laid to rest in the little village churchyard at Tithby [close to Wiverton Hall] on Tuesday. At the express desire of the deceased, the body had been taken to Leicester for cremation, and the ashes, which were enclosed in a small earthenware casket, were conveyed direct to Tithby. The casket was placed, in accordance with the deceased lady's wishes, in a small grave in close proximity to the monument erected to the memory of her youngest son.*

Lina showed her independent spirit to the end, as cremation was unusual at the time (probably because of the Christian belief in resurrection) and had only been formally recognised in law as recently as 1902. Also, it is interesting that Lina chose to be buried with her son George, at Tithby, rather than with her husband at Langar.

Finances Are Stretched

At this point (and probably before, because of Lina's diminishing sight), Mary Anne must have taken over all of Lina's duties connected with the Thoroton Society. Only four months later, on 13th June 1912, the Society visited Annesley Hall. The report of the time stated that most of the visitors arrived by train and the family arranged horse drawn brakes (carriages) to collect them. It was a fine day and the gents in their top hats, with the ladies in hats of feathers and flowers: *"all looked like lords and ladies"*.

In the morning, the vicar of Annesley gave the visitors a talk on the local history, and they then visited the Hall and gardens. After lunch, the party went on to Felley Priory and other sites in the area. Local historian Frank Lyons stated:

> *One of the [Chaworth-Musters] sons was supervising the preparation of the cricket pitch for a match that weekend [this was probably the annual staff vs family*

match]. The sun glinted from a distant stretch of water. The clock chimed over the stables. The summer heat was reflected from the walls of the hall. All seemed secure beyond question.

However, this bucolic scene is a world away from what was happening elsewhere. RMS Titanic sunk in April 1912, with the loss of more than 1,500 lives; there was increasing labour unrest and a three-month National Coal Strike, followed by striking garment workers in London; and growing violence from suffragette attacks, culminating in Emily Davison's protest and her death – trampled by the King's horse on Derby Day in 1913. And almost exactly one year later, the Great War broke out.

Meanwhile, at Annesley, family life carried on, although Patrick no doubt realised that expenses needed to be further curbed in the wake of recent Government policy. In 1909 Lloyd George's Liberal Government introduced a 'People's budget', which was enacted in April 1910. It was controversial, being the first budget in British history with the expressed aim of redistributing wealth more equally among the (male) population. Lloyd George sought to undermine the power and possessions of the old, landed elite; his target made clear in a speech of his in October 1909:

A fully-equipped Duke costs as much to keep up as two Dreadnoughts; and Dukes are just as great a terror and they last longer.

Lloyd George's objective was primarily achieved by introducing higher rates of tax (including a 'supertax') on incomes above £2,000, £3,000, and £5,000 pa (equivalent to over £179,000, £270,000, and £448,000 pa respectively today). More controversially, the Budget also included a proposal for the introduction of complete land valuation and a 20% tax on increases in value (capital gain) when land changed hands.

Both measures would mean that families like the Chaworth-Musters, who were likely to have an income of over £4,000 pa from mining and their remaining estates, would face a much higher annual tax bill. In addition, the National Insurance Act came into force in 1911, meaning that employers had to pay towards sick pay cover for their employees and in 1917, after much debate, the Government also introduced a minimum wage for agricultural workers.

These measures would have meant that Patrick and Mary Anne were, once again, forced to reduce expenditure. In the 1911 census, the household comprises Patrick (51) and Mary Anne (48), plus all their daughters and Bob (14). The other boys would have been away at Boarding school – perhaps Bob was visiting or home ill at the time. Patrick's occupation is listed as "landowner, farmer, and colliery proprietor". The total servant numbers had reduced substantially from 31 in 1901 to only 14: nine, mostly junior, women in the house, with perhaps the older housemaid acting as *de facto* housekeeper. In addition, there were five servants listed in tied cottages: the butler, John Vernon, a hallboy, bailiff, chauffeur, and groom.

Another reason Patrick and Mary Anne might have been trying to curb their expenses, was knowing that three of their daughters were to be married within the next two years – a significant expense for any parents – but especially for those whose status meant they had to lay on a 'society wedding'.

Daughter Elsie Marries

First 'past the post' was their second daughter, Elsie, aged 27 (1885-1954), who married 27-year-old Gervase Gwynne Milward (1885-1968) of Sherwood, Nottinghamshire. The wedding took place on 30th April 1912 at All Saints Church, Annesley conducted by the

vicar, Reverend Kynaston and the couple travelled to London after the wedding breakfast, which was held at Annesley Hall.

From this photo (above) we can see that Elsie bears a resemblance to her mother – the same deep-set watchful eyes and thoughtful expression. She was generally considered the prettiest of the four daughters, whilst Gervase (photo above) is the epitome of the dashing Edwardian gentleman in looks and bearing, though slender and no taller than Elsie.

The papers reported that:

> Both contracting parties come from families well known in the county. The Milwards come from East Bridgford. The bride wore a superb dress of white satin with old lace trimming, having a Court train of figured crepe de chine, a bouquet of lilies and a veil of rare old family lace.

Elsie had three bridesmaids, all cousins, plus Gervase Milward's sister as maid of honour. They are pictured (below) on the steps leading to the lawns at Annesley. PTA Musters reports that Elsie was running First Aid classes for the young women of Annesley and Mary Anne issued invitations for them all to come to the

wedding, which was a kind and inclusive gesture for what would be classed a 'society' wedding. Denis Pearson[14] wrote in 1995 that one of the girls, Miss Clara Hunt, had kept her invitation in its envelope, together with the hymn sheet from the wedding, for over 80 years.

Gervase was a Lieutenant in the South Nottinghamshire Yeomanry and during the Great War, served as a Captain in the King's Royal Rifle Corps, as did his brothers-in-law Pat and Bob Chaworth-Musters. The couple lived at Field House, Tyringham, Newport Pagnell, where Elsie helped initially as land agent but ended up being paid full-time to run the estate (with the help of Mrs King), whilst Gervase served in the army. Mrs King was part-German and Elsie used her actual name of Konig in letters home.

The couple had two sons – Gervase (Gerry) Milward (1916-1985) and Herbert Roderick (Rod) Milward (1927-2012), born when Elsie was the advanced age of 42. Elsie was a great letter writer and took on the task (along with her mother) of keeping the family updated on everyone's news. PTA Musters reports that her brothers, particularly Phil, referred to her as the 'Family News Bureau'.

Apart from prolific letter writing, we know from her son Rod that his mother spent time in the Great War working in hospitals in Nottingham and Mansfield. Like the rest of her family, she was hard-working, with a strong sense of duty. Also, according to Rod, she was stubborn, like the other Musters. Elsie died on 15th October 1954, aged only 69 and Gervase in 1968, aged 83.

Patrick, 1902

Patrick, 1912

---

14. Denis Pearson, *Annesley through the ages.*

The newspaper has inset photos of Patrick (then 52) and Mary Anne (49). We can see that Patrick (photos above) has aged somewhat in the past ten years and is stouter with little hair but sports an impressive set of trimmed 'salt and pepper' whiskers and his usual twinkle about the eyes.

Mary Anne, 1902   *Mary Anne, 1912*

Mary Anne is still slender but has aged markedly since her fresh-faced appearance in the 1902 family photo, only ten years' before. However, she seems to have blossomed in another way and now looks every inch the 'Squire's lady', sporting a very dashing multi-feathered hat.

Daughter Rita Follows Suit

Just under a year later, on 10th April 1913, the couple's eldest daughter Rita (pictured below), aged 29 (1884-1954), married the 16 years' older John Joseph Baldwin Young, aged 45, (1868-1950).

Mr Young came from Kingerley Hall in Lincolnshire, where his father was a modest landowner and farmer. John was a solicitor in Mansfield, Nottingham. He had never been married and had lived mostly with his parents in Lincolnshire and latterly, in Handsworth, Yorkshire. He may have met Rita through a connection with her father who was a JP and Magistrate. John was Catholic, so the pair married at St Barnabas Cathedral in Nottingham, with the Bishop of Nottingham presiding, followed by a honeymoon in Scotland. The

Rita

John Young

Nottingham Journal didn't include photos but reported on the wedding, as follows:

> *The bride was gowned in silver brocaded ninon draped with Honiton lace. Her veil was of Limerick lace and was caught up with a wreath of myrtle. She wore an antique paste necklace, the gift of the bridegroom.*

Her seven bridesmaids included two of her younger sisters, Ruth and Lina, her cousin Joan, plus three of the groom's nieces, who all wore varying shades of pink and violet crepe de chine frocks and carried bouquets of violets. The newspaper reported that Mary Anne wore a royal blue gown, with a dark blue hat trimmed with pale blue feathers.

John Young was spared the Great War due to his age, and Rita told her mother she felt *"quite selfish"* having him at home when so many wives were losing their men to the war. Rita played her part in the war, working in a large Sheffield hospital, as well as writing copious letters to family members. When her parents were stranded in Norway at the outbreak of war, she wrote, offering to house and care for the younger members of the family until they could return home.

The couple moved to a village near Sheffield and John worked for a long-established Sheffield law firm, Wake & Sons, eventually moving to live in The Grange, Eckington, near Sheffield. They had four children in five years:

Patricia Mary Young (1914)
Michael Francis Young (1915)
Margaret Anne Young (1916)
Philip Mervyn Young (1919)

John became JP for Sheffield in 1935 and in 1939 was made Chamberlain of the Sword and Cloak to His Holiness the Pope (one of the highest orders conferred on Catholic laymen). He was a director of five colliery companies from 1933 to nationalisation in 1947. John died, aged 82, in 1950, followed by Rita in 1954, aged 70.

Another Daughter Weds

Even though war was looming, the greater threat to the country appeared to be civil unrest in Ireland. Life carried on much as before for the 'country set' and, as an example, on 14th April 1914 the Nottingham Journal reported that Patrick and Mary Anne *"and the Misses Musters"* had been among 1,200 guests attending the *"pre-eminent ball in the county"* at Welbeck Abbey, the seat of the Duke of Portland, which they had attended in earlier years. The Duke and Duchess held the ball to mark the coming of age of their heir, the Marquis of Titchfield.

Only a month before the outbreak of World War One, Patrick and Mary Anne had another lavish wedding to organise – that of their fourth daughter, 25-year-old Lina, (1889-1963) who married Hugh Lee Pattinson, 26, (1888-1915) on 2nd July 1914. The couple (right) are pictured at Annesley. Lina looks happy and her very dashing husband, Hugh, is smiling broadly.

Lina had seven bridesmaids and there were many guests at the

Back row: Gervase Milward. Jack. Tony. Pat. Bob. Phil. Douglas.
Front row: Jim. Elsie Milward. Patrick. Mary Ann. Lina Pattinson. 'Foulus Pattinson. Ruth. Rita Young. Baldwin Young

reception, which was held partly on the terraced lawns at Annesley. The photo above shows the immediate family members lined up in front of the icehouse (the scene of the family photo taken in 1902).

Looking closer, we see that Patrick (now aged 54) has lost most of his hair, which is now fully white, and is even stouter, with perhaps less of a twinkle than before. Mary Anne (aged 51) also looks stouter, with a matronly bosom, but her hair is still thick and dark, and she looks every inch the lady of the manor, in a layered, lace Edwardian dress and wearing the most extravagant taffeta hat among the family party.

Pictured (overleaf) is the married couple leaving in the family's chauffeured Daimler car for their honeymoon. As we know from letters, Mary Anne worried about these grand events and was generally glad when they were over. But only her close family knew this and would do their best to allay her fears.

Lina and Hugh had 'honeymoon babies', as their twin girls, Bridget and Primrose were born on 21st April 2015, just nine months and two weeks after the couple's wedding. They lived in various rented houses in 1914, whilst Hugh, who was in the army, was waiting to be sent to France.

On the very same day as the wedding (2nd July), the German military recommended that Kaiser Wilhelm II should order the attack on Serbia as quickly as possible. On 28th July, Austria-Hungary declared war on Serbia. Within days, Russia (Serbia's ally),

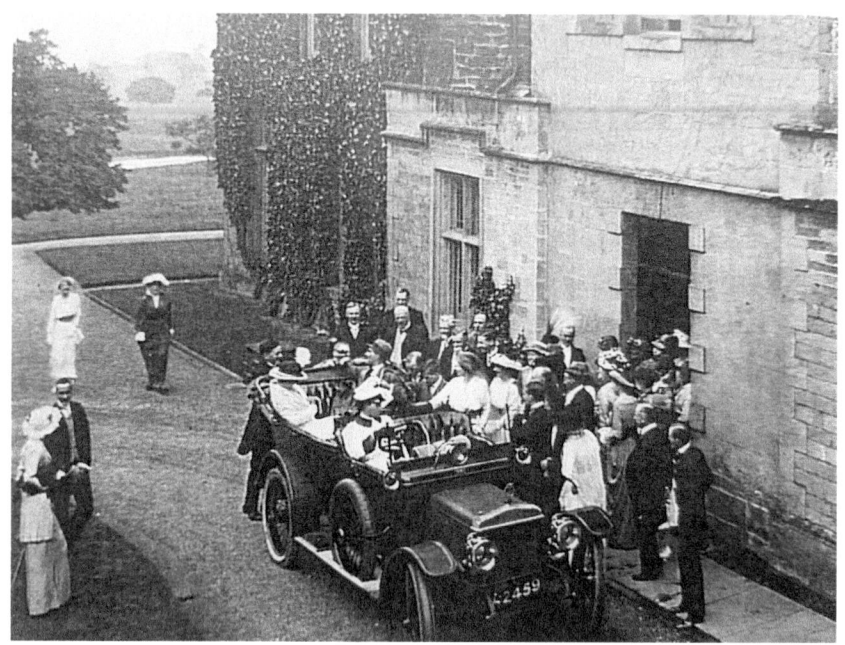

mobilised its forces, followed by France and Germany, and Germany declared war on Russia and France. On 4th August, Germany invaded neutral Belgium and Britain was forced to declare war on Germany. On the happy day of the wedding, Mary Anne wasn't to know this would be the last major party she would ever organise.

'Over by Christmas': War Breaks Out

Patrick and Mary Anne had only recently arrived at their house in Surnadal for the summer after Lina and High's wedding, when war was declared at 9.00am on 4th August 1914. PTA Musters writes that Rita, their eldest child, was 30 when war broke out and very *"aware that she was the responsible family member for overseeing her younger siblings during this time of emergency."* Of the couple's four daughters – Rita, Elsie, and Lina were married and Lina was still on her honeymoon.

Ruth (right) was touring in the Highlands of Scotland with her friend Violet Buck. Violet apparently wanted to remain there, whilst Ruth was *"dying to come south."* We know from letters that Ruth arrived back at Annesley by 17th August.

Lina and Hugh were due to join their parents in Norway on 6th August, sailing from Hull, but she wrote to Mary Anne on 4th August from London, to inform her of the disruption to travel and give her early views on the excitement of the war:

> *They stopped us sailing up the Solent in the usual way and sent us all around the Isle of Wight. It was rather exciting in St Malo – a great deal of the Marseillaise and 'God Save the King' and hand shaking and cheers. I am sorry for the poor women with all their people going off. I suppose it probably means very little to live on whilst they are away... I am very excited at being in the midst of it all.*

Patrick set about trying to get a passage home as soon as he could, though it would take some weeks. He wasn't to know that he would never again return to his beloved Norway.

Food Shortages and Price Rises

The outbreak of war resulted in disruption to supply chains and panic buying, causing shortages of food and fuel. Over the course of the war, inflation drove prices up. Average retail prices more than doubled between 1914-18 and most households had to reduce their expenditure as a result. *Country Life* magazine led the way in setting an example in August 1914, stating:

> *The rich ought to live more sparingly, so that they may not consume food that otherwise might be available for the poor. Let it be understood that indulgence and luxury is not only a foolishness but a crime.*

Landowners could cope with disruptions to food supply better than most, as they usually raised poultry and livestock, grew vegetables and fruit, and had access to rabbits and game. Milk from any cows they might own largely had to be sent to a local centre for distribution, but quite often they would keep back a cow to supply milk for their household. But imported goods like sugar and tea, and domestic goods like timber and fuel became scarcer as the war went on, as the latter were diverted to manufacturing. In 1917, Lady Cynthia Asquith[15] noted:

> *We are beginning to feel the pinch of war in material things...[these] last days each hostess's brow has been furrowed, mentally weighing meat, bread, and sugar.*

Whilst Patrick, Mary Anne and the staff at Annesley may have been buffered by food gleaned from their land, three of their daughters lived in London or the south of England and would have felt the shortages more. This is reflected in letters from Elsie in Newport Pagnall to Mary Anne in Norway. On 5th August she wrote to say:

---

15. Pamela Horn, *Country House Society*.

> *The beastly grocers have already put up prices on all old stocks. Poor Mrs Konig is absolutely in tears. Her mother lives four German miles from the Russian front in Silesia, so she can get no news of her. What she feels most is the terrible way Germany has behaved – she says they must have all gone mad. I don't suppose you will be able to get back from Norway – but you will, at any rate, have the consolation of not eating up the English food supply!*

Clearly Mary Anne replied in much the same vein, complaining of shortages locally in Norway, as Elsie wrote to her on 10th August, ending her letter with something to comfort her worried father:

> *I am much disturbed to hear you are short of meat. We are economising but have hopes it will not come to really short rations. Tell Papa not to worry – we are all right so far – as his children all have their heads screwed on better than other peoples' children!!*

On 17th August Elsie updated them on the family's whereabouts and hoped they would soon return to England. Thoughtful as ever, Mary Anne had clearly passed on kind thoughts to Mrs Konig, which Elsie thanked her for:

> *I daresay you will be able to get over any day now as the papers all report the North Sea clear. I've no idea where Pat and Tony are, except abroad. Ruth and Violet arrived at Annesley today I believe. Food prices have gone down again here. Mrs Konig is much more cheerful now. She was very pleased with your message.*

We know Patrick and Mary Anne finally arrived back in England by 1st September from a letter sent by Elsie that reached her mother at Annesley:

> *How are you getting on at Annesley? Pat's [her eldest brother] letter is his most interesting I have ever read [it was a rare uncensored one, delivered by hand]. There is no doubt Pat is a fine fellow!*

Son Jack Marries Quietly

Shortly after the couple returned from Norway, their second son John Neville (Jack) quietly married 18-year-old Daphne Wilberforce Bell on 19th September 1914 at Chelsea Registry office, London. Daphne was born in Ireland in 1895 and lived in Grafton, Yorkshire until 1911. I've found no mention of the wedding in family letters or newspaper cuttings, so I suspect that it happened quickly, as Jack was already in the army and knew he was likely to be posted abroad very soon.

PTA Musters reports that Jack had earlier brought Daphne to Annesley to introduce her to the family, but it seems that his sisters weren't too sure what to make of her. This is perhaps because Daphne was very young and unsure of herself, and the couple had not known each other for long. However, the family's doubts were unfounded, as Jack and Daphne went on to have a long and successful marriage.

The Gentry Lead the Recruitment Drives

War fever had already gripped the country, with optimistic predictions based on the British government's propaganda machine that with a 'big push' at the outset, it would all be over by Christmas. At the outbreak, the British Army was a small force of 247,000 soldiers, of which half were serving overseas in the British Empire.

It was supported by 224,000 recruits and 269,000 Territorials (the reservist force). Lord Kitchener, the newly appointed Secretary of State for War appealed for volunteers, using an advertisement that quickly developed into the famous poster campaign: 'Your country needs you'. The initial response was overwhelming, with over 1,186,000 volunteers enlisting in the first five months of war being declared.

The landed gentry with their long history of military service were at the forefront of the drive to sign up. Many (Patrick included) were linked to the county yeomanry and many of the first Army officers were drawn from their ranks. *Country Life* magazine appealed to all hunting men and polo players to *"join either the Army or the Territorial Forces"*. The major public schools and universities provided many new recruits, serving both as officers and in the ranks.

Many landowners encouraged their sons to join up if they had not already done so. The Earl of Derby (Lord Stanley) was a fervent example, stating[16] *"If I had twenty sons, I should be ashamed if every one of them did not go to the front when his time came."* The Chaworth-Musters did not need to coerce their sons to join up, as they were either already in the army or headed that way, all possessing a strong sense of duty to King and country.

Eldest son Patrick (Pat) was already a regular soldier, having been commissioned as Second Lieutenant in the King's Royal Rifles on 1st October 1907. Second son John Neville (Jack) had always intended to go into service and was educated at the Royal Naval College, Osborne, on the Isle of Wight. When war broke out, Jack got a commission into the South Notts Hussars. Third-born son, Anthony (Tony), was also already in the army. Having received his senior education at the Royal Military Academy in Woolwich, he was commissioned as Second Lieutenant, 71st Battery, in the Royal Field Artillery on 23rd December 1911.

Fourth son Philip (Phil) had only left school the summer before and had to wait six weeks to join the Army, as he was in Norway with his parents when war broke out. He had returned to England in mid-August but then fell ill. He was finally commissioned as a Second Lieutenant, 28th Brigade of the Royal Field Artillery on 16th September 1914.

Fifth son Robert (Bob) joined the South Notts Yeomanry straight from school in 1914, then once he reached 18, in July 1914, he was commissioned into the 12th Battalion King's Royal Rifle Corps. Sixth son Douglas was at school aged 16, when war broke out and joined the South Notts Yeomanry. He was commissioned into the Royal Field Artillery as soon as he could, aged 18, on 11th May 1916. Finally, James (Jim), the youngest, was only 13, and still at Rugby School, and so was fortunate to miss the Great War, although he did serve in WWII from 1940-1945.

Many landowners also encouraged (or bullied) their estate workers to sign up, and over 400,000 domestic servants entered the war. Again, the Earl of Derby set a leading example. A landowner and leading Conservative politician, he had been appointed as Director General of Recruiting for the war effort, and in a covert threat to his employees, he stated: *"When the war is over, I intend, as far as I possibly can to employ nobody except men who have taken their duty at the front."*

---

16. Pamela Horn, *Country House Society*.

The Earl of Wemyss[17] issued an ultimatum to all his employees in August 1914, to join the army or leave his service. Some, like the Duke of Bedford were milder and promised to pay half the weekly wages to the men's families who chose to serve, if they were away (this was on top of their forces salary).

Patrick Chaworth-Musters did not bully his workers and was known to have looked after them and others in the Annesley area. When Patrick died, Mr Bonner, a friend, and the Chairman of Petty Sessions, said he was told that:

> *Every man who served in the Army in the parish of which Mr Musters was a Squire was remembered weekly by a parcel from Annesley Hall whilst on service.*

Country Life ran campaigns aimed at shaming the rich into ensuring they did not employ any male servant who was fit to fight for their King and country. Adding to this, informal pressure was brought to bear by women handing out white feathers (a symbol of cowardice at the time) to men of serving age, if they were not seen in uniform.

However, the initial flood of volunteers stretched the army's ability to kit out and train them. The recruits were given a perfunctory medical examination, including registering their height and weight (which, initially, had to be least five feet six inches tall and with a chest measurement of 35 inches), and checking for any obvious defects in eyesight, teeth, and lungs.

A network of depots and camps was set up throughout the country to train them, including in the use of the .303 Lee Enfield rifle and bayonet. Many of these camps are referred to in letters from the Chaworth-Musters' children, including those in Woolwich (London), Aldershot (Hampshire), Bulford (Wiltshire), and Diss (Norfolk). Training was a shock to many, as Henry Williamson of the London Rifle Brigade[18] said:

> *During our training in Crowborough it was a month of great heat...We carried 60lb of ammunition, kit and our rifle. We got blisters, but we did about 15 or 26 miles a day, with ten minutes' halt every hour. We lay on our backs gasping; water bottles were drunk dry.*

---

17. Pamela Horn, *Country House Society*.
18. https://www.henrywilliamson.co.uk/.

Volunteer numbers fell sharply in 1915 after the dreadful slaughter was revealed in newspaper reports and letters home, and around 40% of the men who did come forward were unsuitable on health grounds. In May 1915, to bolster numbers, the army reduced its minimum height requirement to only five feet three inches and raised the age limit to 40 years of age. In October 1915, the 'Derby Scheme' (created by the Earl of Derby) was introduced, whereby men enlisted on the promise that they would only be called up if essential, and married men would only be called upon when all available single men had been enlisted.

However, as the war dragged on and casualties grew, by January 1916, there was compulsory enlistment of all unmarried men and childless widowers between the ages of 18 and 41. In desperation, in May 1916, compulsory enlistment was extended to married men between those ages and in April 1918, the upper age was raised to 50 (or to 56 if the need arose).

The Family Rallies Round

In the first weeks of the War, Patrick and Mary Anne were stranded in Norway and relied on letters from their daughters for news of their boys. On 10th August 1914, Rita wrote to Mary Anne and the early enthusiasm for war shines through in her comments about her younger brother Phil:

> *Dear Mother, I expect you are feeling very anxious and fussed about our boys and I am not able to tell you much in a wire... It is really a dreadful affair and I am afraid it is going to be a long one.*
>
> *Pat has written from Aldershot saying he was heading off to France or Belgium or 'I don't know where'. I am so distressed that Phil is not able to do anything [he was in Norway with his parents]. It will be such a pity for him. Bob and Douglas have joined the yeomanry as motorcycle dispatch riders.*

Her sister, Lina, wrote about the same time to Mary Anne telling her that Bob was with his motorcycle dispatch riders in Norfolk, their son-in-law Gervase (Elsie's husband) was with the British Expeditionary Force, and son Tony with the 41st 71st Battery, RFA, both in France. She added:

> *They are only allowed to write letters by printed post cards [many examples of which are in the family collection]. The papers are so heavily censored, however now a little is coming out as they have got the Expeditionary Force over successfully and they found the French papers were not censored and were publishing what they wanted. Food [price] is rather high, but everything is fairly as usual as they have published that all the sea is open and safe except around Belgium, France and Denmark and in the North Pacific.*

Lina wrote again to Mary Anne on 16th August to say that her husband, Hugh, was likely to become an instructor in musketry. She added: *"I am sorry Phil is ill. I expect he is at Annesley now and will find Ruth there."*

The Home Front

It was a chill, dull morning in October 1914 and Mary Anne, surrounded by yarns of dun-coloured wool, stretched her numbed fingers, stiff from constant knitting.

Looking at the low clouds, she shut her eyes, trying hard to picture her two sons and two sons-in-law in France. Their frequent letters were comforting, with stories of plentiful food, camaraderie and, sometimes, boredom from lack of action. But only two months into the war, other stories were filtering through of the mud, rats, food shortages and, worse, the appalling slaughter. In September, her eldest son Pat had made light of a wound to his chest from a sniper's bullet, which had taken him out of action for a blessed (to her) month.

The drawing room door swung open, and Patrick hastened to the side table where the day's post was usually laid out.

"It's 11 o' clock, surely the post should have arrived by now?"

Mary Anne watched Patrick pacing the room. He was anxious by nature but, with two sons in action and two more in training, he had every reason to be.

"I'm sure Vernon will bring it as soon as it arrives dear" she said, patting the sofa next to her. "Come and sit with me – I want your view on the Thoroton Society."

Patrick managed a weak smile and sat, just as Vernon entered, carrying a silver salver. Leaping up, Patrick grabbed the letters and quickly scanned each envelope before ripping one open. Reading rapidly, he moaned: "Dear God, Tony's injured!"

Mary Anne tensed but remained silent as her husband read aloud. The letter was from Tony's Commanding Officer, Major Scott. Her husband read, throat constricted: "I am very sorry to say that Tony is very seriously injured, with a shrapnel bullet through the head. His skull is fractured."

Mary Anne turned sharply to face the window. It had become her job to keep Patrick's spirits up, but at times like this, it took all she had. She dreaded this coming Christmas and thought it would be *impossible to wish goodwill to* all *men, especially those in the opposing trenches who were intent on harming her sons. Her dreams now were full of her precious boys being smashed by bullets, falling silently and unseen, amidst the tearing noise.*

* * *

War Work at Home

In August 1914, most unemployed women in Britain got to work – often as part of local sewing and knitting parties – making socks, scarves, gloves, waistcoats, and blankets for the troops. Millions of items were shipped to France. The women also volunteered in hundreds of supply depots, which served as collection and distribution centres for the donations of clothes, bandages, medicines, books, cigarettes, handkerchiefs, soap, and stationery.

Many wives and daughters of landed gentry got 'war fever' and were involved in Army recruitment drives, hosting afternoon concerts or teas to raise funds, and encourage local men to enlist. As the war progressed, some offered their homes as hospitals or convalescent homes for the wounded. And they set up local Red Cross branches, where volunteers rolled bandages, made swabs, or packed parcels for prisoners of war.

We know that Patrick was heavily involved in war work. Soon after he and Mary Anne returned from Norway, he was frequently seen driving his Daimler or Humber cars on Red Cross work — collecting or delivering parcels. Mary Anne's daughter Lina also played her part, assisting at a hospital in Folkestone in the early part of the war, before she had twin girls in April 1915, and her sister Rita also helped the Red Cross at the outbreak of war.

The British Red Cross and the Order of St John worked together in the UK to send out parcels to registered British and Empire prisoners in Prisoner of War camps. Each parcel weighed 10lb and prisoners could expect one every two weeks. They were greatly prized, as each one was like a mini-Christmas present and generally included:

- Three tins of beef
- 1/4 pound of tea
- 1/4 pound of cocoa
- Two pounds of biscuits
- Two tins of cheese or loaf goods

- One tin of dripping
- Two tins of milk
- Fifty cigarettes.

They contained enough food to keep two men going for approximately a week and for many, they made the difference between health and malnutrition. By the end of the war, the organisations had sent out almost 2.5 million parcels.

In addition, local groups sent 'comfort' parcels of food, clothing (socks, scarves, underpants) and games (cards and dominos) to troops in the trenches, usually to their local forces. Socks were usually stuffed with cigarettes, tobacco, a pipe, or peppermints in the toe. We know from reports that the Chaworth-Musters were involved in sending both Red Cross and comfort parcels.

It is likely that Mary Anne got the village clothing club and the WI involved in knitting and packing comfort parcels for troops. Newspaper articles at the time of Patrick's death reported that the couple were responsible for sending around 4,000 parcels from Annesley Hall to the trenches (which is an average of 20 each week for four years – a substantial effort for a small village). The sons also wrote that they met several men from local villages (such as Bulwell), who were serving in nearby trenches, many of whom thanked the family for the parcels they had received.

Apart from this war work, we know from letters home that Mary Anne and Patrick also welcomed family members for extended stays. Daughter Lina and her twin girls, and Jack's wife Daphne (with her baby daughter Audrey), stayed on several occasions for a month each time, for which Jack was grateful, stating that Daphne was *"rather depressed"* about things.

Food shortages at home became a serious problem as the war wound on, as it took men and horses (over 500,000 of which were requisitioned) away from farm work. To make matters worse, in 1917, Germany began a campaign of submarine warfare, targeting merchant shipping, which affected UK food imports. By Spring 1917, the situation was so dire, that the UK was estimated to have only around three weeks' supply of imported food left. Apart from foodstuffs, imports of nitrate fertilizers were hit, and the subsequent reduction in agricultural output forced up prices and resulted in food hoarding. To combat the shortages, people were encouraged to grow their own produce and keep livestock in their gardens, allotments, and other available areas of land.

One of the national campaigns encouraged housewives to make bread and cake using potato flour, as there was a shortage of imported wheat from USA and Canada. We know that the Chaworth-Musters did their bit. Phil wrote to his father on 6th April 1917 to say he was: *"All for you growing potatoes on the terrace, without cutting up the lawns which have taken years to grow."* However, as major landowners, the Chaworth-Musters would have been shielded from shortages to a large extent.

By 1918, the British were sending over 67 million lbs (30 million kg) of meat to the Western Front *each month* to feed troops, and malnutrition was becoming more common in poorer communities at home. To counteract this, the Government introduced compulsory rationing in London early in 1918 and extended it nationwide by the summer. Also, in 1918, The Local Parks Committee was asked to consider removing flower beds and growing vegetables in parks instead. This was in addition to the existing practice of growing potatoes on park land.

The family contributed however they could throughout the war and in 1921, The Hucknall Dispatch paid tribute:

> *As is well known, the Chaworth-Musters family played a noble part in the last war, and the family did excellent work towards providing comforts for the troops and prisoners of war. The Hall in the park was visited by groups of American airmen when located at Hucknall.*

The airmen referred to were based at Hucknall Aerodrome, which opened in 1916 as a training depot of the Royal Flying Corps (RFC). In 1918, various squadrons operated from the airfield, becoming absorbed into the Royal Air Force (RAF) when it was created on 1st April 1918. In August 1918, a detachment of the United States Army Air Service arrived and stayed for three months, engaged in aircraft and engine repairs. It would have been these airmen who visited Annesley Hall.

The Couple's Men at War

The following chapters cover each phase of the war, as experienced by the couple's sons and one son-in-law, including excerpts from letters sent by them to their parents and siblings. Soldiers tended to adopt a light tone when writing home, playing down the attacks and any injuries sustained and instead grumbling about the cold, mud, rations, and discomfort. Just in case the truth slipped out, it was the unit Officer's job to censure other rank's letters, a job they disliked doing. Reflections that were terrible and realistic were usually confined to private diaries (although writing these were a breach of military discipline if discovered).

The Chaworth-Musters boys' letters, whilst similar in tone and often using the cheery platitudes used by many officers and men at war, do reveal the individual characters of each man. The experiences of several of the brothers intertwined in the early days, so I am examining their stories but first we start with a brief pen portrait of each son and one son-in-law at war.

Patricius George Chaworth-Musters (1888-1915)

The couple's eldest son and heir Patricius (Pat) was born in Norway on 14th June 1888 and moved with his parents back to England in July 1889. He was educated at Rugby School from 1902 and Sandhurst. He was commissioned, aged 19, as Second Lieutenant, 1st Battalion, King's Royal Rifle Corps, on 9th October 1907. He saw service with the KRRC in Cairo, Egypt and on 1st June 1910, was promoted to Lieutenant.

Pat's letters to his parents generally portray a cheery character who is happy with his lot, grateful for small comforts and keen to play down any misery or danger. He reported on events in a matter-of-fact way in an almost illegible scrawl (like that of his brother Jack) but he wrote far fewer letters than his brothers, often sending field service postcards instead. This was probably because at the outset of the war, communication lines were not as established.

John Neville Chaworth-Musters (1890-1970), DSO, OBE

John (Jack), the couple's second son, was born at Annesley on 27th November 1890 and educated at Rugby School, Eton, and the Royal Naval College on the Isle of Wight.

When the War broke out, rather than join the Navy, Jack (then aged 24) got a commission in the Nottinghamshire Yeomanry, also known as the South Nottinghamshire Hussars. His regiment was initially based in Hungerford, then came under the control of the 2nd Mounted Division in September 1914 and moved to Diss in Norfolk for training.

Jack's letters display a resolute and generally positive nature throughout the war. He writes with great emotion about his brothers, shows concern for his parent's mental welfare and expresses the most affection of all the sons, except perhaps Douglas.

Anthony Chaworth-Musters (1892-1987)

Patrick and Mary Anne's third son, Anthony (Tony) was born at Annesley on 3rd April 1892 and educated at Rugby School, before spending two years at the Royal Military Academy, Woolwich, from 1910. He was commissioned as Second Lieutenant, 71st Battery, Royal Field Artillery on 23rd December 1911.

Tony's 71st Battery became part of the 36th Brigade RFA, which was mobilised at the outbreak of war on 4th August 1914 at Ewshot, Hampshire and was brought up to strength with reservists and drafts from other units. He saw action near his brother Pat, and they met up regularly in the early days of the war.

There are few letters (all very neatly written) from Tony but those mentioning him reveal him as a positive, cheery chap, down-to-earth and always thinking of others.

Philip Mundy Chaworth-Musters (1895-1917), MC

The couple's fourth son, Phil, was born at Annesley on 9th April 1895 and educated at Rugby School from 1909-1913. He comes across as the most characterful and colourful of all the sons. In 1910 his Housemaster, Mr S Bradby wrote twice to Mary Anne about Phil (then aged 15). Both letters reveal his character:

Anthony Chaworth-Musters

> *In some ways he is one of the most impulsive, reckless, light-hearted and irresponsible young men I have ever come across... yet for all this, there is a frankness and a something which I haven't been able to analyse, which are very attractive.*
>
> *There is a good deal of the stuff in him out of which principle is made – if only he can be made to be responsible. He will always be liable to do silly and reckless things but I don't think he will do bad things and even if he did, I shouldn't despair of him.*

When war broke out, Phil was in Norway with his parents. They stayed but he travelled from Bergen to Newcastle on 23rd August 1914. He went straight to the Royal Military Academy in Woolwich, where he chose to join the Royal Field Artillery, like his elder brother Tony. He then went home to Annesley to await orders and was reported as being ill for a spell.

His war letters show a sparky, irrepressible character. He was a prolific and untidy letter writer, generally incredibly happy to be

Philip Mundy Chaworth-Musters

at war, although after two years he becomes more outspoken and critical.

He comes across as the impulsive, light-hearted but likeable young lad his Housemaster described. Phil was referred to by Sir Henry Newbolt (a poet and historian, who in the war, became Controller of Telecommunications at the Foreign Office) as *"typically and lovably English"*. His sister Lina added: *"That quite well sums up his appeal to those who know him very well."*

Robert Chaworth-Musters (1896-1918), MC

Patrick and Mary Anne's fifth son, Robert (Bob) was born at Annesley on 24th July 1896 and was educated at Rugby School and Sandhurst Military Academy. Bob may not have enjoyed school life as much as his brothers, as he decided to leave in 1913 (aged 17) to go into banking, and went to work in Manchester for the company Wilson, Latham and Co. Mr Bradby, Bob's Housemaster, wrote to Mary Anne several times that year to persuade her to keep him in school for another year:

The headmaster said to me yesterday 'what a charming boy he is and what a pity he's leaving'... I should have much valued his quiet and wholesome influence in

the house. A boy of that kind, in that position, does so much to keep the general atmosphere sweet.

On the outbreak of war, Bob joined the South Notts. Hussars as a Private, acting as a despatch rider (aged 18) in the Motorcycle Scout Corps, based in Diss in Norfolk. His sister Elsie reported that Bob was upset at having to salute his brother Jack and brother-in-law Gervase, both recently commissioned officers! In February 1915 he chose a commission in the 12th Service Battalion, King's Royal Rifle Corps (like his eldest brother Pat) and, after training in Aldershot, he landed in Boulogne, France in July 1915, as part of the 60th Brigade in the 20th (Light) Division.

Like his housemaster's character assessment suggests, Bob's correspondence reveals a gentler soul, who is far less enthusiastic about the war than his 'gung-ho' brother Phil. Perhaps his father and eldest brother felt Bob needed 'toughening up' a little, as Pat wrote to his mother in December 1914, when Bob had been in training for three months to say:

I got a letter from Bob today; he already seems much more sensible. I think it has probably done him good. What does Father think?

Bob's prolific letters are neatly written, detailed and very atmospheric about the action he experiences. Despite his lack of enthusiasm for war, Bob stuck doggedly to his duty, with minimal complaint, suffering long-term ill-health caused by appalling conditions in the trenches over three gruelling years of war.

Douglas Chaworth-Musters (1898-1957), MC Bar

The couple's sixth son – and the final one to serve in the Great War – was Douglas, who was born at Annesley on 2nd June 1898. He was

Douglas Chaworth-Musters

educated, like all his brothers, at Rugby School and hoped to go into farming. But, with the war in full force in 1915, on leaving school he joined the Royal Military Academy at Woolwich and became a cadet. He was commissioned as a Second Lieutenant in the Royal Field Artillery (like his brothers Tony and Phil) on 10th May 1916.

He was fair-haired and blue-eyed, like his father, and, like his brothers, a very good-looking chap. Douglas' war letters are prolific, detailed and considered, showing much affection for his parents and siblings and with the best handwriting of all the sons – small and neat. They reveal a young man who appears very sensible, calm, compassionate and understated in manner.

Hugh Lee Pattinson (1888-1915)

I include son-in-law Hugh, as he was close to the family and died in the War. Hugh was born in Newcastle-upon-Tyne on 21st August 1888 and was educated at Rugby School (like most of his brothers-in-law, which is possibly how he came to know the family) and the Royal Military College, Sandhurst. He was nick-named Foulus by the Chaworth-Musters family but known as Tersh, short for Tertius by his own family.

Hugh was a serving officer when war broke out, having been commissioned as 2nd Lieutenant in the 3rd Battalion Royal Fusiliers on 6th February 1909, promoted to Lieutenant on 14th February 1914, Temporary Captain on 28th September 1914, and finally Captain on 9th March 1915.

He served overseas in South Africa, Mauritius, and India, returning to England on leave in May 1914, to marry Lina Chaworth-Musters, expecting to go onto India after that. The couple's honeymoon was cut short and in August 1914 he was posted to France as Adjutant to the 3rd Battalion, Royal Fusiliers, attached to the 9th (Service) Battalion, Northumberland Fusiliers.

James Lawrence Chaworth-Musters (1901-1948)

Although he was fortunately too young to take part in the Great War, we conclude this section on the couple's sons with mention of their youngest, James (Jim), who continued the family's duty to King and Country by serving in the Second World War.

Jim was born at Annesley on 1st July 1901, educated at Rugby School like his brothers but, unlike them, didn't join the services and instead read geography at Caius College, Cambridge University in 1920, before becoming an explorer. In the Second World War, like his Great Uncle George, Jim became a naval officer.

He was perhaps the greatest 'eccentric' among the couple's eleven children. Being the youngest, he had to go to bed well before most of his siblings, much to his annoyance, and PTA Musters reports that when very young, Jim would stomp upstairs complaining loudly, *"I assabolootely refuse to go to bed."*

1914: The Western Front Takes Shape

The couple's eldest son, Pat, was stationed at barracks in Aldershot when war broke out and wrote to his parents on 19th July 1914: *"This is quite a picnic at present. You need not get alarmed. I don't know if you are back from Norway yet."* They weren't.

He kept a diary that ran from 12th August to 2nd September 1914 which is in the family collection. Written in pencil, in a consistent style, he probably wrote it up (or transcribed it) during his convalescence from his first injury. It covers his departure from Farnborough via Southampton to begin active service with the King's Royal Rifles Corps in France. On 12th August 1914 he wrote to his father in sombre mood, clearly shocked by the desolation of the trenches in France:

> *I have got here to this most Godforsaken place. I've never seen anything like it. I don't know what will happen to me. I'm afraid the poor old first battalion has been almost wiped out. Another white flag affair [a surrender] from the reports.*

Tony's first war letter was to Mary Anne on 16th August 1914, as he was about to be sent to France. Thinking of his parent's concern, he writes poignantly and with foresight:

> *Don't you worry about us, we shall be alright and after all, there is no better way of giving one's life. So, don't get worried about us.*

Shortly afterwards, his 71st battery, Royal Field Artillery, was sent to France with the British Expeditionary Force, disembarking at Boulogne on 18th August 1914. Little is known about Tony's active service duty as there are no letters from this period, but as part of the Second Infantry Division, 36th Brigade, the 71st Battery War Diary shows he was immediately plunged into several serious battles, including the Battle of Mons on 23rd-24th August 1914. He was stationed five miles south of Mons and in the thick of it straight away. This is corroborated by Pat's presence at Mons at the time, when he states he's met up with Tony twice.

The Battle of Mons

The Battle of Mons was the first major action of the war, when the British Army attempted to hold the line of the Mons–Condé Canal against the advancing German 1st Army. Although the British fought well and inflicted disproportionate casualties on the larger German force, they eventually had to retreat.

Pat's battalion had marched through France, into Belgium, arriving at Givry on 23rd August, sleeping in shallow trenches and expecting to be attacked at any time, as the nearby Battle of Mons was scheduled.

The 71st Battery defend Landrecies.
Image: http://www.britishbattles.com/firstww/le-cateau/landrecies-1200.Patrickg.

He wrote that his battalion retreated through various villages over the next few days. On 25th August he rescued a British soldier in Bavai who had been shot in the foot and returned him to the line on a horse. Pat was fighting the next day, giving support to the Berkshire Regiment near Mervilles, followed by an *"awful night. Attacked and lay in the road for three hours in the cold."* He caught *"three ruffians who looked like spies and handed them over to the authorities"* and his battalion captured 20 retreating German soldiers.

Tony was stationed only a few miles away and was also having to retreat after Mons. His Number 1 Corps made it to the town of Landrecies. We know he was involved in a rear-guard battle, as he is mentioned in an account given by ex-Gunner E. W. Jackson,[19] of Nottingham, who served in Tony's Battery. Extracted from a diary he kept; Gunner Jackson describes the action vividly:

> *On Tuesday afternoon, August 25th, 1914... after marching throughout the previous night and all day... we bring our batteries to a halt in the streets of Landrecies... About 9 p.m. we retire to the barn to snatch a few hours' sleep.*
>
> *Half an hour elapses and our 'number one', Sergeant Kensit, comes rushing into the barn... the German Ninth Corps... had come up through the woods and had almost surrounded us in a surprise attack... We 'jump to it'; we gunners race to the guns and the drivers to the horses. The drivers are ordered to harness up and make preparations for a 'lightning' move.*
>
> *Rifle-fire could be heard, and pretty close, too. The 3rd Battalion Coldstream Guards had thrown barricades across the streets and were doing their best to hold up the enemy's advance. The order then came for Nos. 1 and 2 guns of each battery to stay behind, whilst the remaining twelve, four from each battery, make their getaway, if possible.*
>
> *Being attached to No. 1 gun of the 71st, I, of course, had to stay with the gun. Captain Cree volunteers to stay with us.*
>
> *Point Blank. Fuse nought, time shrapnel, load," barks out Captain Cree. "Fuse nought, time shrapnel, load," echoes Lieutenant Chaworth-Musters.*
>
> *Blimy [sic], Peter, this is _ _ _ healthy," murmurs my mate, 'Ding-dong' Bell. "Fuse nought'll burst any distance up to fifty yards after leaving the muzzle of the gun."*
>
> *Captain Cree walks over to us. He tells us that in the event of the great odds opposed to the Coldstreamers' breaking through, we are to fire the round in the breech, and then 'hang on' as long as possible with our rifles. Captain Cree then told us that he did not expect any of us would ever see England again. We suspected it ourselves... Speaking to us, not as officer to man, but as man to man, he said that although we might not have been in the habit of offering up a prayer since we were*

---

19. Jim Grundy, Small Town, Great War 1914-1918 Facebook page.

little children, he asked us as a request, not an order, to go down on our knees and ask the guidance of Almighty God in our desperate plight. We all did so.

The suspense was awful. One hundred yards or so in front of us the Guards are fighting hand-to-hand. Rifle fire, the clang of steel meeting steel as bayonet parries bayonet, comes plainly to our ears...

The street is red with stabbing flashes and blood. "Stand to, they're through," someone shouts. Our number one stands ready to give the order 'fire', but the order does not come. It is a false alarm. The Guards are still holding out. Now comes a fresh burst of rifle fire. Reinforcements are arriving. The German attack breaks down and we move off about 3 a.m.

... Early on Wednesday morning we came into touch with the rest of the 36th Brigade. Lieut. Colonel Hall told us that he was very pleased to see us, as we were really left behind as a sacrifice to save the remainder of the guns.[20]

This detailed account shows the extreme danger Tony was facing, so much so, that his Commanding Officer told them to pray and not expect to survive. Typically understated, there is no letter home from Tony to shed light on this danger or his probable fears at the time.

By 29th August, Pat had also retreated to safety, met up with his brother and was more cheerful:

I saw Tony yesterday – he is very fit apparently. I could give you lots of news, but I'm not allowed to. I am very flourishing at present.

The Battle of Villers Cottérêts – Pat is injured

Pat's next major action was soon to come, supporting the 4th (Guards) Brigade in the Battle of Villers Cottérêts on 1st September. The battle took place in the dense Forest of Retz and was a muddled affair, with German brigades firing on each other. Pat's Battalion was stationed at the edge of the forest.

It would have been a great shock for his parents when the next they heard of him was a letter from the Advance Base Post, to say

---

20. Nottingham Evening Post, 15th November 1934.

that he had been wounded. Pat had been kneeling, hoping to see a target, when he was hit in the chest by a stray German bullet (the Battalion war diary erroneously states he was wounded in the neck). He was taken by wagon to a temporary hospital at Betz, about 20 km away, where he was bandaged up and slept.

Lieutenant JBW Pennyman,[21] a machine-gun officer, was also shot in the chest in October 1914 and his account gives an idea of the difficulty of being treated at the front at this time:

> *Next thing I remember was a sensation like a blow from a cricket ball. It knocked me clean down and I remember shouting as I fell, bleeding profusely at the mouth... I was wounded at about 14.00 hours but couldn't be got back till 19.00 and came to as I was being treated... Evacuation was difficult and protracted: we travelled in spring-less lorries. I and four other officers were put in the ticket office [of the station] where we lay all night. Next morning... our stretchers were put into carriages. A stretcher is a very cold, hard thing to lie on for the best part of a week.*

Pat's experience was probably similar, as four days after being wounded, he had not yet been fully treated, and even ten days' later, his chest had still not been X-rayed. His letter of 5th September to Mary Anne seeks to reassure his anxious parents, although his postscript is very poignant.

> *You will have seen in the papers that I am slightly wounded. I got hit on 1st September by shrapnel in the chest. It must have been pretty well spent, as it doesn't hurt me at all. It has not been properly looked at yet, so I don't know if the bullet is still there or whether it bounced off. It is a most extraordinary thing that except when they put iodine on it to disinfect it, it doesn't hurt me in the least, not as much as if I had cut my finger.*
>
> *I saw Tony on 3rd. He has not been in action yet, I think [incorrect, as he had been, at Landrecies], and he is still going strong.*
>
> *PS: Don't worry about me because I was never fitter in my life.*

---

21. John Sadler & Rosie Serdiville, *Tommy at War*.

Pat added that he didn't know if they would keep him in the Advance hospital, send him to recover on the French coast or back to England. The newspapers Pat refers to were indeed seen by his parents, as the family collection contains a newspaper cutting of the event kept by Mary Anne, containing a quote from a Corporal who was with Pat when he was wounded:

> *He [Corporal Wilson] was particularly struck by the Officer's cheerfulness after being shot in the chest. Lieutenant Chaworth-Musters lay on an ambulance wagon and smilingly encouraged his men to go on.*

Pat's experience typifies the process for treating casualties at the time. If wounded, a soldier would pass down a series of care points: stretcher bearers would carry those who couldn't walk to the Regimental Aid Posts and once assessed, they would go to Dressing Stations, then Casualty Clearing Stations and finally to an Advance Base Hospital.

The most serious cases were sent to Britain by train and Red Cross hospital ship. There were also convalescent units in France (often private hospitals founded by aristocrats), which offered respite from the stress of trench life, with decent beds, hot food, baths, books, and games. Early in the war, troops usually stayed about ten days, after which they were assessed to see if they were fit to return to the trenches. This time shortened as the war ran on and men were in shorter supply.

Pat's diary states that he travelled by wagon and train to an Advance hospital in Le Mans for two days and then by train onto a convalescent hospital for a week's stay. He wrote to his mother five days later, on 10th September 1914 from there – Lady Dudley's (wife of the Australian Governor-General) private Australian Voluntary Hospital in St Nazaire.

Perhaps because he was out of immediate danger, Pat is uncharacteristically frank about the state of the fighting. He asked Mary Anne to send his letter round to the family members, saying it is probably the only one that would get through the censors – it did as it was hand delivered:

> *I am not coming to England as far as I can gather. I am going on quite alright. I am not considered bad enough. I am and was up to 1st September the only officer here in*

> the regiment. [This ties in with an account[22] of the Battle of Villers Cottérêts, which states that 20 officers from Pat's brigade were either killed or wounded in the fighting].
>
> The French are the people who are no good, as far as we can see they do nothing. Every time we have wanted to go for them [the Germans], the French have refused to join with us. The French are not great dashers. People who have been up against the German infantry, they are not great heroes and shoot very badly – but their artillery is wonderful.
>
> As regards my wound, I was kneeling on the edge of a wood trying to see something to shoot at when I was hit. Whether the bullet is in me or not I don't know as I cannot yet get X-rayed. I am in no way incapacitated. I walk about and everything in the usual way.

Mary Anne must have been disappointed that Pat seemingly wasn't coming back to England, but his condition was soon found to be more serious than he thought, as he was sent home on the SS Cestrian to Queen Alexandra's Military Hospital in Millbank, London, on 18th September. Eleven days letter, he wrote again to Mary Anne from Princess Henry of Battenberg's Hospital, in Mayfair, London, seeking, once again, to reassure her and urging her not to put herself out to visit him:

> The doctors tell me that that I shall probably be able to come home Thursday or Friday, so come tomorrow if you like. But it is not really worth getting tired all about nothing and spending a long time on the train because I am perfectly alright in every way... I'm going to be sent to Kitchener's army.

Kitchener's army was the largely volunteer force of around 500,000 men who were meant to be trained ready for active service by mid-1916. However, heavy British losses meant they were used before then, with their first major action being the Battle of Loos in September-October 1915. Pat was most probably sent to command a battalion as, although he was still relatively young at 27, he was an experienced officer, having served since 1907.

---

22. Britishbattles.com.

Pat was spared being involved in the Battle of the Marne from 7th-10th September, as he was in hospital recovering. Tony may well have been involved in this counterattack by Allied troops along the Marne River, which forced the German Army to retreat. Whilst the Allied victory ensured Germany had no hope of a quick victory in France, it led to four years of trench warfare stalemate on the Western Front.

The First Battle of Aisne – Tony is injured

We know that Tony was next sent into battle around the river Aisne, near Reims and was involved in the First Battle of Aisne between 12th-15th September 1914, which was the Allied follow-up offensive, as the Germans retreated after the Battle of the Marne. The Allied (mostly French) troops crossed the 100-foot-wide river Aisne at night, trying to make for a crest and plateau. The next day, bright morning sun and little ground cover meant they were mercilessly raked by German gunfire and had to dig trenches.

Trench warfare was new to both sides at this early point in the war and the Allied troops did not have entrenching tools, so had to scour nearby farms for make-shift implements. In time, they dug proper trenches about seven feet wide with camouflage and dug-outs braced with timber. However, this took time, and the Germans skilfully used shells, hand and rifle grenades, periscopes, and flares against the Allied troops, causing huge casualties in the Aisne battles (over 250,000 French and 13,000 British killed or wounded).

Tony was involved in this race to dig in by the Aisne. On 4th October he was guarding a gun position whilst digging parties worked on the trenches and was injured by a German shell.

Commanding Officer Lieutenant-Colonel Davies's diary records the event:[23]

> *October 4th – again some shelling at the same part of our trenches and A Company, who were holding it, had one killed and nine wounded [including Tony]. The Germans are now using high explosive shrapnel which, bursting fairly high, throws pieces backwards as well as forwards, and gets men although they may be well covered from the front.*

---

23. Steven Berridge, http://www.lightbobs.com/1914-the-battle-of-the-aisne.html#.

Only a month after hearing of Pat's injury, Patrick and Mary Anne received a letter on 6th October from the 71st Battery's commanding officer, Major CW Scott, saying that Tony had been injured two days before. He tries to be optimistic, although is clearly preparing them for the worst:

> *I am very sorry to say that he [Tony] is very seriously injured with a shrapnel bullet through the head. His skull is fractured. There is no reason whatsoever to despair of him. The doctor is a very clever surgeon. He is conscious but rather drowsy.*
>
> *I cannot tell you how sorry we all are about it. I have had Tony under me for eighteen months and would rather have lost anyone than him. He is one of the most cheery, gallant fellows I have ever met and was wounded in a most gallant action.*
>
> *He was in charge of an isolated gun which was shelled whilst men were digging a trench. Several were wounded. Tony went down the unfinished trench and found one wounded man and pulled him in. While attending to him, another shell was fired, wounding him. You have the sympathy of every soul in the brigade, for Tony with his cheery smile, was a great favourite.*

So, only two months into the war and Patrick and Mary Anne now had two sons injured, Tony critically, with a fractured skull and sight loss. It must have been an enormous shock and strain for them. Major Scott wrote again two days later (8th October 1914):

> *He is as well as can be expected. No unfavourable symptoms have shown themselves, he's quite conscious now. He takes an interest and his sight is coming back. The doctors say it will be a week before they can give any definite opinion.*

Mary Anne wrote to Major Scott's wife, thanking her for his letter. Mrs Scott replied, sympathising: *"I am very sorry for your anxiety; it is trying to be so far away and to know so little."*

The following day (9th October), Major Scott updated the family:

> *I am sorry to say that Tony was not so well yesterday afternoon. However, he improved towards the evening. He is quite sensible and can talk to one about ordinary things although he was a little drowsy and tired very quickly.*

Tony's younger brother Douglas showed the letters about Tony to Mr Bradby, his Housemaster at Rugby School, who had also taught Tony. Mr Bradby wrote to Mary Anne on 10th October expressing sympathy about both Pat and Tony being wounded and giving Douglas leave to go home mid-term to be with his parents at this anxious time:

> *It is comforting to think he [Tony] is being taken good care of and you must be proud of his bravery and courage... Certainly, the school will not be able to reproach the Chaworth-Musters with having failed their country in this hour of peril. I only wish all of us had been equally ready and willing.*

Daughter Lina, who was working in a hospital in Folkestone wrote to her mother about Tony on 17th October 1914. The letter is sympathetic but practical, and shows how life had to go on in wartime:

> *I am afraid he sounds most awfully bad and we shall have to expect the worst, which I make myself do but somehow, I feel he will be alright. He appears to be in very good hands and I only hope it won't be necessary to move him.*
>
> *I should think Tony would be a splendid person out there as he never grumbles and takes everything as it comes... I suppose the nurses would read his letters to him...*
>
> *Thanks for the partridges. Send picture papers, I'd be grateful for them for the hospital. I would pay the postage. I hope you are not worrying fearfully.*

Lina had guessed that both parents would be seriously worried about the situation. Tony was in hospital in France for a time, then shipped to Queen Alexandra's Military Hospital at Millbank, London. He stayed there until 11th November, when he was discharged to

Mrs Rupert Beckett's Hospital for Officers, also in London, to convalesce. Whilst recovering, he was promoted to Lieutenant, 71st Battery, RFA on 23rd December 1914.

Tony's health was assessed on 26th January 1915.[24] His wound was described as healed although leaving a depression two inches long, ½ inch wide and ½ inch deep. But it was noted that his visual depth of field was severely affected, which meant he could not serve as a gunnery officer and was classed as permanently unfit. He subsequently experienced headaches, vomiting and epileptic fits and did not serve on the Western Front again. The next we hear from him is in April 1915.

Meanwhile Pat was also in hospital in England. In total, he was given nearly two months' away from the Front to recover and visited his parents and young brother, Douglas, at Rugby school. Mr Bradby wrote to Mary Anne on 14th October:

> *Patrick came to visit. His brother [Douglas] is very proud of him always, and it seems such a little time, since he came here as a young boy. Now he is a good soldier and told us so many interesting things of the campaign in France.*

We know that Pat was recalled to active service on 25th November 1914. He wrote to his mother from the RAC Club in Pall Mall to say he was on leave for one night but was likely to be recalled soon. He left for France the next day and wrote to his father on 8th December:

> *We have got here at last and I have rejoined the battalion. I cannot tell you exactly where we are, but we are on the line where the BEF has been the whole time, only well in the rear. Phil's division I believe are in the trenches. Post arrives every day about 11.30 am and we feed very well.*

Brother Phil Arrives in France

This is the first mention in letters of their brother Phil. After being commissioned to 124th Battery, 28th Brigade, Royal Field

---

24. Trevor Torkington, https://ww1lives.com/lieutenant-anthony-chaworth-musters-survived-the-war.

Artillery in September, he was sent to Bulford training camp, near Salisbury. He wrote home on 2nd November, saying he was about to be sent to France and asking for supplies: *"Please send me mittens, woollen leggy things, riding breeches..."*

On 7th November he wrote again, saying he had arrived in Le Havre, France and reveals his 'gung-ho' spirit:

> *Don't know and can't say where I'm being sent. I am hugely elated to be going tomorrow. PS: I will avoid bullets as much as possible without funking I hope.*

On 11th November Phil reported: *"I am quite comfortable but very bored here, waiting for somebody to get knocked out so that I can get a job."* By 'knocked out', he means injured or wounded, which shows a degree of spirited self-interest! By 19th November, his Brigade had been moved to the Front in Belgium but would have just missed the First Battle of Ypres. Ever cheery, Phil wrote to say:

> *Arrived within eight miles of German lines. So far I have not come across any hardships of war and have been very comfortable and I am in excellent health.*

It's likely that eight miles from the Front, Phil was in decent billets, as reports from the front-line trenches in this area were very different. The weather had become much colder, with rain from mid-November and snow and heavy frost after that. Frostbite cases were common, and the physical strain increased for the troops, standing all day in trenches half-full of freezing water, falling asleep standing up and being sniped at from opposing trenches as little as 100 yards away.

The next day (20th November) Phil was promoted to Second Lieutenant and, perhaps because of this, he wrote to his mother asking for a massive list of things to be sent to him, including gloves, coats, mufflers and boots. He does have the grace to add: *"So sorry to bother you with all this."*

Phil often asked his parents for extensive supplies, but later letters reveal his purpose, saying that they are not just for him but for 200 men in his Battalion: *"I know it's a tall order."* He explains that they dish them out among the men by drawing lots, which shows that he was aware of his wealth and privilege and, like his parents, went out of his way to help others.

Meanwhile, Pat was back in France but also not seeing much action and he sent a series of field post cards in November, all saying the same: *"Nothing much doing, no news to report."* On 17th December he wrote separately to his parents about a local man, Private George Morley, who served alongside him in the King's Royal Rifles. He asked his mother to track the last known address for Mr Morley and write to say that he fell downstairs in his billets and fractured his skull. He states he is *"alive but in a bad way."* Sadly, he later had to ask his father to write a letter of condolence to Private Morley's wife, as the soldier had died, leaving six young children. The Hucknall Despatch newspaper later said of Pat:

> *He nobly took his share on the field of battle, and it was through him that news reached Hucknall of one of its earliest losses – Private George Worley, who was also in the King's Royal Rifles.*

By December, Phil had been moved up to the Front, and was involved in 'local operations', sniping and shelling nearby trenches, trying to disrupt the enemy and make small gains where possible. He wrote home on 13th December, and despite the hardships, his zeal still shines through:

> *I've only had one bad day so far... it rained, sleeted and hailed all day. We were shelled by shrapnel intermittently. The dug-out was full of water up to the seats and all my clothes were sopping wet.*
>
> *I was rather lucky not to be touched [injured] tonight as I was caught out once or twice but luckily we had no one hit. There is an awful lot of amusement to be got out of this fighting and I have really been very happy since I have been here. I think really we have a very easy time compared with infantry who are very uncomfortable and I expect in a very bad way now.*
>
> *I have come to the conclusion that the war will last at least a year from now. It seems to be all rot about the Germans being beaten. They are just as happy as ever as far as we can tell.*

His pleasure in fighting continued and on 18th December he wrote to reassure his parents:

> *Please do not worry about me at all during Christmas as I am leading a very happy, healthy outdoor life and really enjoying it very much. Of course we get shelled sometimes but the shells have a wonderful knack of keeping out of the way and are always a source of excitement when we get bored. The worst thing about this country is that you can never get a bath. I have not had one for nearly five weeks. However, I wash sometimes.*

The final remark echoes that of his sister regarding his personal hygiene – she had earlier commented on his *"usual soiled neck"*, when visiting him at school!

Their First Christmas in the Trenches

Christmas 1914 arrived – a date when many thought the war would be over. Princess Mary, 17-year-old daughter of King George V and Queen Mary led a public appeal to raise funds for the 'Sailors & Soldiers Christmas Fund', to ensure that every soldier, sailor and 1,500 nurses at war received a Christmas present. The gift was small brass tin, which held cigarettes, a pipe and pipe tobacco, a photograph of the Princess and a Christmas card printed with the King's handwriting: *'May God protect you and bring you home safe'*. For non-smokers there was a tin of sweets and some writing paper, and for the nurses, chocolates.

In total, they delivered 426,000 boxes, all arriving by Christmas – an amazing logistical feat. Nurse Evelyn Luard[25] movingly described handing out 25,000 of the tins on Boxing Day morning:

> *The men were frightfully pleased; it was so unexpected. The processions of hobbling, doubled-up, silent, muddy, sitting-up cases who pour out of the trains want something to cheer them up, as well as the lying-downs.*

Pat and Phil would have received the King's present but, also, being officers from a wealthy family, they had other gifts from their parents and would also order goods such as small primus stoves from the Army & Navy Stores and have them delivered to the Front. Pat wrote to his parents on 26th December, thanking them for their

---

25. John Sadler & Rosie Serdiville, *Tommy at War.*

letters and presents but asking for further practical supplies – a tablet of carbolic soap, torch and batteries, and underclothes. He clearly had a difficult Christmas:

> *We have just got back from four days in the trenches. It is a very bad form of amusement. We were in trenches about forty yards from the Germans, luckily so close to them that they could not shell us. I hate trenches as you cannot get any sleep. If you go to sleep, all the men do too.*
>
> *The Germans are absolute experts at sniping. They spend all the time shooting day and night. They waste tons of ammunition and do very little damage, which is a good thing.*

Trenches had dug outs, reserved only for officers, while other ranks had to scrape shelters or 'funk holes' in the sides of the trench and try to grab some sleep. Even with the dug-outs, sleep and comfort were clearly hard to come by. Harry Patch,[26] of the Cornwall Light Infantry confirms this:

> *Our living conditions were lousy, dirty and insanitary… There were rats as big as cats and if you had any leather equipment the damn things would gnaw at it. For four months in France I never had a bath, and I never had any clean clothes to put on.*

Trench life affected morale badly. So, after four days in the trench, troops were rewarded by three days in reserve (out of line) in billets. These were sometimes nearly as poor as the trenches but, being well behind the front line, less dangerous. Troops might have the chance of a hot bath, clean clothes, and a decent meal – although this wasn't guaranteed. Wages (a shilling a day for an infantryman), were paid on the first day in reserve and were generally spent on cigarettes, wine and, often, women.

Officers generally had a far better time in their billets. Phil was most likely in billets when he wrote on 27th December to say: *"I had a happy and comfortable Christmas. We are wallowing in food."* Pat's letter to Mary Anne on 28th December, after his miserable stint in the trenches, echoes Phil's:

---

26. Ibid.

> *The amount of food we get here is absolutely astounding. Luckily, we are billeted so we can eat and eat and eat. A German we captured told us they got cold pea soup once a day, poor wretches. We are all putting on weight frightfully as we get the minimum of exercise.*

However, for the men in the trenches, the food was dire. As veterans recalled:[27]

> *Mostly we had Fray Bentos corned beef and dog biscuits, as we used to call them [made by Huntley & Palmers] ... And there was Maconochie's stew maybe once a month [a fatty meat stew containing sliced turnips and carrots in a thin gravy]. We got bread sometimes – and water, and what they called tea for breakfast, lunch and supper. In reserve we used to get to sit down at a table, but the food was just the same as in the trenches.*

Soldiers often complained that their tea tasted either of vegetables or petrol, as it was carried to the front lines in cooking vats or old petrol cans. Food arrived in straw-lined boxes to try to retain the heat but it was always cold. Sometimes a group of soldiers managed to buy a small primus stove between them. When they could obtain the fuel, which was always in short supply, they could heat up their food and brew some tea.

Food for officers in the trenches was much the same as for the troops, although it would be supplemented by parcels from home and the Chaworth-Musters often mention parcels of cake and game. However, with access only to primus stoves (as requested, for example, by Phil) in trench dug-outs, it meant the best meals were had in billets.

---

27. John Sadler & Rosie Serdiville, *Tommy at War.*

1915: STALEMATE AND DESPAIR

At the beginning of January 1915, Phil wrote home to say that he couldn't get leave for three months, adding: *"I had a little fright today as a Little Willie landed about 50 yards over me, of course as it was going over me it sounded as if it was going to hit me."*

The Little Willie was the first prototype British tank, which became the Mark I, though it was still affectionately known by its protype name. However, from Phil's description it sounds like he was talking about a shell, rather than a tank, so it must have been a misnomer on his part, as armoured tanks were not used by the British until mid-September 1916.

Their brother Jack, meanwhile, was still training in Norfolk, with time to shoot game. On 2nd January, he wrote asking Mary Anne to *"Ask Father to send my gun and 100 cartridges."*

Pat Gravely Wounded

Pat wrote to his mother on 5th January and seemed cheery:

> *I am quite alright in the trenches now. I wear gum boots and waterproof trousers; it is most successful... We do 24 hours in and 24 out. We are up against a very medium lot of 'Boches' here. They are not half the fellows we were against before.*

The terrible irony of Pat making light of the *"very medium"* enemy soon became clear when a telegram arrived at Annesley on 8th January from his Commanding Officer, Lt Colonel WS Knox Gore of the 59th Division:

> *Pat wounded. It was such rotten bad luck; one of our own Lyddite shells dropping short, burst in a dug-out where Pat and others were this evening. One killed and*

two wounded. There is, I believe, no danger about Pat's wounds, but he is hit in the side (not very deep), on the side of the head and in the arm (about the right elbow). The last is the most serious.

He was most awfully plucky about it all as the pain must have been, I'm afraid, bad and was talking quite cheerfully all the time. Sickening luck. He had been so pleased with himself when he came out of the trenches last time and said that he enjoyed sniping at Germans much more than partridge shooting!

The Battalion diary records the following for 8th January:[28]

About 3.45pm one of our own Lyddite shells unfortunately dropped into 'C' Co's trenches killing Captain F C Norbury and wounding badly Lieutenant P G Chaworth-Musters and 2nd Lieutenant B F Whiteley.

So, Pat's earlier attempt to reassure his parents was to no avail and, ironically, he had been injured by 'friendly fire' in an incident at La Bassée. Pat's upbeat character shines through in Knox Gore's telegram – not only had he acted *"cheerfully"* throughout but his comment about sniping vs partridge shooting is classically Pat. One can only imagine the worry the couple faced over the next few days, as they waited for further news.

Mary Anne displayed her anxiety by immediately writing to ask Phil not to be too foolhardy or gung-ho. He replied on 12th January and shows his cheeky, irrepressible side when talking about taunting the pious new Lieutenant:

I must say your letter worried me a good deal as my physical courage is in my own humble opinion about the only asset I have as an officer worth two ha'pennies.

I am well and pretty happy, though I am bored that we have got nothing to do. I have not yet seen one of these Germans, which is rather feeble, if we do not get a move on before long I shall go blind with old age and never see one at all.

---

28. Trevor Torkington, https://ww1lives.com/lieutenant-patricius-george-chaworth-musters26-died-of-wounds.

> *We have a new subaltern...very pious and religious. I raise grand discussions with him by pretending I am on the point of becoming a R. Catholic! He rises every time, much to my joy.*

Meanwhile, unknown to Phil when he wrote that letter, his parents had received worse news about Pat. The divisional Chaplain wrote from the No.1 Casualty Clearing Station in Bethune on 10th January, which arrived on 11th, to say that Pat:

> *Has been severely wounded and the doctors fear that blood poisoning is or may be the result and it is a matter of life and death, but the only hope is the amputation of the right arm. Pat readily consented and wounds do not pain him at all.*

He added a PS later that day before posting: *"Your son has done very well. The amputation was successful, and he feels better today."*

Patrick and Mary Anne must have felt desperate and confused but still hopeful, as within two days and two letters, Pat had gone from being in *"no danger"*, to a position of *"life and death"*, then to doing *"very well"*. The next day (12th January), the couple received a further letter from the Chaplain informing them, with deep regret, that their son had died of Sepsis from his wounds late at night on January 11th, 1915. He was to be buried in a war grave in nearby Bethune. A later letter from Sister Caven who nursed him, placed his death at 12.40am on January 12th. This may be true, but his death is officially recorded as being on 11th January. The chaplain added:

> *He told me how dreadfully you would all feel his death if he did not survive and he did not wish his brother [mentioned as a gunner, so it was Phil] to be saddened by coming to visit him.*

The Battalion's diary of 12th January records:[29]

> *A very quiet day both as regards shelling and sniping. We were very sorry to hear during the morning that Lt Chaworth Musters had died of wounds in Bethune.*

---

29. Ibid.

The Family Mourns

So, only five months into the war and their first-born boy had been killed; just one of many thousands who had already died. Still training in England, Jack was shocked to receive news of his elder brother's death. Apart from the sadness, he would realise that he was now the heir to the family estate – if he survived. He wrote a heartfelt letter to his mother on 14th January 1915, which expressed concerns for his father's mental welfare:

> *It was a most awful shock to get your telegram today... I am most awfully sorry about Pat and I am sure both you and father are pretty cut up about it. I wish I could cheer you up a bit. It is rotten luck after having escaped once.*
>
> *When I got your wire today, I felt that if I had a German of any sort near enough, I should slay him in cold blood without the least confrontation. Somehow it made me feel it was a much more personal matter now.*
>
> *Try to keep Father from getting too depressed if you can. I know you will find it hard as you will feel it as much yourself, if not worse. I'm afraid I can't write what I feel but I think you will know.*
>
> *With all of my sympathy.*
> *Your loving son Jack.*

His separate letter to his father on the same day was shorter but in the same vein:

> *It was awful about poor Pat and does seem such rotten luck. I expect you are all very miserable at home and it makes me feel very sick when I think about it. I can't get leave for a week or so but I will put in for it after that.*

Strangely, news was slower to travel the very few miles in France from where Pat had been to where Phil was stationed, and by 17th January he had only just heard that Pat had been injured but not yet that he had died. He wrote to his mother:

> *I am most awfully sorry of course to get such bad news about Pat. I will ask [pray] for him now. If it were*

> *not for disasters like Pat's I should not mind being at war all my life. I think it must be worse for the people at home than for us.*

The next day, now having heard of Pat's death, Phil wrote again. His letter is matter of fact, and accepting of the war and its consequences, though somewhat over-optimistic that his parents would remain cheerful:

> *I have just had the news that poor old Pat has died. I wish it had been one of us younger ones but still I suppose it is all for the best in the end. I was afraid he was dead as soon as I got the first letter and I felt it at once. I think we must draw consolation from the fact that he died in the best way anyone can die, fighting for his country.*
>
> *I am quite well here...I am sorry I could not see Pat in hospital. Rita tells me they tried to find me but of course this is no time for that sort of thing and I am sure that P would rather have had me working [this was true, Pat hadn't wanted Phil to visit]. I shall be back in a few days and I hope I shall find you and father both well and cheerful.*

Letters saved by Mary Anne show the true picture of Pat's death. One arrived from a friend he was with at the time: *"[Pat] was perfectly conscious and wonderfully brave, though in great pain."* He collected all Pat's personal effects and sent them on to his parents.

Mary Anne received a series of letters from two ward Sisters who nursed Pat at the Casualty Clearing Station. The first was from Mrs Caulfield, a sister who spent the most time with him. She reported that Pat arrived at 9pm on 9th January, they got him into a comfortable bed, with plenty of hot water bottles and his condition began to improve. After the operation to remove his right arm, stoic Pat told her:

> *Do you know, I think it was the happiest moment in my life when I got into the operating theatre and I knew that I was going to have my arm off. I felt I should get alright then and the loss of the arm didn't worry me in the least.*

John Singer Sargent's painting of No 41, Casualty Clearing Station, 1917, courtesy of IWM, London. © IWM (Art. IWM ART 1611)[30]

Mrs Caulfield added:

> *He was always plucky, cheery, grateful, thoughtful of others around him, unselfish, brave and hopeful to the last. How proud you must be to be the mother of such a son!*

Sister Watkins wrote saying that he was nursed in a ward with other officers he knew and described his passing, which must have been very moving for his parents to read:

> *He died peacefully. He was conscious to the last and his breathing was shallower. He said that he had no pain. He got so thirsty at the last. I kept making him drinks of orange juice, which he liked so much. He said, 'Thank you Sister, beautifully made.' The Chaplain and I stayed with him until the end. He took everything very philosophically and the last thing he said to me was 'This is a queer go isn't it Sister?'*

---

30. https://www.iwm.org.uk/collections/item/object/23728.

There was an exchange of letters between Mary Anne and Sister Watkins, with Mary Anne thanking the nurse for her hard work and kindness to those in her care.

Meanwhile, in the immediate aftermath of Pat's death, the Chaplain had been busy. He arranged Pat's funeral, with a coffin and cross of wood in Bethune town cemetery. He sent photos of Pat's grave (see below); fresh earth mounded up in the foreground, with three stark white crosses outlined against a dark sky. He added an arrow pointing to Pat's grave, attached a hand-drawn sketch to show its exact position in the cemetery (which was among the French fallen) and included a letter of sympathy in French to Patrick from the Mayor of Bethune.

Pat's original grave in Bethune cemetery, which was later replaced with a permanent headstone (right) by the War Graves Commission

Patrick received a moving letter from Pat's Colonel, Edward Northey, which, despite using the usual stock phrases, took time to explain how he had lost his only brother at Ypres, had been wounded himself and his father had died of shock from the war:

> *I was so terribly shocked and grieved at your boy's death. He is one of the best officers that I have lost in the last few days... of them all, one of the best and dearest was your son – I cannot tell you how brave and splendid he has been all through. He had done wonders in making a good Company out of new and nearly raw material: he*

> *was popular with us all and beloved by his men ...He was gallant and splendid and died a soldier's death.*

Although the Colonel's letter reads like many others written at the time, Patrick and Mary Anne no doubt found some comfort in reading it. They received a stream of condolence letters from family and friends. These excerpts are typical. Penn Sherbrooke, Patrick's brother-in-law, wrote to him on 14th January:

> *I know quite well what the blow will be to you and Pollie [Mary Anne's name from her service days] in losing an ideal son in every way...the loss of one of those men whom England can least spare at any time, let alone now.*

His wife Kitty (Patrick's sister), wrote to Mary Anne: *"I always thought so much of him."* It is interesting that these close family members both call her Polly and perhaps that was how she was known informally to close friends – the name given to her when she arrived at Annesley as a servant may have stuck throughout her life.

Putting on a Brave Face

Following Pat's death, the couple were kept busy with various tasks – informing family and friends of the news, arranging receipt of his personal effects, ordering a permanent headstone, and writing letters of thanks to the hospital staff, the Chaplain, his fellow officers, family, friends, and the private secretary of the King, from who they received a telegram of condolence. However desperate they felt, parents were expected to show little public grief, as it was considered weak and unpatriotic.

Pamela Horn reports that Lady Ettie Desborough,[31] a society hostess, lost two sons in the space of two months, in early 1915. She was determined to show a brave face and carry on as usual, and her close friend, Lady Cynthia Asquith, admired the way she appeared *"absolutely normal in company."* But as soon as the two women were alone, *"tears pour down her cheeks, and she talks on and on about the boys, and yet preserving such wonderful sympathy for others."*

Other families commented in their letters and diaries that they lost themselves in war work, seeking to numb their pain by constant

---

31. Pamela Horn, *Country House Society*.

activity. The same was true for Patrick and Mary Anne, who continued their work and had nearly full-time jobs keeping in touch with their ten children based throughout England, on the Western Front and at boarding school. In some little way, this 'busyness' probably helped overcome the initial grief.

Charles Masterman, Liberal politician, and head of the British War Propaganda Bureau 1914-1917 said that *"the flower of the British aristocracy"* had died at Mons and the First Battle of Ypres in 1914. At certain points in the war the average life expectancy of an infantry subaltern on the Western front was about three months. The majority who were killed were aged 18 to 24, especially young and inexperienced officers. Their son Pat was only 26 and one of the flowers that Masterman referred to.

In January 1920 Pat was posthumously awarded the 1914 Star, accompanied by a letter to his parents from the War Office thanking them for the *"services rendered"* by their late son. Most recipients were officers and men of the pre-war British army, who landed in France soon after the outbreak of the War and who took part in the First Battle of Ypres and Retreat from Mons, hence the medal's nickname 'Mons Star'.

Tony Is Transferred to the UK

Meanwhile, back in the UK, Tony having been classed unfit to return to the Front, was based at Bulford camp, in Salisbury. He was clearly frustrated with this, but it must have been a huge relief for his parents. Tony wrote to Mary Anne on 11th April 1915:

> *I am attached to a battery. They won't give me one till I am fit for duty, as they don't think light duty entails being battery commander, so I have at present got rather a soft job.*

The army decided on a role for Tony, appointing him as Officer of a Company of Gentlemen Cadets at the Royal Military Academy in Woolwich on 15 July 1915, where he stayed until the end of the war. He seemed to have thrived in the role and Phil wrote to his parents praising his brother:

> *I met a fellow who was at Rugby [School] with Tony and was instructed by Tony [at Woolwich Academy]. He*

> *said that Tony was the best gunnery instructor they had had there and that his class always got the best marks in the exam.*

Tony was rewarded with a promotion to Captain on 8th August 1916 and to Company Commander on 1 January 1918. In April 1918, he again volunteered for active service. A letter on 10th April 1918 from the army's Assistant Director of Medical Services states that Tony had been seen by a medical board and the doctor said it is *"quite obvious that some further examination should be made"* and he would arrange this. As a result, Tony was not considered fit enough to go on active service as, apart from anything else, he suffered occasional epileptic fits due to his injury.

In early 1915, Phil and the couple's son-in-law Hugh were in action in Flanders, getting a week's leave every few months. Phil clearly had time to cook and tend to rabbits, and play with his cat, which he had brought back from England with him. This was not unusual and cats and stray dogs were much prized. They helped catch rats and provided companionship and amusement for the troops. Phil later also acquired a dog he called Pich.

Phil diligently wrote home every two days, enjoying the exchange of news with his parents and siblings. On 13th March in a letter to his father he remarked: *"I hope mother is alright although she is not allowed to write."* And on 22nd April said that he was missing letters from home, as Mary Anne was still unable to write, only finally thanking her for a letter on 27th April. This means that Mary Anne was unable to write for over seven weeks, but whether it was a simple injury to her hand or arm, or something more seriously confining, we don't know.

The Second Battle of Ypres and First Gas Attacks

By 13th March 1915 Phil was about to be busier and wrote to tell his father that he had moved: *"I suppose you understand about the snipers. I am only about 250 feet from one of the gates."*

It is likely from this description, subsequent letters, and the timing, that Phil was now stationed on the outskirts of Ypres, in readiness for the Second Battle of Ypres. The town had medieval stone gates leading to the old, fortified centre, only one of which now remains, Lille gate. Phil's letter could be referring to his position near the Lille gate, where he was clearly in danger. German snipers were generally admired for their marksmanship and bravery but also hated for their accuracy and the British considered sniping 'unsportsmanlike', thinking that the killing should be confined to formalised attacks.

On 16th April, Phil told his mother:

> *I am very pleased with life at present as I was actually complimented by my Major yesterday, I think for the first time in my life.*

Phil's confidence would be required, as he was about to be involved in various separate actions that together comprised the Second Battle of Ypres, which was fought from 22nd April – 25th May 1915 for control of the strategic Flemish town of Ypres. Earliest of these was the Battle of St. Julien (24th April – 5th May), which was noted for the first mass use of chlorine gas by Germany, on the Western Front. Phil may have obliquely referred to the battle when he wrote to his mother three days later, on 27th April:

> *I am flourishing though we have had quite a warm time recently. The papers of course lie freely about what has happened, but everything seems to be alright now.*

Though on 7th May he added: *"The Germans do not look as if they were beaten yet out here."*

On 27th April he told his mother: *"I have been keeping a journal though I only write it up occasionally with the idea of making an account from it after the war."* He asked her to send him a notebook, so that he could copy his extracts and send it back, which he did. Keeping a private diary was a breach of military discipline, so it is surprising that Phil openly wrote about keeping a journal. Maybe as a Second Lieutenant, his superiors turned a blind eye.

On 25th May, Phil wrote to report a further gas attack: *"We got gassed yesterday but as we are so far away it was not bad."* He was lucky not to have been in the front line, as the evidence confirms he was near the Battle of Bellewaarde (24th–25th May 1915) – the Germans' last attempt to take Ypres. On the morning of May 24th, they drenched the Allied lines with chlorine gas along a 12 km front.

When yellow-green clouds drifted towards the Allied trenches, the French officers, assuming at first that the German infantry was advancing behind a smoke screen, alerted the troops. But when the cloud reached the trenches, soldiers began to complain of chest pains and a burning sensation in the throat. Word was passed to the troops to urinate on their handkerchiefs and tie them over their nose and mouth. Recollections of the attack from Private W A Quinton, 2nd Battalion,[32] Bedfordshire Regiment show the horror:

> *After the gas attack the men came tumbling from the front line. I have never before seen men so terror stricken, they were tearing at their throats and their eyes were glaring out.*

The Daily Chronicle (26th April 1915) had reported on the earlier use of chlorine gas at Ypres:

> *Among those who escaped, nearly all cough and spit blood, the chlorine attacking the mucous membrane. The dead were turned black at once. They [the Germans] made no prisoners. Whenever they saw a soldier whom the fumes had not quite killed, they snatched away his rifle and advised him to lie down 'to die better'.*

If in the direct line of a gas attack, men would choke, vomit green bile, and mostly die. Those that lived could take weeks to recover and their lungs were often irreparably damaged. Phil was luckier, as he was clearly not close enough to the front line at the time, though he added more detail in his letter of 25th May:

> *It hurt my eyes a bit and made them swim a good deal, but it smelt only good. In fact, the first thing I thought in the morning when I got out of my hut was what a delicious smell!!*

As Phil mentions, soldiers soon learnt that the gas had a very distinctive smell, resembling a mixture of pineapple and pepper. After the first attacks, Allied troops were supplied with masks made of cotton pads soaked in urine; ammonia neutralised the chlorine. Others preferred to use a handkerchief, sock, or flannel body-belt, dampened with a sodium-bicarbonate solution, which they tied across their mouth and nose.

Officers like Phil were luckier, as they could often call on wealthy parents. He wrote to his father on 1st June 1915, asking him

---

32. Imperial War Museum, Private collection, Documents 6705.

to send *"a respirator with goggles for gas, as my eyes are being affected."* This level of protection would have been a year away for other ranks.

By June 1915, soldiers received rudimentary smoke hoods and from February-August 1916, were issued with increasingly sophisticated anti-asphyxiation box respirators, in time for the Battle of the Somme. The British Commanders condemned the use of gas, but sadly, it was the start of a chemical arms race on both sides that lasted throughout the war.

On 28th May, after the Second Battle of Ypres ended, Phil wrote in his typically understated and cheery way to report that:

> *Officers, and men were killed and wounded. Horses too. It was rather a nasty affair, but I am flourishing.*

That battle became for the British what Verdun had been for the French: there was no tactical gain and cost an estimated 200,000 British and Irish lives.

Phil Becomes a Gunner

On 9th June Phil changed Brigades, becoming a Second Lieutenant in 28th Trench Mortar Battery, Royal Field Artillery. He was most likely a Gun Position Officer (GPO), which meant he was well behind the front lines but still subject to German counter-battery fire. Clearly, he didn't much like this role and preferred being in the thick of the action. He wrote to his father explaining:

> *I've moved seven miles back to learn about mortars. Of course, it will be dangerous work, but I do not like this half soldiering here.*

There may have been an incident with his Commander Major Kinsman, over a misunderstanding, as Phil wrote to his father on 15th June:

> *I do not think I am really leaving the brigade in disgrace, but I dare say you know more about that than I do; anyway, everyone seems very nice and polite to me and the new commander of 124, would certainly have me back if there was a chance.*

Later in the same letter he relayed a remark about him that had come second-hand from Major Kinsman:

> *He is an awfully good boy, only twenty-one but a splendid fellow and as cool and brave as anything. He is very fit and keen on his work.*

Whatever the circumstances, Phil reported to his mother that he was now: *"A commander of a trench howitzer battery attached to 48th division"* and asked her to send him a Lifeguard periscope. Invented and patented by Edgar Duerr, this periscope was considered lifesaving, as it enabled front-line soldiers to observe enemy movements from 50cm (20 inches) below the parapet, providing them with a view of up to 91m (100 yards).

Phil was clearly well thought of to be commanding a howitzer battery at only 21 years' old. The howitzer was one of the most effective guns used by the British during the war. Royal Garrison Artillery Officer Monty Cleeve[33] outlined what it could do:

> *It fired upwards in a curved trajectory, dropping down out of the sky to take out guns and destroy enemy trenches. Attacks were carried out daily, usually firing about 800 to 1,000 rounds per day during set periods, with the eight to twelve men it took working in a rota of four-hour shifts.*

Phil grew to enjoy the role, although on 16th June he wrote saying he was disgruntled:

> *They have taken away most of my gunners and given me infantrymen of the baser order instead.*

This was because in mid to late 1915, many units were switched to those of the 32nd Division, a newly arrived volunteer formation. The idea was to strengthen the inexperienced Division by mixing in some regular army troops; even though by now, many of the pre-war regulars had died and the regular battalions themselves were often largely composed of new recruits.

Phil clearly has a job on his hands to train up these new recruits in double quick time. By the end of June, however, he was clearly

---

33. Imperial War Museum, https://www.iwm.org.uk/history/voices-of-the-first-world-war-gunners.

proud of his work: *"You can see my bombs all the way and they go off with a biggish bang"* and added: *"I imagine I am quite the youngest and most junior battery commander. So far I have been pretty successful."*

Bob Arrives in France

Phil's younger brother Bob arrived in France on 22nd July 1915 (two days before his 19th birthday) as part of an advance party, so the couple once again had two sons on active service in the war. He had been promoted to Lieutenant on 3rd February 1915. Writing home from where he was stationed, Bob's first letter reveals the shock of the situation that faced him.

He reported that he was very seasick on the boat over, that a sergeant in his unit had shot himself in his billet (military records suggest it was an accident,[34] but this cover-up often occurred to spare the man's family and the Battalion's reputation) and *"some other men have gone mad"*. He added that the place was *"desolate"*, and they were short of men of *"military age"*. By that comment, he presumably meant they lacked experience, although he would be counted among that group, having only signed up a year before, and not having yet seen any active service.

Unlike his brother Phil, Bob didn't ask for much in the way of provisions, even requesting that his family send him fewer cigarettes each week and no more chocolate! Bob spent his first month at the Infantry School of Instruction and was therefore lucky to miss the battle of Aubers Ridge in May 1915, which was particularly savage and costly for the Allied forces. After that he was stationed only about ten miles from Phil, near Armentieres.

Brother-in-law Hugh Pattinson Is Killed

In August, only a month after arriving in France, Bob heard the sad news that his brother-in-law Hugh Pattinson had been killed. Phil was particularly close to Hugh, and being based near him, the pair often met up for lunch or tea in the billets. Hugh was superintending a working party digging communications trenches at Houplines, about two miles from Armentieres.

Trenches were very primitive in 1914, as everyone thought the war would be short. By 1915, they realised it was going to be a long

---

34. Trevor Torkington, https://ww1lives.com/captain-robert-chaworth-musters-22-died-of-illness.

haul, so they had to 'dig in'. Communication trenches were dug at an angle to those facing the enemy and used to transport men, the wounded, equipment, and food supplies.

It is estimated that there were around 15,00 miles of trenches constructed in total in the Great War. Digging was hard and filthy work. As the conflict wore on, the trenches were made narrower and shallower, to save both time and resources, and because the ground conditions couldn't support anything big.

In the Houplines area at the time, digging only two feet down, men would hit the water table, so the trench needed supporting with timber and corrugated iron, topped by sandbags – all of which needed constant maintenance.

Soldiers of "A" Company, 1st Battalion, Cameronians (Scottish Rifles) in the trenches at Houplines, 1914. Image courtesy of Robert Cotton Money, IWM Q51558.

The white zigzag pattern made by the sandbags formed an easy target for German gunners and distances between the opposing lines could be half a mile or only 20 yards away, making the work doubly dangerous.

Men were ordered to keep their heads down during the day to avoid snipers and not give away their position and, if the trench was not deep enough, they had to crawl through the mud. At night they worked on repairing, extending, and building new dugouts. This was a grim experience as the war went on, as a soldier recounts: *"The ground was like a huge graveyard, and we were continually unearthing dead Germans."*

Snipers were a constant and deadly presence, as was random shelling, as both Pat and Tony knew, to their cost. Whether Hugh was careless or just unlucky, he was shot in the head by a sniper whilst supervising the trench work and died on 3rd August 1915, aged 26. Phil telegraphed his father on the night Hugh was killed, relaying the sad news. He also wrote a longer letter to his mother the next day, containing more details:

> At 8pm he [Hugh] took out a couple of working parties on trench work. He was hit about 8.20pm. A bullet from a land rifle far back in the German line had gone through his brain. He lived for ten minutes but was quite unconscious, but he smiled slightly at first. He could not have possibly suffered any pain.
>
> I saw him at tea yesterday afternoon, and he was in great form. I am writing to Lina and Mrs P [Hugh's mother] but I find it rather a hard task. The curious thing is that he was not on a dangerous job. They were quite 800 yards behind the firing line, and he was the only casualty.
>
> I have been to see the place where he fell and I have also seen his body. The funeral is tonight at 6pm. I am quite sure he is alright. He looks quite peaceful in death, but it is Lina and the twins I am so worried about.

On 13th August he reported to Mary Anne that:

> Lina wrote a very nice letter and seemed as well as can be expected. The day Hugh was killed was one of the quietest I ever knew.

Hugh was buried in the Cite Bonjean Military Cemetery, in Armentieres and Phil displayed his kindness further when he wrote to say: *"I failed to get photographs of Hugh's grave, but I sent Lina a sketch of it instead and also a plan of the cemetery."*

The Major (second in command) of the Battalion wrote:

> I would like you to know that this is an irreparable loss to the Regiment and particularly to this Battalion. Personally, I would rather have lost a Company. He was wonderful at his work, and everyone loved him and worked his best for him. Taken all round he was the most efficient fellow I have ever worked with.

Such letters were typical of those received by officers' families, who generally got a letter from the commanding officer, often together with personal letters from fellow officers. By contrast, families of other ranks often only got a terse official letter informing them of the date of death and general cause in the briefest of terms (e.g., wounded in action) and explaining that if any personal effects were found, they would be forwarded, and the family notified to collect them.

Hugh's loss would have been a great sadness to Patrick and Mary Anne. He was the second family member to die in the War and was very well-liked. He had only been married to Lina for 13 months and, tragically, had not yet had the chance to meet his four-month-old twin daughters, Bridget and Primrose.

Lina and her daughters were living in London when Hugh died and went to stay at Annesley for some time. Lina never remarried, and survived Hugh by 49 years, moving to Hartley Wintney in Hampshire between the wars, then to Moreton-in-Marsh in the Cotswolds (like her sister Ruth). At the end, she suffered a severe stroke, and eventually died on 25th July 1963, aged 74.

Hugh's death rattled Phil and he commented: *"It is strange how I am passed over time after time and more important people taken."* Bob was also touched by Hugh's death and wrote home: *"I am very sorry to hear that Foulus was killed. It was rotten luck and wretched for Lina."*

Phil and Bob Keep in Touch

Phil kept in touch with his brothers, exchanging letters, and started to meet Bob regularly, as he was also stationed nearby. On one occasion Bob cycled over eight miles to see Phil (and back again) and one gets the impression that they were particularly close. This mention from Phil is typical of many examples in their letters:

> *Bob came over again the other day and we went out to tea in A [likely to be Armentieres]. He's very flourishing and cheerful nowadays, far more so than before when he had had rather a bad time.*

Phil seemed to have a quieter few months from August to mid-December 1915, as his letters don't speak of any action but of his animals. His puppy died of distemper and he lost some pet rabbits. On 28th September he said:

> *I am quite well and not very busy and in no danger, but I am rather anxious about Bob. It may all be quiet where he is.*

On 22nd October Phil reported on having received a six-page letter from Tony about his engagement:

> *I have never had such a long letter from him in his life. He seems to be very happy. I hope it will stand the test of time alright.*

This remark makes it sound as if the engagement was rather sudden and perhaps Tony's fiancée Popsy was either not well known to the family or not considered the 'right sort'.

Phil was right to be concerned about Bob, as though he was only eight or so miles away, he had indeed experienced a 'busy time' in the Autumn of 1915. By the end of August, he was on the front line near Armentieres for a long stint of mining and sniping at German trenches, with daily counterattacks taking place. The remarkable book, *Tommy at War,* includes many testimonials from men in the trenches about the terror of the next attack. They report on the endless waiting and bombardment of their artillery, followed by the call to 'make ready' and fix their bayonets.

The Battle of Loos – Bob Soldiers on

Apart from the constant danger, there was great discomfort. Armentieres was notorious for its high-water table and troops spent time shoring up sodden trenches, whilst being soaking wet most of the time. Bob endured this until November 1915, with brief periods of respite in billets. In September he reported home:

> *I've got pretty bad foot rot. I'm going to be sent to the hospital for a few days. I got it for having my boots on too long and being in a foot or more of water. I am getting gum boots ordered from stores.*

Bob was made the Lewis Gun Officer for the battalion, in charge of the machine guns and was involved in the Battle of Loos near Ypres, which lasted from 25th September-8th October 1915. He wrote home on 23rd September, to say that he was going into the trenches that day, then on 27th wrote to say: *"I expect you'll hear something soon but I cannot reveal what"*, followed by a Field Post card (a usual sign of being in action and being unable to write a letter).

He later wrote to say he'd had a *"pretty warm time"*. As ever, this was an understatement, as he was recommended for (and later awarded) the Military Cross for his role in the battle, which included capturing a German soldier and being slightly gassed.

Following Loos, Bob remained in action, engaged in patrolling, mining, mortaring, and sniping to prevent the Germans taking parts of the British line. It was still an active, dangerous time, as he reported in October 1915: *"The Huns have developed a habit of sending off mines which rock the earth like earthquakes."*

Bob was back in hospital briefly in November, having been diagnosed with Trench Fever, which was caused by bites from infected lice. The situation in the trenches had clearly worsened due to the constant shelling as Bob reports (with his notable dry humour):

> *Everything is underwater here. When you are in the water you find deep holes which you unsuspectingly fall into. One of my men got stuck up to his chest and shouted out 'For Gawd's sake, don't let me drown'. We got him out after a bit.*

The men had to spend much of their time repairing the trenches, which was hard and thirsty work. The water in nearby streams was undrinkable so had to be brought up in bottles from the battalion water cart, which was often a mile away, so had to be used sparingly each day. All the while, the danger of shelling and sniping was constant, as Bob knew too well: *"I got hit on the back yesterday by a piece of shell as I was bending over digging but it didn't even cut my coat."*

Phil's war warmed up again in December, when it is likely that he was involved in diversionary attacks at Ypres, as part of the Autumn Offensive. Overall, the British suffered heavy losses, especially due to machine gun fire during the attack and made only limited gains before they ran out of shells, which may have accounted for a comment Phil made that they were only allowed to fire four shells a day from one gun.

Phil's letters in December are brief and mention he has been in action (as ever, much to his delight), referring to 27th December especially:

> *I have been most awfully busy lately. I have had a bit of fun and excitement though it probably goes down in the official news as nothing to report.*

1916: The Deadliest Battles

Tony Marries

Phil had hoped to get leave, with Bob, at the end of December 1915 to travel home in time for Tony's wedding, but the war prevented that. Only two months after his swift engagement, Tony got married on 1st January 1916 (aged 24), to Marjorie Caroline Booth ('Popsy', pictured right), aged 22. They married at the Anglican church, St. Martin's-in-the-Fields, in Trafalgar Square, London and an announcement was made in *The Tatler* magazine.

Marjorie was the daughter of the building works manager at Woolwich Arsenal, where Tony was posted as Training Officer in the Royal Military Academy from May 1915 until the end of the war. The RMA was within the Arsenal complex, which at its height, employed around 80,000 people (mostly women) manufacturing armaments for the Great War. This is probably how Tony and Marjorie met and perhaps both the speed of their courtship and her parentage may have accounted for the family's apparent misgivings about the marriage.

Mary Anne was clearly concerned, as Phil tried to reassure her in letter:

> *I do not think you ought to feel that it is a son lost but a daughter gained but I suppose it does seem that way. But of course, I cannot understand it altogether at any age.*

The couple's first child, a daughter they named Marjorie, was born on 27th October 1916 (so, a honeymoon baby), followed by Barbara in 1919 and Diana in 1922. The family's concerns may have had some substance, as Popsy left him after a few years, and he later remarried Mabel Chorsley.

Phil's understated bravery was rewarded in early 1916, when he told his father:

> *I have been lucky enough to get a Military Cross, ... for that busy time on 27 December. I am quite well fed, comfortable and cheerful.*

Reports from Phil in February focus on him relaxing, reports of his dog, and a mention of some action thrown in. His humour (and language proficiency, as with all the children) is evident in a letter on 6th February 1916 to his father:

> *I am trying to learn a bit of Flemish from the beautiful young ladies at the billet. It is very easy, as if you try the English, Norwegian and German and then mispronounce all three in turn you nearly always strike the Flemish.*

Shell-shocked and Rat-infested

After a month in billets, in early 1916 Bob remained near Ypres, an area that had been turned into a quagmire by constant shelling. The trench system was now badly fragmented, shallow, and poorly maintained, with remnants separated by gaps of up to 80 yards (73m) of mud. The shelling was clearly taking its toll on Bob, as in February 1916, he wrote from the billets:

> *The most appalling big shells keep going over. I am back today after having had five days up there. The five days seem about six years to me, you get so infernally muddled by the shells and things.*

He wasn't alone in his 'muddle'. Lieutenant John Walcote Gamble,[35] wrote:

---

35. https://www.durhamatwar.org.uk/material/832/.

> *The effect of the whole show on one's nerves defies definition, but with all those millions of tons of high explosives flying about, it seems as if something must break in the head – but one just hangs on and hopes.*

By December 1914 as many as 10% of British officers and 4% of enlisted men were suffering from 'nervous and mental shock', with the term 'shell shock' first being published in 1915 in *The Lancet*. At first, shell-shock casualties were rapidly evacuated from the front line – in part because of fears about their unpredictable behaviour. But as casualty numbers increased, men were only evacuated if physically injured or displaying extreme behavioural symptoms. As an example, at the Battle of the Somme in 1916, as many as 40% of casualties were designated as shell-shocked.

By 1917, the situation was dire and medical officers were instructed only to give shell-shocked men a few days' rest away from the front line, but on their return, to spend time *"talking calmly and taking an interest in them."* In the heat of a battle and with all the deprivations we have heard about, one can imagine how ineffectual this course of action was. Saul Dibb's moving film *Journey's End* (2017) shows the damage of war to the individual in the characters of the alcoholic, mentally disintegrating commanding officer, Captain Stanhope, and shell-shocked junior officer Hibbert.

Stoic Phil was experiencing much the same action in February but seemed as sanguine as ever:

> *Been a bit of a fight. Bombs were dropped but no great damage and no gas. My dog is in the photo – worst mongrel you can imagine but a nice fellow all the same.*

He was hospitalised in Rouen for nearly four weeks from 24th March, following an accident where someone let off a trench mortar and it perforated his ear drum. He recovered and went back to the Front by early May and wrote to tell his father that he might be coming home soon to receive his Military Cross from the King. He added:

> *I am resting again as I have hurt myself by falling down in a communications trench, straining my leg. My dog will not leave the trenches now as there are so many rats there.*

Rats became an increasing horror in the trenches as the war went on. Disposing of food and human waste was impossible and the large numbers of dead could not be properly buried.

In his brilliant and moving memoir, *Goodbye to All That*, Robert Graves writes (realistically) about a new officer's first night in the trenches:

> Rats came up from the canal, fed on the plentiful corpses, and multiplied exceedingly...When he turned in that night, he heard a scuffling, shone his torch on the bed, and found two rats on his blanket tussling for the possession of a severed hand.

For this reason, dogs were popular companions and were encouraged to catch and kill the rats. Phil also wrote to say when next on leave he would get a ferret, to help keep the rats down and he did by 21st June 1916.

Phil returned home to receive his Military Cross on 15th March. The published citation reveals his bravery, which he had not referred to in letters home, other than having had *"an awfully busy time."* It reads as follows:

> *Lieutenant Philip Mundy Chaworth-Musters, 28th Trench Mortar Battery, Royal Field Artillery. For conspicuous gallantry and devotion to duty. In face of very heavy shell fire he bound up a corporal who was badly wounded, took him into safety and then returned and personally worked a gun under circumstances of great difficulty.*

Fortunately for Bob, his Division was relieved in mid-April, and went into reserve around Poperinghe, with the men of each brigade spending around a week on leave in Calais, followed by a month of rest and retraining.

Phil Wearies of the War

On 20th May 1916, the day Phil had been promoted to Temporary Captain – which Tony didn't achieve until August 1916 – he revelled in sibling rivalry. But otherwise, his outspoken letter shows finally how weary of the war he is:

> *I am looking forward to coming on leave as Captain to crow over Tony! I am most awfully fed up with things at present here. The average officer we get for general purposes is a complete funk and as ignorant of all military matters as a new-born child, added to which most of them too proud to learn. I suppose all the decent fellows are killed.*

This level of soldier is perhaps not surprising after two years of intense fighting. At the beginning of 1916 conscription was introduced and many of the infantrymen were young, frightened and in poor physical condition. Whilst this would not necessarily be the case for the officers, they were young and often arrogant, buoyed up by the wartime jingoism fed to them in the newspapers, and largely unprepared for the realities of war.

Phil's letter went on to complain about the generals, who according to him:

> *Sat at home and draw fat screws for nothing to save a few pounds by working men to death and causing general inefficiency. If ever I get through this war and ever live on in the army to be a general, then by Jove I will remember these last few months.*

Whether it was the Allied Generals' fault or not, by mid-1916, the German war strategy was to make the British defend as many points of the trench system as possible, with the aim of causing unsustainable casualties. With less than six months' training, the new recruits were more likely to be caught out.

The battles at Ypres continued, with intense German shelling, mining, and trench raids. Bob wrote that he had missed the Battle of Mont Sorrel (2nd-13th June 1916) as he was: *"On a course and by luck escaped the strafing at Ypres."*

The Battle of the Somme

The infamous Battle of the Somme started on 1st July 1916 and was a bloodbath for the British, with 57,470 casualties – 19,240 of them fatal. It remains the Army's largest loss on a single day. Those back home were kept in the dark about the extent of the slaughter. On 3rd July, *The Times* reported on the first day of battle:

> *Everything has gone well. Our troops have successfully carried out their missions, all counter-attacks have been repulsed and large numbers of prisoners taken.*

But by the end of 1916, when the casualty lists were published in the UK, the country was staggered at the losses. Bob was recalled from rest and retraining to take part in various actions that formed the Battle of the Somme. The artillery bombardment continued and was still affecting him – it may well be that like many others he was suffering from shell shock:

> *The noise that goes on is simply appalling. There is no other word for it. I lived for three days this time in a mine crater – a colossal thing about 50 yards across and 50 feet deep. That is a pretty fair thing to blow up isn't it. It is a most depressing place to live in for some time, especially when you expect another to go up any time.*

He added that he hoped his brother Phil was still in hospital, so out of the action, as it was *"not very healthy down there"*. When the Battle of the Somme started, Phil's Division was enjoying a period of rest and re-fit and was in GHQ Reserve but was soon called into action. Phil's Division saw action in The Battle of Bazentin Ridge on 14th-17th July and The Battle of Pozieres Ridge from 23rd July to 7th August.

But, as Bob hoped, Phil had indeed been lucky. He had been injured and, as a result, missed both battles. He wrote from hospital on 4th July to say that he was being allowed to get about *"a good deal now. Allowed to bathe. I am afraid they will keep me some time yet or they may put me on light duty."*

On 13th August Phil wrote again from hospital to say he was doing a machine gun course and was on light duties. He acknowledged his luck:

> *It was a rather lucky accident as I might have easily got strafed [machine gunned] in the finish [of the battle].*

We don't know the nature of Phil's injury, but it must have been fairly serious, as he finally left hospital around 27th September (after a 12-week convalescence) and reported that he was:

> *Quite alright but I must not be knocked about at all and have volunteered to help look after convalescent men until I'm fit to go to the front line.*

Meanwhile, Bob's Division was hard at it, working in the mud of the forward area, which was still covered in the bodies of the dead from previous assaults. He said it was *"a deuce of a time"*. In August and September 1916, the Germans started using phosgene gas shells, which may have affected Bob's lungs. In the Battle of Morval from 25th-28th September he experienced more shelling, gas, and trench raids by the Germans. He wrote a long, detailed letter home to say he'd had *"About the worst time I've had over here"*. He added that he was in the last great advance and he reports on the British tanks, which were new to the war: *"like great monsters... terrifying."*

On 28th September Bob wrote home in his typically modest and funny way to announce he had been awarded the Military Cross for his time in Ypres:

> *I have got my MC alright and I got the goose, which was very good indeed.*

He was presented with his medal a month later (aged only 20), and the *London Gazette* citation on 20th October 1916 stated:

> *Military Cross, Temp. Lt. Robert Chaworth-Musters, K.R.R.C. For conspicuous gallantry during operations. He moved constantly up and down his trench under heavy shell fire, in order to encourage his men, and several times crossed over [broken trench lines] to an isolated company though sniped at every time. He also brought in a wounded man.*

Bob's last major battle was also the last one on the Somme – the Battle of Transloy at the beginning of October. By now, his Division was operating at 50% of normal strength, the Brigades fighting on exposed flanks, with a gap of around 350 yards (320m) between Brigades. They were relieved on 8th October, after 1,112 were killed, wounded, or missing and they had taken 192 German prisoners. Their Corps Commander, Lieutenant General Lord Cavan, praised the men for their part in the Somme battles and added:

> *I have asked the Army Commander and the Commander-in-Chief not to take away the 20th Division if they can help it, and they have promised to do their best. I would not lose the 20th Division for crowns and crowns.*

Phil had a quieter time of it in October as he continued as an instructor, and he wasn't sent to the front line until November. He wrote home: *"I am so pleased he [Bob] got an MC too as he seems to have been having a pretty warm time."*

Phil and Bob met in late October, ate a good lunch, and had their photo taken (Phil is on the left). Bob appears very slender for his height – his jacket looking loose, and writing to his father on 7th November, Phil altruistically expressed his concern about his brother:

> *I'm safe enough here. Bob seemed pretty flourishing, but I think he has had about enough of it. I suppose you cannot make up any old bird to get him a safe job?*

After their efforts on the Somme, Bob's Division spent two months out of the line resting, retraining, and absorbing much-needed replacements. Having had enough of trench warfare, Bob asked for a transfer to the Royal Flying Corps but was concerned he might be rejected (which he was) because he was severely underweight. The intense fighting and trench conditions had, by now, taken its toll on his health. As a result, in November he was in hospital in Amiens for several weeks with laryngitis and flu, and wrote to his father on 13th November to say:

I can't get back to England as my heart and lungs are now affected. If they weren't I could.

Whilst Bob's health would have been of concern to his parents, at least he was safe from the fighting in hospital. Meanwhile, it's likely that Phil was involved in the Battle of Ancre (one of the last phases of the Battle of the Somme) in mid-November, as he was uncharacteristically silent and was told off by his parents for neglecting to write home. In early December Phil reported he had been into hospital with a temperature but that it was a false alarm, and he was out and expected to *"go up the line this week."* On 13th December he referred to his involvement in the Battle of the Somme, which was now at an end:

Dug all night and was through the Somme battle. Tell Mother it's pretty quiet and comfortable.

As he was writing to his father, he also felt able to tell him of his paramours (as he did regularly):

I called on the beautiful lady I told you of last March, twice. She was equally charming and attractive. Wishing you a happy Christmas.

In December, Bob returned to action on the front near Le Transloy, which by then consisted of a series of dangerously isolated posts (due to the fragmented trench system), some only 10 yards (9.1m) from the Germans. The British troops had to hold the line, repulsing repeated German attacks.

1917: Gas, Tanks and Skirmishes

Another Christmas came and went and 1917 arrived. Phil had now been on the Western Front for two years and three months, which is a major feat. Young lieutenants and captains were often the first to scramble over the top of the trenches, setting an example to their men and, as a result, their average life expectancy at this point was just six weeks.

Phil was protected to a degree, having been in gun batteries for much of the war, and injured for some of the time. However, as a captain, he would have been in more dangerous forward positions, so he could observe the fall of shot from the guns under his command. As such, his survival that long was remarkable.

Phil's letters from February to June 1917 speak little of action, although his February leave was cancelled, due to him having a bad cough and cold. Life was not all bad though, as in billets he confesses to his father:

> *I have met another beautiful young lady this rest but am not about to succumb, as her beauty is all the attraction she has.*

In January 1917 Bob wrote to report that he had spotted a German aircraft chasing a British one and had downed it with three 50-round drums from his Lewis Gun, fired from his shoulder. The plane landed behind British lines and the pilot, Max Winkelmann, got out but was shot dead, through the neck, by a German sniper.

By 16th February, Bob's health suffered further, and he was in hospital close to his Battery with laryngitis. A week later he returned to his Battalion and was promoted to Temporary Captain. In March 1917, the Germans retreated from the Hindenberg Line and the British advanced, involving Bob in further attacks in April.

By then he was clearly at the end of his tether and looking to the future. Writing to his father about the possibility of joining the regulars after the end of war, he complained he would lose rank if he did (he had just been promoted to Captain) and added:

> *In any case, I don't want to be a soldier. I don't like it and I consider it a mug's game. If there are no wars you don't get on and if there are, you probably get killed for your troubles. There are plenty of better things to do.*

He also complained about the enemy:

> *... the wanton destruction by the Hun of villages. If you hear anyone talking about the Hun being a fine fellow you ought to tell them about these villages... Wait till we get into Germany. I shall blow up everything I can see if I can get the explosive.*

In April Bob was sent to the 15th Army Corps School for sniper training. This was a quieter period, defending the line against patrols and raids. However, the line was once again a series of isolated posts, as the trench system had been comprehensively wrecked. Stationed near a *"very big wood"*, life seemed a little better for Bob, despite the fighting. In his letter of 26th May he asked for his father's field glasses to be mended for him as:

> *I've moved to a place with more action... They [the field glasses] are invaluable out here – I can't do without them. I saw a nest today with young ones – of the bird I enclose a description... I have been getting gooseberries out of gardens. Will you not send me any chocolate and tinned stuff now, but some lettuce, asparagus, cucumbers etc would be very nice, also a little vinegar and salad oil as it is difficult to get here.*

These are very dainty requests, and one wonders just how the fresh food would have survived the journey from England! Phil, after a quiet spell, was in action again. His Division was involved in the Second Battle of Arras in May and was part of the Second Battle of Messines on June 7th-14th, when the British blew up 19 deep mines and recaptured Messines Ridge (about 10 km from Ypres).

The regimental history records[36] that:

> Excellent work was performed [in the run up to the attack] by the trench mortars in destruction of the enemy front and support lines, wire and trenches under Capt. P. M. Chaworth-Musters, MC... The former fired an average of about 100 rounds per day per mortar... in spite of more than one direct hit on their emplacements. Something like a record must have been created by these trench mortar batteries in firing 1,250 60-lb bombs from the 2-inch trench mortars in one day, besides 108 9.45-inch bombs.

This excellent work was confirmed in a newspaper article later that year, when it was reported that Phil *"had won the encomiums of the General for his valuable work preparatory to the Messines battle."* Phil also wrote to say that he was involved in two or three operations that were particularly successful and that he'd received congratulations from the Divisional Commander for the men he commanded. He was granted leave after the Messines battle on 17th June and passed through London to visit relatives on his return.

Douglas Arrives in France

Douglas also joined the Royal Field Artillery, like his elder brother, Phil. He was sent for training in 1916 and by early 1917 was stationed near Salisbury Plain, doing *"experimental work"* as he called it, for some of that time. Whilst Douglas was training, Phil wrote home on 20th March to say:

> I had an amazing letter from Douglas the other day. He seems to be a great character nowadays. I have several fellows who know him and they all have some funny story to tell about him.

By 5th May 1917, Douglas was a Second Lieutenant in France with 504 Battery of 65th (Howitzer) Brigade, RFA, although he was not yet at the front line. He was fortunate to have missed the various battles of the Somme in 1916, when his Division was in action and suffered 11,000 casualties in just 43 days of fighting.

---

36. Trevor Torkington, https://ww1lives.com/captain-philip-mundy-chaworth-musters-22-killed-in-action.

The 65th Brigade formed part of the 12th (Eastern) Division throughout the war and Douglas was involved in supporting the Division's infantrymen around Ypres, who mounted several raids and small-scale attacks. The infantrymen spent much of their time on trench repair work, as the area was full of shell holes and disconnected trenches, with few dug-outs and poor communications.

Douglas' early letters home describe him as being comfortable and so well fed that he asked his mother not to send food parcels, as they had *"tons to eat."* He started seeing action around 5th June 1917, saying he was *"rather busy"* and might not be able to write home for a while. He was in the line for much of June, returning to billets for a week of rest and said he hoped to meet up with Phil, who he knew was stationed close by.

The pair met for dinner on 7th July and Phil wrote to his sister Elsie to say that 19-year-old Douglas was *"very flourishing and bloodthirsty, with a mind of his own."* Hopefully this comment didn't get back to his poor mother, who would have been even more alarmed to hear that of the three sons she had in action, two were displaying 'gung-ho' behaviour.

Phil Runs out of Luck

On 12th July Phil said forlornly: *"I've got a bit of a cold. Beastly weather."* Tragically, that was to be his last letter home, as his luck ran out after 31 months on the Front. On 18th July, in the run-up to the Third Battle of Ypres (more commonly known as Passchendaele), the British artillery regiments, including the RFA, begun a massive bombardment, together with an aerial attack. Phil was killed – hit in the chest by a stray 'friendly fire' British shell on 18th July 1917 at Hooge, 4km east of Ypres. This was Patrick and Mary Anne's second son to have been killed by a British shell, a dreadful irony when they were so proud to be fighting the enemy.

The Brigade's war diary records this but makes no mention of it being a British shell:

> *The Brigade sustained severe military and personal loss in the deaths of Capt. P.M. Chaworth-Musters MC, RFA (DTMO) and Lt. A. Davoren RFA who with the DTMO, 8th Division were killed by a shell. Second Lt. W T Voss RFA was seriously injured in the face by the same shell.*

Phil was buried at Poperinghe New Military Cemetery, near Ypres in Belgium. His family later had his headstone inscribed with the words *"Beloved to you be light and life and joy always."*

Douglas was greatly affected by Phil's death; they were close and had met up only ten days beforehand. He informed his parents and brother Bob of Phil's death, attended his funeral, and went out of his way to pass on letters and condolences from those who knew him. His letter of 19th July is especially poignant:

Photo courtesy of Marvin & Samme Templin

> *Phil was killed yesterday instantaneously by one of our own shells. They [his Battery] were all very upset about it and were undoubtedly all very fond of him. From what I have seen since I've been here I'm sure he was a great deal braver than most people here and to have stuck it as long as he did and then show no signs of nerves is a thing which very few do...*
>
> *His poor old dog Pich is waiting for him and jumps up eagerly when anyone comes in. I'm sure they will find him very hard to replace. I am quite sure that he is quite alright over the other side and did not suffer at all.*

The phraseology about instant death and not suffering was standard fare for the time, to spare parents and siblings at home, and we don't know whether this was the case for Phil.

On hearing of his death, Bob wrote to his parents in a relatively cheery manner, trying to console them but mentioning the danger of friendly fire:

> *I was very sorry to get a letter to say that poor old Phil had been killed. I know that all his people will miss him very much as he was such a good fellow out here and knew his job absolutely. But still, as Douglas says, I am*

> sure we will all meet somewhere. Don't be upset because it was by our own shells again, as I am afraid it always is bound to happen and does very often. I am glad to see that it was instantaneous as he can't have felt anything.

Phil's elder brother Jack, serving in Egypt, wrote to his mother:

> I am most awfully sorry to hear about him [Phil]. I cannot too quite realise it, as I hadn't seen him for nearly three years. Try to keep as cheerful as you can.

Again, we have a son urging his parents to be cheerful. Jack was clearly worried about his father's mental state as he asked after him, saying that he'd not heard from him in about a fortnight, and said about Phil:

> It really is awful as he was doing awfully well. I had begun to hope that he had got a cushy job at last.

Douglas' initial letter was followed by a flurry of others to his parents. He forwarded a letter written by a fellow officer and friend:

> You must be so proud as everyone in this Division has been. He was a very gallant soldier and the best type of a young English gentleman. His work has been splendid.

On 22nd July Douglas wrote to his mother, enclosing a letter from Phil's servant who said he would look after Phil's dog Pich *"as long as he is able."* He mentioned finding Phil's diary in his jacket pocket, which he returned. He added: *"He was loved by all the battery officers."*

Douglas stated that he had visited Phil's grave and on 28th July, wrote with further news on his death: *"He was going round the trench battery and was right in the front line opposite Hooge."*

On 23rd July, Mr Bradby, Phil's former Housemaster at Rugby School, wrote to Mary Anne. His letter is emotional and sympathetic, going beyond the usual platitudes; the last sentence especially probably better reflected the pain that Mary Anne and Patrick felt:

> Your news has been a very hard blow. I was always very fond of Phil. His gallant and unconquerable spirit, his

> *immense zest in life and love of fun were always a delight while he was here. He was always so light-hearted and so absolutely free from anything like envy or meanness. I always thought he would be one of the people who would come through alright. ... I know how crushed you must be feeling and indeed my heart is very heavy for all of you...*
>
> *There are moments when I feel as if the burden of this war were almost intolerable – as if we simply couldn't go on bearing it any longer and your burden is so much heavier than mine. I have loved them all, but they were not my children.*

Mary Anne wrote to Phil's commander, Captain Cunningham, and received a reply on 1st January 1918 that mentions Phil's dog Pich had attached itself to another Captain. He also shed further light on Phil's death:

> *Your son was on a recon of the front line trenches with a view to bringing the mortars forward. He was consulting a French map when a shell burst directly over them. Three were killed outright and the fourth blinded. In your dear son Phil we all lost a friend and a leader, exceedingly gracious and courageous, one who had more than the respect of all of us and the heartfelt affection of some of us, who were privileged to know him well enough.*

After three and a half years of a dreadful, prolonged war, Patrick and Mary Anne had lost their eldest son Pat, their son-in-law Hugh, and their nephew Roger (the son of Patrick's brother, George, and a pilot in the RFC, who was killed in action in July 1917). In addition, their son Tony had sustained severe injuries that would blight his life, and now they had lost a second son, Phil, aged only 22.

Having six sons serving in the war, they came to the attention of the local press and a moving and lengthy article appeared in the *Hucknall Dispatch* on 2nd August 1917 under the headline *"A family of heroes: two lives sacrificed."* It outlined the service of each son, containing photographs and included the following foreword:

> *If ever the history of the Great War is written from a local viewpoint, a place of honour must be accorded in its pages to the noble part played by the family of Mr and*

> Mrs J. P. Chaworth-Musters of Annesley Park, inasmuch that their six sons all resolved to fight for England on the outbreak of war. Sad to relate, two of them have died for England during the past three years of war...

The article ended with a tribute to the family:

> Such a record as the above must certainly form one of the outstanding features of this war, and this locality has indeed, something to be proud of. And whilst the sons are fighting to overthrow Kaiserism, both Mr and Mrs J.P. Chaworth-Musters, are doing a noble work by assisting in the sustenance of prisoners of war from the Annesley neighbourhood, whilst their sympathy to wives or parents who have lost husbands or sons is genuinely expressed.
>
> Indeed, they are indefatigable in their labours on behalf of the local lads, especially those who are captives or wounded, and in the villages their names are mentioned with a gratitude for their many kind deeds.

As Patrick and Mary Anne knew all too well, life had to go on, as they still had three sons in action (two on the Western Front and Jack in the Middle East) and Tony serving in England. Fearing that the war would run on, Bob wrote to his parents warning them about his youngest brother, still at school: *"Don't let Jim join up until he's forced to."*

Douglas wrote home on 16th August to say he had suffered a gas attack but that the ammonia tablets Mary Anne had previously sent had helped lessen the effect. It is most likely that he was awarded the Military Cross for his role in the raids around Arras in August 1917. The citation appeared in the *London Gazette* on 26th September 1917:

> MC, 2nd Lt. Douglas Chaworth-Musters, R.F.A. For conspicuous gallantry and devotion to duty during an intense hostile bombardment of his battery. When an ammunition store was hit and set on fire by an enemy shell, he removed the burning ammunition and extinguished the fire, by his prompt and gallant action preventing the fire spreading and causing very serious damage. On the following day, although heavily gassed by a shell which fell

within five yards of him, he refused to report sick, as his commander would have been single-handed.

Douglas' letters of the period are – like those of his brothers – typically modest and make no reference to this act of bravery, only that a shell fell outside his latrine door, and he was slow to put on his respirator, so caught a whiff of gas which left him choking.

Bob's Division was in action around 131 km away from Douglas, southeast of Amiens, which in his words was *"a ghastly place with hundreds of dead Bosches"* lying around. Despite a rest and retraining period, Bob's health continued to suffer and by the end of July 1917, he had been removed from the front line to serve as an instructor in the nearby 3rd Army Musketry Camp.

The original School of Musketry in Hythe, England, had been such a success that the British army established a series of sniping schools behind the lines, with instructors such as Bob teaching advanced skills in firearms and marksmanship. It meant that British infantryman on the Western Front were, in part, able to offset the early superior machine-gun power of the German army. The Hythe school's success had coined the phrase 'the mad minute', highlighting the British soldiers' ability to fire their rifles 15 to 20 times in only 60 seconds.

Bob stayed at the musketry camp until December 1917 and was busy most of the time, although he wrote home relaying how he'd built a cement-floored pen and was raising pigs and chickens.

The First Battle of Cambrai

In mid-November 1917, Douglas' Division was involved in the First Battle of Cambrai, which was the biggest German attack since 1915, although it ultimately ended in stalemate. In a second phase of fighting on 30th November, the Germans started an intense early morning artillery barrage, followed by a hard and confused fight as their infantry advanced. The result was heavy losses of up to 50% of the Division's units.

Because of the shortage of manpower, Douglas was promoted to Lieutenant and Acting Battery Commander on 10th November and in April 1918, learnt that he would have been made overall second in command, but for the fact he was too young (he was still only 19 years old). Following this news, he made a rare but mild complaint in a letter home, saying this was *"rather annoying."*

Douglas was given leave home after Cambrai and enjoyed a Winter game shoot at Wiverton with his father. On his return to France in December he was moved to a *"better spot"* near Amiens, and was now in the same army as Bob, who he cycled 25 miles to visit in January, staying with him for a couple of days. The rain had been almost continuous since November and the wet, mud and cold made conditions miserable. However, in his letters, Douglas was as sanguine as ever and said their dug-out had a stove and was *"nice and warm."* Conditions would, of course, have been worse for the non-commissioned ranks. He also mentioned spending some of his time in the wagon line, tending to the horses, which he enjoyed.

Malaria and Dysentery: The Middle Eastern War

I don't think a great deal to it. I'm being bothered by flies and bitten by mosquitos... I am fed up with the war and wish the d——d thing would finish.

Before we cover the last year on the Western Front, we'll examine Jack's war, which largely took place in the Middle East. When war broke out, Jack joined the South Nottinghamshire Hussars, and his regiment came under the control of the 2nd Mounted Division in September 1914. In early March 1915, after six months' training in Norfolk, Jack's Brigade received a warning order to prepare to move to the Middle East. The headquarters and units sailed from Avonmouth near Bristol in early April 1915, and his Brigade arrived in Alexandria, Egypt on 24th April 1915. They joined the Egyptian Expeditionary Force (EEF) to conduct campaigns in Egypt, interspersed with tours in Gallipoli in Turkey, and Salonika in Greece.

Jack wrote home on 29th May 1915 to say he'd been in Egypt for a month and was camped on the beach in tents, plagued by pests. He'd also seen the pyramids and the sphinx but found them very disappointing, tourist-ridden, and filthy.

He wrote again on 8th August to say he was going on active service. On 10th August 1915, the Division received orders to reorganise as a dismounted (infantry) unit bound for Gallipoli. Most of the Division sailed from Alexandria and landed at Suvla Bay, Gallipoli in Turkey on the night of 17th-18th August 1915. However, Jack fortunately missed the worst of the brutal Gallipoli campaign, as some men stayed behind, primarily to look after the horses and go on reconnaissance patrols around Egypt.

Jack was one of those lucky few that remained behind, in his case, acting as Embarkation Officer. On 27th September 1915, he wrote from the military HQ, based in the Savoy Palace Hotel, to say he was due to be sent back to France to join the Western Front but first was *"going to Gallipoli tomorrow with 2 Field Battery, South Notts Hussars."* He also mentioned the happy news that his first child, a daughter Audrey, was born in early August.

Suvla Bay, Gallipoli

*British soldiers dug in at Chocolate Hill,
Suvla Bay, Gallipoli 1915[37]
Image courtesy of the National Army Museum, London*

Meanwhile his Division had participated in the Battles of Suvla Bay, the Battle of Scimitar Hill and the attack on Hill 60 on 21st August 1915. It sustained heavy casualties, which were soon exacerbated by losses due to sickness. The ever-reducing numbers of men forced a major reorganisation of the division, which was probably why Jack was sent to Gallipoli from HQ, rather than to France.

Any letters from Jack in this period are either missing or were not written, as there is nothing on record between late September 1915 and January 1916, but it is likely from his 27th September letter, that he was in the thick of things for over three months.

Conditions in Turkey were appalling. Suvla Bay was overlooked by high ground held by strong Ottoman forces and was under constant artillery and sniper fire. The terrain and close

---

37. National Army Museum, https://collection.nam.ac.uk/detail.php?acc=2000-08-94-67.

fighting meant the dead could not be buried and the heat resulted in swarms of flies and vermin. Of the 213,000 British casualties in Gallipoli, over 145,000 were due to sickness – the chief causes being dysentery, diarrhoea, and enteric fever.

This diary description of conditions at Suvla by Trooper Leonard Bullwinkle,[38] 1st-3rd August 1915, highlights the terrible conditions:

> *Water and mud in trenches is plentiful and it is cold and damp at night. The bodies in long grass in front of trench smell horribly. Flies in millions. Got the squirts a little this morning... we shall soon have a good crop of disease.*

The Gallipoli campaign ended in failure for the Allied forces, so by November 1915 the commanders decided to retreat, and Jack's Division was evacuated to Egypt in late December. Jack's promised move to France was delayed, and he wrote to his father on 29th January 1916 from Alexandria. The letter was mainly about finances – how he was short on his allowance and his wife Daphne was struggling, but added:

> *I am fed up with the war and wish the d——d thing would finish. I nearly got 'strifed' but luckily the bullet was spent.*

Horseback Patrols in Egypt

Jack was still clearly on active service as he put it, *"in Egypt and moving about a bit"* on reconnaissance patrols to help defend the Suez Canal from attack. In January 1916, his Brigade was renamed the 7th Mounted Brigade and moved to Salonika, to help defend neutral Greece against a feared attack from the Bulgarians, although this never materialised. It had been a freezing winter in Greece and the army was not properly equipped, as a diary entry of Captain Noel Drury,[39] 6th Battalion, the Royal Dublin Fusiliers, 27th-28th November 1915 reveals:

---

38. National Army Museum, https://www.nam.ac.uk/explore/gallipoli.
39. National Army Museum, https://ww1.nam.ac.uk/stories/captain-noel-drury/#.YHW5FuhKhPY.

> *Very bad night – no shelter from the cold and wet...*
> *Our overcoats are frozen hard, and when some of the men*
> *tried to beat theirs to make them pliable to lie down in,*
> *they split like matchwood. The men can hardly hold their*
> *rifles as their hands freeze to the cold metal...There are*
> *many bad cases of frost bite in hands and feet.*

Jack made light of this in a letter home, saying that it hadn't been too bad, apart from two days when there were floods and blizzards and they had to sleep in the open at night. He also reported that he'd nearly been 'strifed' again. Perhaps things weren't too bad for him, however, as he added that although he'd been on three different fronts so far – Salonika, Suvla and the Suez Canal defences – he'd only experienced three weeks of fighting.

The British army used cyclists (incredibly) and cavalry to patrol and defend villages in the Struma Valley against attacks from the Bulgarians and Turks, and Jack and his 7th Mounted Brigade were involved in these operations.

Following the freezing winter, the troops then had to suffer a ferociously hot summer and many succumbed to heatstroke. Private George Veasey,[40] 8th Battalion, Oxfordshire and Buckinghamshire Light Infantry, described this in July 1916:

> *Marching is very hot and tiring and we get a thirst*
> *which no amount of drinking will satisfy... Our bottles are*
> *filled before moving off and no man must drink until the*
> *order is given... The water men have difficulty in keeping*
> *up the supply, which has to be carried in leather bags on*
> *the mules...*

Both sides evacuated the valley in the height of summer, owing to the prevalence of diseases like malaria, which alone caused 160,000 British casualties during the Salonika campaign. Jack also succumbed, as he wrote home on 29th August 1916 to say he was *"in hospital for week with malaria – sore throat and touch of fever."*

The Bulgarians did not attack Salonika and the Allies advanced north and west during 1916, establishing a front line that ran from the Albanian coast through northern Greece, to the Aegean Sea. Jack reported in April 1917 that he'd seen no fighting of late and felt

---

40. National Army Museum, https://www.nam.ac.uk/explore/salonika-campaign.

hopeful that the war would soon be over now that the Americans had entered the arena.

In June 1917, Jack's brigade returned to Egypt, as part of the Desert Mounted Corps (DMC) and after arriving on 4th July, he was stationed in Cairo to strengthen the offensive, following the lost campaign of the Battles of Gaza.

Only a month after Jack's return to the relative haven of EEF HQ, he heard of his younger brother Phil's death in France, and wrote separately to both parents on 15th July 1917, trying to console his distraught mother. It is sobering to think that for such a close family, Jack hadn't seen his brother for several years.

The postal service for the EEF appears not to have been as reliable as for those serving on the Western Front. Jack complained about not hearing from his father and on 29th September 1917, had to defend himself from the same complaint from his mother:

> *Mother, I have just got two letters complaining bitterly you haven't heard from me for ages. I don't know what it is about as I wrote to you every month.*

The Gaza to Beersheba Offensive

Jack was circumspect about war at this point. He was certainly about to get busy, as he took part in the major offensive against the Gaza to Beersheba line. To prepare for the Gaza offensive, the Brigade issued each man with an officers'-style saddle wallet, in which they could carry three days' rations and some spare clothing. Attached to the saddle were two nosebags containing two days of grain for their horse. A third day's grain and two days' rations for the men were carried with the Divisional train.

Every two weeks the forward division would move en-masse towards Beersheba; leaving in the afternoon, they rode all night to be in position on the high ground in front of town by dawn the next day. They remained there all day and returned to their base the following night.

These long-range patrols (which were often attacked by Turkish aircraft and artillery) got the men and horses used to desert travel, with no water available for the horses from the afternoon they left until they returned (over 24 hours later). This routine continued until the end of October 1917, when the Corps moved forward for the coming offensive.

The offensive started on 27th October 1917, the very day that Jack was promoted from Captain to Major, in command of a larger number of men. The EEF began a heavy and almost continuous bombardment of Gaza and launched successful attacks on several trench systems. Jack's Desert Mounted Corps was involved in a series of battles, including the Battle of Beersheba on 31st October. The Gaza to Beersheba line was finally broken on 7th November, and the Ottoman Seventh and Eighth Armies were forced into retreat, allowing the EEF to capture Jerusalem in December 1917, ending the long stalemate in Southern Palestine.

The DMC divisions were in a bad shape at this point, having fought for several days without any rest and were short of water – some of the horses had been without water for over 84 hours, and food for men and horses was also in short supply. Jack wrote to his wife Daphne on 25th November 1917, showing his usual understatement, and saying that he'd been *"hard at it for a month."*

> *On October 31 – Gaza, took Beersheba. We started about three days before. Lots of fighting... The Aussies took about 300-400 prisoners. We've ridden all over the country. Our horses are about finished... no rest, not much to eat and sometimes no water. I know what thirst is now as we were sixty hours on one water bottle full. It was beastly hot at the time, and we were fighting in steep hills... We had one good scrap... My horse was killed the other day. He had his leg shot off by an HE [high explosive shell]. Luckily, I wasn't on him at the time. I don't think I would have missed this stink for anything, although it was beastly hard work for a bit.*

He had been unable to write letters for over five weeks, which coincides with the progress of the battle, but he seemingly had enjoyed it. It is interesting that he wrote only to his wife – perhaps he didn't dare worry his parents further with news of the serious battle after the loss of two sons and one seriously injured.

Jack's positive disposition shines through in another section of the same letter, despite highlighting the food shortages the Brigade experienced:

> *The country here is really quite nice, lots of orange groves and we live on Turkish bread, raisins and Jaffa*

oranges at present but I don't get much fresh meat. We had a bit of old cow the other day which was excellent and also some chickens, which were the height of luxury.

In January 1918, the British held a line of trenches to the north of Jaffa and Jerusalem. The DMC was withdrawn to Gaza to rest and refit and most of its yeomanry regiments were retrained to serve as infantry or machine-gun companies. On 3rd April 1918, Jack's brigade merged with the Warwickshire Yeomanry, to form the B Battalion of the Machine Gun Corps. This was done in response to the German gains in the Spring Offensive in Flanders, as there was little role for cavalry on the Western Front.

Jack Sets Sail for France – with Near Tragic Results

Plans were put in place to transfer the Brigade to France and Jack embarked on HMS Leasowe Castle on 26th May 1918, along with over 2,900 troops and crew, to sail to Marseilles. They never reached their destination. The ship was part of a convoy of six and about 100 miles out from Alexandria she was struck on the starboard side at 12.25am by a torpedo fired from a German submarine. A vivid account of the event is given by a survivor:[41]

> *The engines stopped almost at once, but the ship remained on an even keel, settling slightly by the stern... Around forty boats and rafts were thrown overboard, and troops began leaving the ship. By 1.30 am around 2,000 men had been evacuated...*
>
> *Rescue operations were carried out until about 2.00 am, when the ship sank rapidly at the stern. Many men jumped into the sea in the last few moments and were picked up from rafts, including the Battalion commander, Major Sir St. J. Gore. However, 102 men lost their lives including eight officers and forty-four other ranks from the South Notts. Hussars. Most of them had been waiting on the forecastle when the ship upended.*

---

41. Rosemary Collins, Radcliffe on Trent WW1.org.

*Survivors from HMS Leasowe Castle on a rescue boat.
Photo reproduced by permission of survivor's descendants, courtesy
of Radcliffe WW1 website.**

*http://www.radcliffeontrentww1.org.uk/a-timeline-1/a-timeline-14/.

Some of those who perished would have undoubtedly been Jack's friends, colleagues, and men, who he had fought alongside since 1914. Captain Sutton[42] described his experience:

> *Nearly all of us were asleep. I was subconsciously aware of a sudden jar... I went straight to our emergency station and found the other men arriving. They were awfully good on the ship, and there was no panic... I climbed down about six feet of ladder, held my breath, looked at the black water, and dropped quietly in. I had a swim of about thirty to fifty yards... we rowed and rowed round in circles till a motor launch came and took us in tow, and then we arrived in an auxiliary ship of war...A few minutes after, the ship went down with a rush. We made off back towards Alexandria with over 1,100 survivors on board... On the quay we were given clothes, army issue, and the Red Cross gave us tea and biscuits.*

Rosemary Collins continues the story:

---

42. Scotlandswar.co.uk.

> *Nothing was seen of Captain Holl [the ship's captain] after the disaster. He had been last heard giving the order, 'Every man for himself'... During the hour and a half that the ship floated, whenever the Chief Officer reported to him, Captain Holl said: 'Do your utmost; they must be saved.' Several times he came down on to the boat deck, encouraging and exhorting the men to further efforts, always cheerful, always hopeful.*

Jack wrote to Daphne about the event and, despite the evident drama and danger he experienced, he typically underplayed the situation:

> *Ship torpedoed. Spent an hour in the water and nine hours on a life raft at night. Got back to Alexandria that night and had a drink in biggest hotel. In pyjamas and him [a man Jack rescued] in pyjama top and pair of slacks covered in blood and a pair of old boots.*

Jack failed to tell her that he had saved a half conscious and injured man, Philip Warwick, from drowning. Daphne received a letter from the man's grateful wife, and she passed on the woman's thanks in a letter to Mary Anne:

> *Mrs Warwick says: 'After the ship was hit, she seemed OK for about one and a half hours and then suddenly sunk in four minutes. Philip was streaming with blood and picked out of the water by Jack, who was on a raft. He was splendid. Philip says he couldn't have survived without the aid of Jack.' They were then rescued by a Japanese destroyer.*

Jack was awarded the Distinguished Service Order (which is just below the Victoria Cross in order of merit) on 3rd June 1918 for his conduct in Egypt. After rest and recuperation back in Alexandria, Jack and his unit re-embarked in mid-June, sailing to Taranto in southern Italy (arriving on 21st June 1918) and were then moved by train to Étaples (near Boulogne) in France. The rest of his war in France until Armistice Day is covered below.

1918: The Tide Turns

> *[To Mary Anne], I do hope you are better and not in great anxiety for the boys. I hope they are in a quiet part of the line.*

In 1918 Bob's condition worsened (not helped by a poor winter). In January he was confined to bed in the 56th Casualty Clearing Station in Gezaincourt, 30 km from Amiens: *"They say I had diphtheria... I'm not allowed up."* Douglas visited his brother, who was by now seriously ill, and was moved in February to Lady Michelham's convalescent home in the Grand Hotel du Cap Martin, near Nice. Here Bob reports enjoying tea dances and watching the sea and local wildlife. His health was assessed and, considered too unwell to return to the Front, in March 1918 he was posted to light duties at the School of Musketry's HQ in Hythe on the Kent coast.

Despite this precaution, Bob's health deteriorated further, and by April 1918 he was staying at Langstone House, a convalescent home in South Hayling, Hampshire. Here he undertook gentle activities (including trying his hand at sand yachting) and wrote to his father about investments and marriage, considering the best age to marry was about 25 (he was then 22). Dr Beddard's note at the time of his full assessment on 29th July makes sober reading:

> *He has diphtheria leading to pleurisy. Is a stone underweight. His organs are sound. His lungs are not.*

Following this assessment, Bob wrote to his father with the bad news and although he was clearly concerned, he tried to reassure him:

> *I'm told I have a smouldering tubercle in my chest. I can get rid of it in two years if I keep well and feed up. I've*

had it for five years apparently. Has there been any in the family before? There is not the slightest need for mother to get fussed over it.

Although far from well, Patrick and Mary Anne would have taken some comfort from the fact that Bob was now safe in England, together with Tony, leaving only Douglas in action in France and Jack in Egypt.

Douglas Fights in the Spring Offensive

From March to September 1918, Douglas was involved in the Spring Offensive, where the Germans attacked the Western Front at several points, desperate to defeat the Allies before the United States could fully enter the war. The offensive included the Second Battle of the Somme, the Third Battle of Arras, and the Battle of Amiens. Douglas' Division played a role in the Battles of the Hindenburg Line and the Final Advance in Artois. However, by the end of September, the Division was still only 26 miles from where the offensive had begun in August – for a loss of 6,229 officers and men.

At the time Douglas wrote home to say that he'd been *"monumentally busy"* and had *"five hours sleep in five days... almost dropping asleep at moments."* PTA Musters relays a story told by Douglas' eldest son, Pat. Although he rarely spoke about the war, Douglas had recalled a time in March 1918 (so probably when he was on the Somme), when Germans broke through the line and the exhausted British troops were falling back, half asleep on their feet and many without orders from their missing commanders. Douglas seized a rifle and bayonet and 'persuaded' the tired men to turn and form a defensive line.

Sir Arthur Conan Doyle mentioned the Division's role in his book *The British Campaign in France and Flanders*, stating that in March and April 1918 they:

Withdrew from the line in glory, for it is no exaggeration to say that they had fought the Germans to an absolute standstill.

For his part in this effort, Douglas was awarded a Bar to his Military Cross (in effect a second Military Cross) on 26th July 1918.

Amazingly, he had only just turned 20 years old. With his typical modesty he said that he couldn't think what he'd done to earn it. The official citation again commented on his calm manner and stated:

> Lt. Douglas Chaworth-Musters, M.C., R.F.A. For conspicuous gallantry and devotion to duty. He took command of his battery when his commanding officer was wounded and commanded it with skill during several anxious days. By his constant calm and gallant demeanour he did much to maintain the spirit of the battery.

Meanwhile, the strain on Patrick and Mary Anne of four years of war must have been immense. We know that Mary Anne had several spells of ill-health, where she was confined to bed and not allowed to write. On 20th June 1918, Jack's wife Daphne wrote to a clearly worried and ill Mary Anne to say:

> I do hope you are better and not in great anxiety for the boys. I hope they are in a quiet part of the line.

Jack Arrives in France

Jack was sent to France in July 1918, to help with the 'final push'. He wrote home on 2nd July 1918 to say he had arrived in France, having sailed past the Riviera and Italy, mentioning that submarines had fired at their ship on the way. Having no use for cavalrymen in France, he retrained as a machine gunner at Étaples, which was the most important base for the British Army's infantry. New troops held at the base were 'toughened up', while awaiting dispatch to the Front. Wilfred Owen described the camp as the *"bull ring"* because of the brutality of the instructors (many of whom had not served at the Front) and the harsh conditions, which led to a mutiny by a small number of troops in September 1917.

Jack did not stay at Étaples long and was in hospital briefly in July. In August 1918, his brigade was renamed as the 100th Battalion Machine Gun Corps, and he went into action. He wrote on 3rd August 1918 to say: *"Been in Flanders five days. Somewhere near the line."*

Jack was most likely involved in the Battle of Amiens, which began on 8th August 1918 and was a co-ordinated 'all arms' attack, combining infantry, artillery, tanks, and aircraft. By the end of the advance, a gap of 15 miles (24 km) had been punched in the German line south of the Somme and Allied casualties were relatively light, with around 6,500 killed, wounded, and missing.

Jack's letter home on 22nd August 1918 confirms this: *"Quite a hard time of it but not many casualties."* After Amiens, the Allied forces began the 'Hundred Days' offensive, a series of attacks along the line, which drove the Germans back. Jack alluded to this in his letter of 19th August, saying he was *"Walking back towards Germany."*

Bob's Health Deteriorates Further

Douglas got leave home in August, and Bob travelled up from Hampshire to London to meet up and see him back off to France. From there, Bob reported to a London hospital where he was X-rayed, and his earlier diagnosis of consumption was confirmed. His doctor's note of 10th August stated: *"Pleurisy, diphtheria, night sweats, lost a stone in weight. TB – 4 months in a sanatorium."* He was sent back to the sanatorium at Hayling Island and on 15th August wrote to his clearly increasingly worried mother:

> *I don't see what you have to worry about, as far as I can see it would be a very good thing if I had got a touch of it, as it can easily be got rid of in a year or so and if I haven't I shall be back in France with my battalion shortly, which is so much more risky and unpleasant.*

Bob deteriorated further and was now finding blood in his phlegm. So, in late August 1918 he was moved to the isolation ward at Queen Alexandria Military Hospital, Cosham for investigations. In September he wrote, hoping he would be allowed home for a visit, as it had been eight months since he had been to Annesley, but sadly this wasn't possible.

After his August leave, Douglas was back in France *"in the old place"*, so probably near Armentieres, although about 15 miles behind the line, and at rest for part of the time. He was involved in the Fifth Battle of Ypres from 28th September to 2nd October, writing to say it had been *"pretty warm"* but although there was an attack on 28th, he didn't have to go 'over the top'.

In October, Jack was sent to the General HQ Machine Gun School in Wisques, Flanders for a month's training on the Vickers

Medium Machine Gun. The consensus was that the German army was defeated and couldn't last out much longer, and that surrender would soon come.

Meanwhile in hospital in England, Bob seemed to be on the mend. He had put on 5lbs in weight and hoped, finally, to be allowed leave home. But just before this happened, in early October, he wrote a few quick lines to his mother:

> *I have just got an attack of flu or something, so cannot travel. I expect I'll be alright by the end of the week.*

Tragically, this was to be Bob's last letter as, like many thousands of servicemen and millions of civilians worldwide, he had contracted the 1918 Pandemic (H1N1 virus), known as Spanish flu. Although serious enough in itself, because of his already TB-weakened lungs, Bob developed pneumonia and died on 10th October 1918, aged just 22. His parents had the final agony of losing their third son to the conflict. The terrible irony is that, despite his continued ill-health, Bob had managed to survive three years of active service in some of the major battles on the Western Front, to die just one month short of Armistice Day.

With the German Army on the run and the end of the war in sight, Jack and Douglas would have been shocked to hear the news of Bob's death. Bob was only two years older than Douglas and they were close. On 14th October 1918, Douglas wrote to his mother:

> *I don't suppose there is much that I can say. I suppose no one was expecting it were they? It seems such a shame, just as we were imaging him coming home safe for good. I hope you and the rest are not feeling too bad about it. Please do not worry about me at all.*

Having had time to reflect, he wrote to Mary Anne again three days later:

> *I shall miss him [Bob] very much and a great deal more when I come home and find him not there. We had quite decided to stick together after the war. I hope you and the others are cheering up a bit, it is the only thing to do.*

Similarly, Jack wrote with great emotion to his mother and separately to his father, on 12th October 1918:

> *It really is awful and came as a great shock to me. It does seem most rotten after all he had done in France. I don't know why it is, but all the best fellows seem to go. I am afraid that you and mother must be feeling pretty bad about it and I only wish I could help you out. I don't quite realise yet how much we have lost but we shall miss them most awfully when we all get back.*

Bob's Commanding Officer, Lt Col G I Parrie wrote to his parents:

> *He was a most valuable officer. Although very young he was a born leader of men and could do anything with his platoon, which was about the best in the battalion. He was extraordinarily popular with the officers and men.*

Bob's funeral took place at 2.30pm on Tuesday 15th October 1918 at Annesley All Saints Church and his parents placed a memorial brass plaque in the church, which simply read:

> *Died in Cosham Military Hospital after four years and two months' service. October 10th 1918, aged 22 years.*

His death is also recorded on the family memorial, which movingly states that their sons were lost *"In the morning of their lives."*

Although the end of the war was close, Douglas was in action throughout October, mainly at the Second Battle of Cambrai, and reported that many horses were killed, officers wounded, and that currently, he was the sole officer in his section. Fortunately for his grieving parents, Douglas didn't have much longer in danger, as the Armistice was declared on 11th November 1918. On Armistice Day Douglas wrote to Mary Anne:

> *You do not need to worry anymore about me at any rate. I wish all the others were alright though to see it... I shall get out of the army just as soon as I can.*

After Armistice Day, Jack was posted back to Egypt and wrote on 17th November from the General Helouan hospital in Giza:

> *I'm having sulphur baths and am supposed to drink the water. It's perfectly filthy. How are things at home now? I wish I could be at home now and help you shoot the game.*

It's likely the baths were to rid Jack of scabies, a common complaint in WW1 caused by lice from blankets and clothing, that created skin sores. Treatment was twice daily sulphur baths, which removed the scabs, followed by iodine applied to the skin, and in Jack's case, sulphur drinks too. Most cases were cured within a week or so. The following day (18th November) Jack wrote to his father and had clearly had enough:

> *The show is over at last. I don't see how I can get home. If you could write a letter or two saying you wanted to see me about business affairs I could put in for leave.*

Unfortunately for Jack, he doesn't seem to have been granted leave, as a month later he was still in the army and had been sent back to Flanders, though he was in better spirits. He wrote to his father from Ciney, 30 miles north of Namur, in Belgium, on 16th December, where he had got in some wild boar shooting and played rugby:

> *In winter quarters. Mother sent preserved fruits for Christmas. We had quite a cheery Christmas and some of us were cheerier than was altogether necessary!*

Jack finally returned to England to be reunited with his wife, daughter, and family in January 1919, and was de-mobilised in March, having lost three of his six brothers, his brother-in-law and a cousin in the war.

Douglas Marries

Despite having said that he would get out of the army as soon as he could, Douglas must have changed his mind, as he went on to

Molly, photographed in 1937

serve in Ireland and India. It was there that he met Mary (Molly) Bomford-Emerson, who had travelled to India to visit her sister.

The daughter of a GP from Bedford, Molly had been a volunteer nurse in the British Red Cross in France from 1916-1919. The couple married in June 1924 in Bedford. PTA Musters reports that Jack's wife Daphne thought that Molly was *"not quite from a suitable family at all"*, although she seems to have been well liked by everyone. The couple had four children:

- Patricius (named in honour of Douglas' father and elder brother) Chaworth-Musters (born 1925 in Rawalpindi, India, died 2010)
- David Mundy Chaworth-Musters (born 1926, Uttarakhand, India. Died 1933)
- Philip Robin Chaworth-Musters (born 1928, Norfolk, died 2021)
- Juliana Mary Chaworth-Musters (born 1935, Bedford).

After the war, the Government started to reduce the size of the forces and Douglas was one of the victims of the cuts. He left the army in the late 1920s and, on his return from India, began farming at Saxmundham in Suffolk.

After the war, Tony remained in the army working in a desk role at the Ministry of Munitions but in 1920, he was listed as being unable to work, as he suffered further ill-health from his original injuries. He was finally discharged from service on 29th January 1921. Later that year, on 4th December 1921, his sister Lina wrote (perceptively) to Mary Anne:

> *I hope Tony finds a job to suit him. I think he is too mentally active for farming and I don't think there will be much to be made out of it in the future.*

A Nation in Mourning

It will require the whole of the national energy to get things straight again.

Country Life

The Armistice was signed on 11th November 1918 to initial joy and relief in many quarters. Servant Helen Cecil[43] wrote home on 12th November from Great Wigsell in Sussex:

> *I never thought I should live to be so happy as I am today... Everybody was running around for hours and telling everybody else. Hawkhurst is a fine sight, arches of flags, real crowds of people, perfect strangers nearly kissing each other in the streets & the joy bells ringing.*

However, the initial reaction to the Armistice in the various theatres of war was mixed. Colonel Thomas Gowenlock, an intelligence officer in the American 1st Division, based in France, described what happened where he was posted[44]:

> *But at the front there was no celebration. Many soldiers believed the Armistice only a temporary measure and that the war would soon go on. As night came, the quietness, unearthly in its penetration, began to eat into their souls. The men sat around log fires, the first they had ever had at the front. They were trying to reassure themselves that there were no enemy batteries spying on them from the next hill.*

---

43. Pamela Horn, *Country House Society*.
44. http://www.eyewitnesstohistory.com/armistice.htm.

Once the initial joy had subsided at home, Britain became a nation in mourning. Globally, over ten million people had died, an average of 6,000 a day for four and a half years. Another 21 million had been wounded, many of whom would suffer mental or physical damage for the rest of their lives. Nearly seven million civilians died from disease, starvation or were killed in military operations. Britain alone had suffered 743,000 dead and over 1.5 million injured, and almost every family had suffered terribly.

The Chaworth-Musters family suffered more than many. They had lost their son and heir, Pat, fourth son Phil and fifth son, Bob to the war, plus their third son Tony sustained injuries that affected him throughout the rest of his life. They also lost son-in-law Hugh Pattinson, and nephew Roger.

Many senior officers have been derided over history for leading men to slaughter in the Great War but on the ground, the (mostly public-school) officers embodied the notions of service and sacrifice, and of deep patriotism. A wife and mother of a husband and two officer sons who served said: *"These are all my men and I am proud to feel they all held commissions before the outbreak of the war".* Apart from their great sorrow, Patrick and Mary Anne felt immense pride at the sacrifice of their three sons, whose bravery and sense of duty had garnered a total of four Military Crosses and a DSO. Like many parents they would have presented a face of public stoicism to cover their private anguish.

Mary Anne Seeks Recognition for Tony

However, Mary Anne felt a great sense of injustice that the efforts of all her boys were not equally valued. In 1919 she wrote to Tony's Commanding Officer Major Scott to find out why he had not been awarded for gallantry in the field for rescuing a colleague and getting shot in doing so. Tony appears to have been told at the time he'd been recommended for the Victoria Cross but later heard instead, this had been downgraded to the Military Cross.

This never materialised. Major Scott investigated and told Mary Anne that many recommendations made in the early part of the war were overlooked – probably because communications and honours systems had not yet been properly established. He discovered that General Percival had sent a recommendation for the Military Cross and strongly supported Tony's case, but the original application seemed to have been mislaid in 1914.

Showing great tenacity, Mary Anne also wrote to several of Tony's fellow officers, but none could precisely recollect or corroborate what happened at the time (or perhaps chose not to). The MC recommendation was resubmitted in 1919, with Colonel Hall and General Percival strongly recommending it but nothing came of it. Major Scott apologized to Mary Anne but concluded that nothing further could be done and added:

> *I certainly think that many men have received high awards during the war for doing much less than he [Tony] did. I hope he is well and strong now, though I suppose he can never hope to be fit for active service again.*

With the war over, life had to somehow go on and the economy and society had to be rebuilt. The men and women who served and survived were encouraged to play a full part in this regeneration. The following letter from Lieutenant Colonel W S Knox-Gore, of the 59th Division was typical of those sent by commanding officers to those who served under them:

> *Now that the time has come for you to leave the Army and go back to civil life, I wish, both personally and officially, to thank you for the service which you have given.*
>
> *You take away with you the priceless knowledge that you have played a man's [sic] part in this Great War for freedom and fair play. You will take away with you also your remembrances of your comrades, your pride in your Regiment and your love for your Country.*
>
> *You have played the game; go on playing it, and all will be well with the great Empire which you have helped to save.*
>
> *I wish you every prosperity and happiness.*

The code of the time is unmistakeable here; the public-school ethos of 'playing the game', love of tribe and country, and the unshakeable belief in the continuity of Empire – when death and killing was the reality.

This sense of continuity was tested soon after the end of the War and for many years to come. In the immediate aftermath there was the global pandemic of Spanish flu that lasted from November 1918 to mid-1920. It is estimated that about 500 million people (one-third of the world's population at the time) were infected and around 50 million worldwide died, including over 228,000 in the UK. There was an unusually high mortality rate among the 20 to 40 age group; the very men and women who had been through so much in the recent war. This is likely to have been caused by the stress and ill-health they had been placed under for four years.

Again, the family was caught up in this tragedy. As we've heard, Bob caught Spanish flu in hospital, which turned into pneumonia and killed him in October 1918. And in November 1918, Douglas wrote to his father: *"I'm sorry you have the flu. Lots of others in the services are getting it bad and dying."* Patrick survived the flu, but the virus noticeably weakened his health and probably shortened his life.

Commemorating the Fallen

Once the initial jubilation of the Armistice had subsided, many were sombre, remembering the dead and aware of the terrible state the country was in. Most pressing was the need to come to terms with the loss of so many men and women. Many who survived experienced an acute sense of guilt, speaking of the 'ghosts in the room' at large gatherings, where former friends would have been present.

In 1919 it was suggested that the body of an unidentified soldier should be brought home for reburial, to become a national memorial for all those killed in the Great War who had no grave. In 1920 the War Office agreed, and at 11.00am on 11th November 1920, the King unveiled the new Cenotaph, designed by leading architect Edward Lutyens, and the body of the unknown soldier was interred with great ceremony in Westminster Abbey.

It is worth mentioning the important work of commemoration undertaken by the Imperial War Graves Commission (WGC). As we have heard, in the early years of the war especially, the dead were left unburied or buried hastily near where they fell, their graves marked, at best, by simple wooden crosses. In 1914, Fabian Ware, a Director of Rio Tinto Company, bemoaned the lack of any official mechanism for locating or documenting graves and he started collaborating with the British Red Cross. By 1915, 50,000 graves had been registered and the WGC was established by Royal Charter in May 1917, with Mr Ware as Vice Chair.

There was public outcry in 1918 when the Government decided not to repatriate the bodies of those who had fallen and, instead, the WGC set about the mammoth task of establishing cemeteries and organising (re)burials and headstones. Between 1920 and 1923, they created over 1,000 cemeteries overseas and were shipping over 4,000 headstones a week, completing their work around 1927. The family archives in Nottingham University contain correspondence and the completed forms sent by Patrick and Mary Anne outlining the details and inscriptions they wanted on their two son's headstones.

Two of Patrick and Mary Anne's three lost sons were buried in different cemeteries in Flanders, so it was important for the couple to honour them locally. Patrick and Mary Anne added a citation to the family memorial plaque in All Saints Church, Annesley. It reads:

> *To the glorious memory of Patricius George Chaworth-Musters, Philip Mundy Chaworth-Musters MC, and Robert Chaworth-Musters MC, eldest, fourth and fifth sons of John Patricius Chaworth-Musters Esq of Annesley Park, Notts, and their cousin, Roger Michael Chaworth-Musters, Lieutenant 50th Squadron Royal Flying Corps, second son of Lancelot George BM Chaworth-Musters Esq, of Field Dalling, Norfolk, He fell in aerial combat in France May 7th, 1917 aged 19. In the morning of their lives.*

They also added a side on the memorial stone in the churchyard to commemorate their boys. The inscription at the bottom reads:

> *He is not a God of the dead, but of the living, as all live unto him. Be thou faithful unto death and I will give thee a crown of life.*

Many public schools organised commemorative ceremonies for fallen former pupils. For example, in December 1920, parents attended a ceremony at Eton school to unveil a bronze frieze running along the wall of the Founder's Quad. It recorded the names of 1,157 Etonians who had perished; an attrition rate of 20% for the school.

Other families derived comfort from visiting the graves of their fallen relatives in war cemeteries. Lady Kenmare visited her son's grave and told her friend Lady Desborough,[45] it was:

---

45. Pamela Horn, *Country House Society*.

> *All so beyond comprehension, the wide battlefields, so awful, so terrible; the strange hush over all that devastation, the grim ruins, the piteous little crosses standing here and there in utter loneliness; one's mind and soul seemed to break.*

Seeking comfort in any way they could find it, there was a noted rise in the popularity of spiritual séances, with many popular mediums booked well in advance. However, the *Bystander* magazine warned of the trickery used to fool grief-stricken wives and mothers that contact had been made with their dearly departed. Madeleine Beard[46] sums up the mood well:

> *Among the men who returned from the war there emerged a conspiracy of silence, a mutual and unspoken understanding that the horrors witnessed on the battlefield should be forgotten. For landed society, the happy world of the years before the war was transformed into one of cynical detachment.... The realisation that landed wealth and influence was no longer unassailable seemed to engender among the survivors a brittle, frenetic outlook.*

This *"brittle, frenetic outlook"* was captured by the antics of 'The Bright Young Things', a moniker coined by the tabloid press to describe a small but high-profile group of Bohemian young aristocrats and socialites in 1920s London. They threw elaborate parties, and some drank heavily or used drugs — all of which was enthusiastically covered by journalists. The group inspired several authors to write novels on this theme, including Nancy Mitford (*Highland Fling*), Anthony Powell (*A Dance to the Music of Time*), and Evelyn Waugh's later novel, *Vile Bodies*.

For most major landowners, there was an attempt to return to a semblance of normality. Chaperones returned to favour to escort younger women to dances and balls. Men had their clubs, which offered drinking, dining and in some cases, gambling. For both sexes, there was a return to the Saturday to Monday house parties with tennis, golf, punting, dancing, fishing, and cards on offer. And, according to the *Field* magazine, many were determined to make a fresh start and by March 1919, many hunts had relaunched themselves.

---

46. Madeleine Beard, *English Landed Society in the Twentieth Century*.

A 'Perfect' Economic Storm

Whilst trying to cope with the grief of his broken family, Patrick's pressing concern was to, once again, stabilise the income from his remaining estates. The Government had introduced the Corn Production Act in 1917 to guarantee minimum prices for wheat and oats and to minimise imports. It resulted in a pay increase for farm workers (as they were a scarce commodity), and a rise in farmers' profits and land productivity. But the reopening of peacetime trade changed this and, in 1921, the Act was repealed. The result was a rapid reduction in agricultural wages – by as much as 40% in one year – and an increased indebtedness of arable farmers.

At the same time, the UK experienced an agricultural depression, as the price of meat and wheat, barley and oats fell in the face of increased competition from Australia, North and South America, now sea trade was re-established. This led to many tenant farmers giving up their tenancies, further reducing the income from landed estates.

Landowners had been prevented from raising agricultural tenancy rents during the war and had only raised them about 15% since 1918, despite a sharp increase in their outgoings. As food prices slid in 1920, landowners were forced to reduce their rents once more, some by as much as 20%, to keep their remaining tenants in business.

An additional burden for landowners came in the form of a rise in income tax during the war and, the introduction of a new super-tax on incomes over £10,000 pa (around £400,000 today), which is likely to have affected the Chaworth-Musters. Income tax rates were increased further in Lloyd George's 1919 budget. In addition, land tax was now levied on gross income rather than net, which proved disadvantageous to landowners who generally had large outgoings for property maintenance and estate improvements, on top of their wider philanthropic commitments in the local community. These outgoings were no longer taken into consideration.

The final blow for major landowners was Lloyd George's increase in death duties on estates, which were raised in 1919 to 40% on estates valued at £2 million or more, compared with only 15% pre-war. Also, the estates now had to be valued at the current valued *sale* price of the land, not the rental price, as before, so the burden of death duties was much greater.

As if this was not enough for Patrick to contend with, the Government imposed increased duties on mineral rights, so those like him, with mining assets were also hit hard. Many were forced to sell land, mineral rights, sell or let country houses, or dispose of other assets such as furniture and paintings. *Country Life* claimed that the record of land sales in 1918 would *"take a lot of beating"* but it was comfortably exceeded by sales between 1919 and 1921. In total, a quarter of all land in Britain changed ownership between 1918 and 1922.

Many large country and town houses were sold and turned into schools, museums, hospitals, and asylums. Successful businessmen (notable among them, war profiteers) bought houses from impoverished gentry and were often regarded with hostility by the retained servants, who (like others in society) felt this 'nouveau' money was inferior to 'old' money.

Despite this, the new entrants generally succeeded in buying their way into high society through the purchase of property, marrying into it, or by buying titles from the Government. Although this had long been possible, Lloyd George pursued it more systematically than others before him, using a network of agents. At the time, Knighthoods were said to cost between £10,000-£12,000 (£394,000-£471,000), baronetcies £35,000-£40,000 (£1.35m-£1.57m) and peerages, more.

Not surprisingly, many of the landed society complained – both about the process and the quality of those entering the peerage. Among their targets were Sir William Vestey (who was described as a wartime tax dodger), Sir Rowland Hodge of Northumberland Shipbuilding Company (who had been convicted for hoarding over a ton of food during the war) and Sir Joseph Drughorn (who was convicted for trading with the enemy). With the benefit of history and hindsight, one might say that many of the landed society who complained at the time made their fortunes in equally dubious ways – principally slave trading and/or the exploitation of both slaves and workers on their land and in their factories.

Running the Estate and the House

The Chaworth-Musters were undoubtedly greatly affected by the war. In terms of their lifestyle, they had lost sons, including their heir, their daughters were mostly married and living elsewhere, and Patrick and Mary Anne were not the house-party type. They didn't pursue the frenetic social life of those in London, or probably even play such a great part in the county set, as before.

Patrick (in weakened health) was grappling with the future of their estates, which must have looked somewhat bleak. He had sold much of the lucrative land and property after his father's death in the late 1880s and 1890s to raise funds for taxes, pay off debts and fund further home improvements, as well as provide for the ongoing living expenses associated with a family of twelve, with six boys at public boarding school.

He had little property left to sell, no estates with associated titles, and was by now living off the income from Wiverton Hall and its nearby estates, and the Annesley estates. In 1904, the Worswick family's lease of Annesley Colliery ended, and a syndicate headed by the Hardwick Colliery Company took over the colliery. A mining engineer's report in 1901 had described the colliery as antiquated, even though it had only been in production for just over 30 years.

In 1921 the main Top Hard seam was abandoned at Annesley Colliery, after having been worked since 1867, and production was concentrated on the lower seam, Deep Soft. Tonnages would have reduced considerably, resulting in fewer royalties to the family. Royalties around the time in Nottinghamshire averaged at 1.7 pence per tonne and in the war years, before the closure of Top Hard, the colliery produced about 730,000 tonnes per annum, potentially resulting in royalties of £12,410, (over £800,000 today). This would drop to around £400,000 pa (in today's money) after Top hard closed. And these royalties would be shared between other directors of ACC and not just the Chaworth-Musters, who would receive far less than this total sum.

In the immediate aftermath of the war, Mary Anne would have her own challenges in running the household. The war had changed everything in relation to domestic staff, with thousands of male servants joining the armed forces and women undertaking war-related work as agricultural labourers, munitions and factory workers, bus conductors, canteen organisers and nurses.

In 1903 Emmeline Pankhurst and others, frustrated by the lack of progress in gaining votes for women, founded the Women's Social and Political Union (WSPU), which ran until 1918. Their efforts contributed towards the implementation in 1918, of the Representation of the People Act, which extended the vote to virtually all men over the age of 21 and allowed women over the age of 30 who owned property, to vote. This would include Mary Anne, who was of the right age and owned their house in Norway.

Although voting equality didn't come into effect for women until 1928 via the Equal Franchise Act, by 1918, about two-thirds of women in the UK could vote, widening opportunities for women. It became increasingly difficult to persuade women, especially young women, into domestic service. They preferred to work in shops, offices, and factories, especially since the Factory Acts ensured they would work shorter hours than they would in service. In addition, they had more freedom in their time off work to socialise, especially with men, than they would in service.

Whilst job opportunities for women were good, for men it was a different story. Thousands of demobbed (and injured or battle scarred) men were now struggling to find work, as the economy headed towards recession.

In 1919-20, roughly 2.4 million British workers went on strike, mostly in the mines, railways, and docks. Mines had been put under Government control in 1917 and there were calls, led by mineworkers, for a nationalised industry, which (not surprisingly) were strongly rejected by the mine owners, so Lloyd George backed off from nationalising the industry. However, the post-war production boom ended, and both exports and coal prices fell rapidly in 1921. Lloyd George handed the mines back to owners, who immediately set about shoring up profits by reducing wages – in some areas by as much as 49%.

Miners went on strike for three months in 1921 but ended up being forced back to work on worse terms than before. This worker unrest continued, on and off, until the General Strike in 1926, which also ended in crushing defeat for the miners and organised labour generally.

Those who were unemployed were initially helped by the introduction of the 'Out of Work Donation' in 1918, which gave short-term relief to the registered unemployed. However, by 1921 the position changed radically, as UK unemployment was now close to 20%. The Unemployment Insurance Act 1921 extended the eligibility provisions, and the length of time benefit could be drawn but claimants now had to show that they were genuinely seeking work and were obliged to accept *any work* paying a fair wage.

So, within a space of just three years, the position may have improved for the Chaworth-Musters in terms of staff. Moving from a shortage of domestics in the war and its immediate aftermath, the 1921 job-seeking clause in the National Insurance Act, meant those seeking dole were encouraged to take jobs in service.

But, whilst the couple may have found it easier to recruit servants, their income would have been hit by the continued agricultural recession, the recent miner's strike, and a subsequent drop-off in coal production. Despite this unrest, the family's philanthropy continued. In 1921, during the miner's strike, Jack gave a piece of ground on the estate for the miners to create a cricket pitch. The Annesley Park Eleven that he formed and skippered for some years was still going strong in 1937.

A Final Wedding

Despite their grief and economic difficulties, life had to go on, and on 27th January 1921, the last of Patrick and Mary Anne's daughters, Ruth (1887-1967), married Colonel Henry Francis Askwith (1865-1938). Ruth was a mature 34 years old, and her husband was 56 (so, only five years younger than her father).

Colonel Askwith was a career soldier in the Royal Horse Artillery (his late father having been a General in that regiment). Henry fought throughout the Boer war, served in the Indian army, and was appointed to the Companion of the Order of St Michael and St George in 1916, for his services to Commonwealth nations. During the Great War, he was made a temporary Brigadier-General, and was involved in many of the major battles on the Western Front, being mentioned three times in despatches. Colonel Askwith was a Deputy Lieutenant and JP, like Patrick, and may have met Ruth via her father.

The couple married in All Saints Church, Annesley, in a simple service. Patrick was sadly too ill by now to give Ruth away, so the duty was performed by her brother Jack, who was the eldest surviving son. The *Nottingham Evening Post* reported on the *"pretty ceremony"*:

> *The dress of the bride, who was given away by her brother Major J N Chaworth-Musters DSO, consisted of*

plain white brocade. She also wore an exquisite lace veil lent by Mrs Milward, her sister, and carried a bouquet composed of white heather and carnations.

The bride was attended by her three little nieces [two being Lina and Hugh's pretty six-year-old twin girls Bridget and Primrose] ... they were becomingly attired in blue velvet frocks, gold lace caps and gold-coloured socks and shoes. Their bouquets consisted of daffodils... The service, which was choral, was marked with simplicity.

The service was followed by a reception at Annesley Hall, with all the family members present, including her father, Patrick, and various cousins. Once married, the couple lived in London, near Harrods, and had no children, spending much of their spare time enjoying horse-racing.

Though Ruth was said to be stubborn and argumentative, she was also noted for being very kind to younger members of the family. Henry died in 1936, allegedly whilst playing an energetic game of Bridge! Ruth lived in Norfolk for many years (near her uncle and cousins), ending up in Moreton-in-Marsh along with her sister Lina, being looked after by her niece, Bridget Pattinson (Biddy). She died on 6th August 1967, aged 80.

Patrick Passes Away

Sadly, Patrick's ill-health was now serious and by the end of 1921, he was confined to bed under the care of Dr Dixon of Eastwood. He died on 12th December 1921, aged 61, of heart failure (specifically a hardening of the arteries).

Average life expectancy for a man in 1920 was 55.6 years, so the fact that Patrick lived a little longer was probably accounted for by his wealth and better standard of living. Mary Anne was 58 when Patrick died and had been with him as partner, then wife, for 40 years. She must have felt immensely sad, as in the past six years, she had lost three of her sons and now her beloved husband, and as far as we are aware, she wasn't that close to her own family in Bedfordshire.

The *Nottingham Evening Post* ran ten column inches on 14th December, announcing Patrick's death, under the headline *"An heroic family"*:

> Practically since the death of his son, Captain Robert CM MC KRR two years ago, the Squire of Annesley had been in failing health and during the last few months had been confined to his room, with Dr Dixon of Eastwood, in frequent attendance... [He] preferred the more romantic life of travel in pursuit of sport. The result was that he was a great naturalist and ornithologist, and at the Hall may be seen one of the largest private collections of eggs in the kingdom. He delighted also in fishing in the Norwegian waters, and amongst the countries he visited may be mentioned Lapland, Iceland, Russia, Germany and well as South America.

Patrick's love of nature and birds was shared by many of his children but especially by Jim, his youngest child, who was an ornithologist and later used the family house at Vaulen as his base. The obituary went on to mention the couple's War efforts:

> Not only did the late Mr Chaworth-Musters and Mrs Musters contribute so largely from their family, but they also assisted the war charities in a very large measure. One of the late squire's duties was to give his Daimler and Humber motor cars for Red Cross work. The people of Annesley and neighbourhood shared in their benefactions, and those lads who served at the war have fragrant memories of the parcels they received from Annesley Hall, the number being compiled at no less than 4,000.
>
> This sentiment was echoed by a work colleague, Mr Bonner, Chairman of Petty Sessions, who made sympathetic reference to the death of Mr Chaworth-Musters, saying he was the oldest member of the Bench, having been appointed JP over thirty years ago. He believed Mr Musters never recovered from the loss of his three sons who were killed during the war.
>
> He was a gentleman who was held in the highest esteem, and his death was undoubtedly a great loss to the district. Mr Bonner added that he was informed that every man who served in the Army in the parish of which Mr Musters was a Squire was remembered weekly by a parcel from Annesley Hall whilst on service.

On 17th December, the *Nottinghamshire Journal* covered Patrick's funeral (albeit in a notably smaller piece than for his father's funeral):

> The late Squire of Annesley was laid to rest in the peaceful cemetery at Annesley All Saints, close to the striking memorial to his three sons, lost in the war. The church had been unable to accommodate the large assembly of mourners, drawn from a sorrowing countryside, with the result that there was a huge concourse round the open grave.
>
> The cortège was an impressive spectacle. The plain oak coffin made from wood grown on the estate was brought from the Hall on a hay wagon. All the bearers

> were farm labourers. They were followed in procession by colliery officials, and numerous tenants, whilst scores of villagers and many who had come from a distance gathered at the church gates. The service in the church was simple yet impressive.

Like his father before him, Patrick's funeral was a simple, country affair, with no elaborate coffin or hearse being used. Mary Anne had the following carved on his memorial stone:

> There is no death, what seems so is transition.

The family also erected a memorial plaque in Annesley Church, which was moving and more personal in nature:

> In affectionate remembrance of John Patricius Chaworth-Musters... A devoted husband and father. A kind and just Landlord. A keen Naturalist and most loyal Subject of the King.

Probate was granted on Patrick's Will in March 1922, with his brother George among the executors. It shows he left an estate of over £124,000 (equivalent to over £5.3 million today). We don't know who benefitted but it is likely that the bulk of the estate was formed of the properties and estates of Annesley and Wiverton, which automatically passed to his heir, Jack. However, Patrick no doubt left some specific provision for Mary Anne, knowing that she wouldn't inherit any money from her own family.

Special wartime legislation had reduced the burden of death duties levied on landed estates in relation to those who had died in the war. It was considered especially difficult if an owner died, quickly followed by that of his heir. This legislation may have helped reduce the tax burden when Jack inherited, as the family's true heir Pat had died during the war.

At the time Jack lived at nearby Wiverton Hall, and chose not to move to Annesley until 1923, after the birth of his last child. Perhaps this was in deference to his mother, allowing Mary Anne time to grieve and stay in the comfort of the home she had known since she was 18 years old. Jack continued running the estate and business affairs, as he had been doing for the past year, whilst his father was unwell.

The photo to the left (above) is thought by some to be of Mary Anne in her late fifties, around the time Patrick died. It can't be verified but there certainly does seem to be strong a resemblance around the mouth and eyes to a photo taken in 1912, when she was 49.

When Jack and his family moved to Annesley Hall in 1923, unusually, Mary Anne chose not to relocate to Wiverton Hall, which was the home traditionally used by family widows (including her mother-in-law, Lina). Instead, she moved to a flat in London and Jack let out Wiverton Hall.

Her flat at 3 Morpeth Mansions, Morpeth Terrace, Westminster SW1 (pictured above), was in a substantial red brick Edwardian mansion block on a quiet road fringed by London plane trees. This choice of home was likely to have been for several reasons. Mary Anne perhaps preferred to live in a home that was a lot less grand and demanding than Wiverton. It also took her out of the local county society, so (unlike Lina), she would not have to continue with the social duties and 'good works' that she may have found a strain without Patrick at her side.

It meant she would be close to her widowed sister-in-law Catherine (Kitty) and widowed daughter Lina Pattinson and her two young girls, who lived in London before later moving to Hampshire. It may also have been a question of economy, with the rent on a modest flat being far less than the running of Wiverton, from which Jack could now gain an income, to help shore up the family's increasingly burdened finances.

Whatever the reasons that drove this decision, Mary Anne would have led a modest life, enjoying overlooking a school and its playground. PTA Musters comments: *"She was well provided for with a convenient flat, and occasionally younger members of the family would be taken to meet her."* Barbara Chaworth-Musters (Tony's daughter) is reported as recalling a visit in London, aged four (so around the time Mary Anne moved to London) to her grandmother, the *"splendid Polly"* (further evidence that her servant's name stuck with her in close family circles).

We also know from a letter Mary Anne sent to the War Graves Commission in 1924 that she continued to spend her summers abroad in Norway, staying with Jim who lived full-time at Vaulen from the mid-1920s, with other family members no doubt visiting.

Mary Anne's Name is Defamed

Shortly after her move to London, there was an unpleasant incident in 1925, word of which may have reached Mary Anne and her children. A family cousin, Rachel Daubney was researching and writing a 'pedigree' of the Norfolk side of the family (the Hamond's – Patrick's Great Uncle). Rachel wrote to Winifred Chaworth-Musters, a distant cousin by marriage to the family, seeking information on the Hamonds.

Winifred was a born-again Christian who, when her naval husband died in 1929, walked round Great Britain for a wager of

£100, saying she would not spend any money on food or accommodation. She won the wager and wrote a book of her travels. After that, she travelled the world, earning her living as a journalist and author, and converted to Islam in 1930. She was made bankrupt in 1931 but lived to the age of 90, dying in Somerset in 1963.

Eccentric or not, her comments made in reply to enquiries by Rachel were far from Christian in tone, being snobbish and untrue, and they caused great offence. The letters form part of the Hamond family archive lodged in Norfolk Record Office in Norwich. Her first letter (1st November 1925) criticises the Hamonds but goes onto slander Mary Anne (whom she also calls Polly):

> *The Hamonds are dear people but they were bankers and have no pedigree – they only had money...we love them but they are nobodies!*
>
> *Polly Musters was a harlot, though of course that fact was ignored by those who liked the history and comfort of beautiful Annesley. I made a great fuss with her and she 'liked' me, only because I wanted to go to Annesley. I thought her really too common for words. Poor Aunt Louisa did the same.*
>
> *If she had no money and no place, her sins would have been ever held before her face!! Forgive me saying this but Jesus told the woman fallen in adultery to go and sin no more. He never meant other women to think they could sin again and be quietly forgiven as she was... we have more right to be in the family records than the eleven children of a Harlot like Polly for she may have lived with other men before living with Patrick.*
>
> *The four sons can never stand up for their mother's honour. Polly's sons could not deny any man or woman, boy or girl, who called their mother a whore – for she is one and will be one till she dies and that branch will chop off.*

Apart from being wildly offensive, her claims are inaccurate. Mary Anne didn't commit adultery, as both she and Patrick were unmarried to anyone else when they began their relationship. There is also no evidence she ever lived with another man prior to Patrick.

Clearly distressed, Rachel Daubney replied:

> *The Hamonds were never bankers. Your remarks about Polly Musters are greatly uncalled for. If you thought I knew all, it was unnecessary to tell me – and if you thought I didn't know it – it was still more unnecessary to tell me. 'Let him that is without sin among you first cast a stone at her'.*

She signed off saying simply *"Yours"*, adding *"for I can't feel any affection for you."* Winifred replied, defending her claim in much the same vein and received a final, firm reply from Rachel: *"This correspondence had better now close."*

Rachel then wrote to other Hamond family members about Winifred, warning them off her:

> *She shouts harlot...about everybody, dead or alive, who has ever had an illegitimate child. It is not a true description anyhow. She knows nothing of anybody's pedigree. I answered her so shortly as to be almost uncourteous. Of course, her father has been in a madhouse for years, so one can't say a great deal that one otherwise would. The mixture of pride and religion is inconceivable and her letters are poisonous to make one feel sick literally.*

Hopefully, word of this exchange did not reach Mary Anne, as it would no doubt have been very upsetting for her to hear that over 40 years after joining the family, there was still someone (albeit eccentric or mentally unstable) who held this view. Instead, Mary Anne lived quietly in London, visiting nearby family and friends, and receiving visits from other family members who were spread throughout the country: Jack was living at Annesley, Elsie in Nottinghamshire, Rita, and Ruth both near Sheffield, Tony in Colchester, Douglas in Suffolk (and later Bedford) and Jim divided his time between Norway and Surrey.

Mary Anne Passes Away

Only nine years after Patrick passed away, Mary Anne died, aged 67 on 1st March 1930, at the home of her eldest daughter, Rita Baldwin Young, at The Grange, Eckington, near Sheffield. The Grange is a fine, double-fronted Victorian house, now run as a care home by Derbyshire County Council. We don't know the exact cause of death or whether she was by now living with her daughter or just visiting. Mary Anne was reported as dying *"early on a Saturday morning, after only a few hours' illness"*, which sounds like she could have had a heart attack or stroke. PTA Musters says Mary Anne was *"much respected and greatly missed."*

Her death is indexed twice, once under Chaworth-Musters and the other as Mary A C Musters, registered in March 1930 in the district of Chesterfield. Her funeral service and interment were at Annesley. The *Nottingham Journal* of 6th March 1930 reported on her funeral:

> *The funeral took place yesterday afternoon of Mrs Mary Anne Chaworth-Musters, whose death took place at the residence of her daughter Mrs Baldwin Young, The Grange Eckinton, Derbyshire at the age of sixty-seven, early on a Saturday morning, after only a few hours' illness. Prior to the interment, a service was held in the parish church, All Saints Annesley, and was conducted by Canon W H Kynaston of Lincoln Cathedral [previously the Vicar of Annesley]...*
>
> *The organist played 'O rest in the Lord' and the 'Dead March in Saul', and the bearers were eight of the old employees of the estate. The hymns sung in the church were 'There is a blessed home', 'Son of my soul' and 'Abide with me'. The lesson was taken from the 15th chapter of Corinthians and the Psalm sung was 'The Lord is my shepherd'. The service at the graveside was conducted by Canon Kynaston. The deceased lady, who until the death of her husband, Mr J P Chaworth-Musters resided at Annesley Hall, where she was highly respected and her good work, during the war in connection with the men serving their King and Country and the families left at home, will be an everlasting memory.*

The newspaper listed the chief mourners, which included most of the family members, Patrick's sister Kitty, and senior members of the Annesley estate. None of Mary Anne's side of the family are listed as attending, and possibly they didn't. Mary Anne was commemorated in a simple manner on the family's memorial in Annesley All Saints churchyard, with no personal inscription, other

than her age and date of death. Humble in life, as in death, perhaps this was as she wished it.

The probate on her estate was recorded on 13th May 1930 and the contents of her Will reported in the local papers in mid-June showed she left a reasonable estate (probably mostly comprising the house in Vaulen):

> Mrs Mary Ann Chaworth-Musters... left estate of the gross value of £6,691, [£333,142 today] with net personalty £5,977 [£297,593] ... She left £50 [£2,489] each to her grandchildren and £100 [£4,978] to one of them. The Military Crosses and medals and two small school running cups 'won by my late sons' Capt. Philip Mundy Chaworth-Musters MC and Capt. Robert Chaworth-Musters MC and 'the polo cup won by my late son, Lieut. Patricius George Chaworth-Musters' were left to her son, Douglas Chaworth-Musters.
>
> She declared: 'It is my wish that my daughter, Margarita Young, and my son, the said Douglas Chaworth-Musters, should go over my clothes and personal belongings, two boxes of papers, the suitcases with tiny mementoes belonging to my late sons, and a tin box containing cups and other mementoes of them, and that any letters therein or such as he thinks it advisable to burn, should be burnt by the said Douglas Chaworth-

Musters'. All her real estate in Norway she left to her son, James Lawrence Chaworth-Musters and subject to several specific bequests, the residue of the property between her sons Douglas, and James Lawrence.

The notable points are that she left nothing to Jack, deliberately and fairly, as he had inherited the bulk of the estate from his father in 1921, being the male heir. What is surprising is that she left the bulk of her estate to her two youngest sons, Douglas and Jim, and nothing directly to Tony or to her four daughters. Douglas by then had been married for six years and had two young children, whilst Jim never married.

More poignant is the fact that she had kept the small school trinkets and mementoes of her dead sons all her life. In his war letters Douglas comes across as the most compassionate and sentimental of the sons, so this perhaps explains why Mary Anne left the trinkets in his care. The family archive in Nottingham University also contains extensive press cuttings that she kept of Pat, Phil and Bob's war achievements and their deaths, which were covered in more than 20 publications, including *The Lady* and *Horse & Hound* magazines.

The final sadness is that she asked for all her papers and letters to be burnt, so that we have no diaries or journals that reveal her own thoughts and words throughout her life. Perhaps this was also a sign that the unconfident girl remained so to the end – a now elderly woman wishing to mask her extraordinary history.

Yet from those humblest of beginnings, Mary Anne had an exceptional life. Patrick clearly broke with the tradition of marrying to further the interests of the family estate or to simply provide the 'heir and a spare'. He married Mary Anne, knowing she had no money or status, and they had more children than their parents, probably because their relationship was a love match with a deep connection, which represented much more than mere duty.

PTA Musters says of her that:

> *Polly was a truly remarkable woman. Her dress sense and accomplishments were impeccable and her relatively humble origins were never guessed by many who came to know and love her. Her grandson Roderick Milward still refers to 'Miss Sharpe' with affection.*

He adds that the Chaworth-Musters of that period were a:

> *Seemingly close-knit family, all of them fluent in Norwegian but with a local Bergen accent. They were self-reliant, outward looking, country-bred and capable young people – very proud of their parents and heritage.*

Perhaps in her earlier years, Mary Anne couldn't believe her luck at having escaped the drudgery of straw plaiting and then domestic service, but her later life was not without difficulties. She appears to have been a simple country girl at heart and perhaps didn't truly want or enjoy the trappings and responsibility that came with her role as lady of the manor.

We know she suffered several prolonged bouts of illness in her later years, from mentions in letters from her children. Her role may also have pushed her further away from her own family, which was likely to have caused sadness. And of course, she had the anguish of losing three sons and having one critically injured in the Great War and the knowledge that this loss contributed to her husband's early death soon after the war.

Nevertheless, Mary Anne was hopefully rightly proud of her accomplishments. She had enjoyed a long and seemingly happy marriage, raised a large and close-knit family, endured tragic loss with great stoicism, and performed her duty to husband, family, and country throughout. Moreover, she was personally admired and loved by those that knew her.

The End of an Era

As the youngest child, we've made scant mention so far of James (Jim) Chaworth-Musters (1901-1948), so we'll cover his life here, as well as round up the lives of the other sons. Jim may well have been a favourite of Mary Anne, being her youngest and a gentle, nature-loving soul. Despite this, he had an interesting life, displaying the family's trademark duty and bravery in World War II.

This photo is of Jim in his naval uniform during WWII, and reveals a kind face, with a twinkle in his eye, and looking remarkably like photos of his father at the same age, although slimmer in the face. He was born at Annesley on 1st July 1901 and educated at Rugby School like his brothers. Fortunately, Jim was too young to serve in the Great War (being eligible only three months before Armistice Day) and, unlike all his brothers, he didn't join the services and instead read geography at Caius College, Cambridge University.

He inherited his father's love of nature and birds, fostered by their summers in Norway, and decided to focus on this as a career. Whilst still at Cambridge, in 1921, aged nearly 20, he took part in his first expedition to Jan Mayen – a Norwegian volcanic island in the Arctic Ocean. The success of the expedition led to him cutting short his studies and joining the Royal Geographical Society, later becoming a Fellow.

After this, he started a serious study of Palaearctic small mammals and birds, undertaking frequent field expeditions, including to Libya (1926), Greece (1931), the U.S.S.R. (1936), Morocco (1937) and Afghanistan (1939); from all these expeditions he brought back material for study and to enhance the national collection.[47]

A collection of his drawings of whales and plants, executed mainly in Norway between 1921-1928, is part of Nottingham University's family collection. Scientific peers stated that Jim's knowledge was deep and his critical judgement extremely sound. He was an authority on the works of early European and Asiatic travellers, including those of Carl Linnaeus, and his publications included a biography of Père Armand David, discoverer of the giant panda. Jim himself discovered a new species of mouse in Afghanistan, which was named after him ('Musterii') and forms part of the Natural History Museum's vast collection.

Mary Anne left Jim her property in Vaulen on her death in 1930, and he continued to live there in the summer each year, until the start of World War Two. In 1939 he was working as British Vice-Consul for Bergen in Norway, representing the Government at key meetings. He was fluent in Norwegian and was well-integrated in the community.

Jim's Part in WWII

After the Germans invaded Norway, landing at Bergen on 9th April 1940, Jim escaped to the Nordfjord area (North of Bergen) on foot, posing as a 'village idiot', to avoid answering questions if stopped. He then went into the mountains and spent six weeks moving from hut to hut on skis. He discovered two British soldiers who had been separated from their unit and, after convincing them that he was not a German agent, they travelled to the coast, persuaded a fisherman to take them to Shetland, and set out across the North Sea. They were fortunate to be picked up by a British destroyer and returned to England. It was said that Jim succeeded in this adventure largely owing to his speaking the regional Bergen dialect like a local, knowing the geography, and by his typically calm and laid-back attitude to unexpected events.

---

47. https://no.wikipedia.org/wiki/James_Lawrence_Chaworth-Musters.

Back in Britain, he quickly joined up. It is said that he considered the army but would be required to shave off his full beard, which he refused to do, so instead became a Lieutenant in the Royal Naval Volunteer Reserve. He was immediately recruited to the Special Operations Executive (a secret organisation in WWII) as a Transport Lieutenant.[48]

The SOE's purpose was to conduct reconnaissance, espionage, and sabotage in occupied Europe, and to support local resistance movements. Jim conducted shipping operations to transport Norwegian refugees to the Shetland Isles to join the Allied forces. Based in Lerwick, he also took part in the first sabotage raids into occupied Norway in May 1940 and continued throughout the year, helping create a weapons depot, and blowing up pipelines, power, and telephone lines.

In March 1941, Jim was involved in establishing the SOE's Norwegian Independent Company 1, (NORIC1) which was officially formed in July 1941 and became known as Kompani Linge, after its first leader, Captain Martin Linge (who died in a

---

48. https://no.wikipedia.org/wiki/Kompani_Linge.

major raid in December 1941). Originally, Kompani Linge undertook commando raids (e.g., on heavy water plants and rail lines), led the Norwegian resistance movement, and conducted intelligence/espionage operations.

Jim also acted as a liaison officer between the SOE and the Norwegian Government in London, for whom he interrogated escapees from Norway to gain valuable intelligence. Kompani Linge was disbanded at the end of the war and, in 1945, Jim was awarded the King Haakon VII Medal of Liberty (also known as the Norwegian War Medal) for significant services to the country. He returned to Norway to receive the medal and was met with acclaim, with the Trondheim newspaper running an article on 23rd October 1945, headed *"Musters from Surnadal"*, and featuring his exploits. His nephew Robin later said that the family knew he was involved in training resistance fighters in the war but that he was reluctant to talk more about his involvement.

Photo of Jim Lawrence's statue at Vaulen, courtesy of Astrid Meland*

* Astrid Meland, CC BY-SA 3.0.

In 2004, a memorial statue was erected at Vaulen for Jim and a plaque commemorated the Kompani Linge's exploits, with many of the company's survivors present at the ceremony, as well as Robin and Bob Chaworth-Musters (Douglas' and Jack's sons). The photos above show the statue and a photo of Jim c. 1942 that it was based on. In this photo he looks every inch the British upper-class eccentric. As evidence of this, PTA Musters records that Jim was an accomplished knitter, especially of socks, and could be found on UK train journeys in full naval uniform, quietly knitting.

In 1946 Jim returned to his peacetime occupation as a zoologist. He was appointed as Assistant Keeper, Mammal Section, in the Department of Zoology at the British Museum and divided his time between London and Norway. He continued his work of preparing a checklist of the Palaearctic mammals, which involved a vast amount of patient research into type localities.

Jim Passes Away Unexpectedly

Jim was working for the British Museum and living in Kensington, London at the time of his early death aged just 47 (his obituaries state it was sudden, so possibly a heart attack or stroke) on 12th April 1948. He never married and had no children.

His brother Douglas travelled from his home in Bedford to London to take Jim's ashes by train to Annesley. PTA Musters reports that when Douglas arrived at Nottingham station to be met by his brother, he called out – to Jack's embarrassment – that *"Jim never travelled 3rd class before in his life!"*. Jim's ashes were interred at Annesley All Saints Church on 21st April 1948, alongside family members, with an address given by Rod Milward (son of Jim's sister, Elsie). Jim was said to be acutely observant, unconventional, outspoken, and always independent and original. Had his parents been alive, they would undoubtedly have been equally proud of him as they were of their sons who fought in the Great War.

Returning now to the couple's other sons, Tony re-joined the forces

Tony in WWII

at the outbreak of World War II, despite being unfit for active service, and worked in an Anti-Aircraft ("Ack-Ack") Command Unit on the East coast of England. The AAC controlled the Territorial Army anti-aircraft artillery and searchlight formations defending the UK. He retired from the army in September 1944 with the honorary rank of Major.

After the war he worked occasionally as a chauffeur and in 1953, he married Mabel Charsley of Wilmington Delaware – widow of Lt Commander John H Charsley RN. PTA Musters states he was a:

> *Dear man, kind to everyone and adored by his three daughters... his children would have fun looking for the place in his head where his war wound had been trepanned!*

Despite his two near-death experiences, Tony lived a long life, finally passing away in 1987 in Hampshire, aged 95.

After the Great War, Douglas gave up his farm in Suffolk and the family moved to Bedford. Around this time their second son David, tragically died, aged only six. Douglas took up beagling (he is pictured left in 1937, aged 39, in his Beagle Master outfit) and shooting.

He was known for being a kind, down-to-earth man who loathed pretentiousness. In June 1939, Douglas volunteered once again for the Royal Artillery and joined an anti-tank regiment, working as an instructor in Northern Ireland before being invalided out of the army and re-joining his family, who were housing evacuee children. He was placed on the reserve of officers in 1943 with the honorary rank of Major and was taken off the reserve list in 1948.

His son described him as much changed by the Great War, not surprisingly, as he was such a young man at the time, bearing great responsibility and had lost three much-loved brothers. Perhaps his experiences took a toll on his physical, as well as his mental, health as he died in Bedford on 2nd April 1957, aged only 59 and was buried in St Mary the Virgin Churchyard, Goldington, Bedford. He lived at the time in a modest semi-detached 1930's house, leaving a total estate in today's value of around £290,000. His wife Molly moved to Lymington and lived until 1983, dying aged 87.

Jack's Life after the War

Jack, as the eldest surviving son, took over Annesley and the estates from his father in 1921. He and Daphne had four children: Audrey (b. 1915), Pamela (b. 1919), John (b. 1922), and Robert (b. 1923). Jack's military career continued after the First World War[49] and he was promoted to Lieutenant-Colonel of the 107th South Notts Hussars Yeomanry Brigade (a reserve regiment) on 12th February 1928 and was made a Brevet Colonel on 12th February 1932, holding the post until 1961.

Between 1939-1941, Jack was made Lieutenant-Colonel of the 150th South Notts Hussars Field Regiment but didn't see active service. However, tragedy struck the family again, when their son-in-law, Major Miles Petre was killed in 1942, followed by their eldest son and heir, John Henry Chaworth-Musters, who died while serving with the 2nd Battalion, Coldstream Guards in Tunisia on 12th April 1943.

Jack was said to be a 'soldierly-looking' man (as the photo above shows), with an upright bearing and direct gaze. But he was also noted for his kindness to his family, staff, and the locals in Annesley. PTA Musters reports that during WWII, Jack was attacked by poachers he found in Annesley Park. When word spread, a representation of miners came from the village to assure him that the poachers must have been outsiders, as 'no local would have harmed the Squire'.

A man of duty and community in the Chaworth-Musters tradition, Jack took on many of the local administrative positions

---

49. Trevor Torkington, https://ww1lives.com/major-john-neville-chaworth-musters-dso-obe-jp-dl-survived-the-war.

that his father had previously held, serving as a magistrate from 1922 to 1963, was appointed as Deputy Lieutenant for Nottinghamshire in 1931 (and again in 1957), High Sherriff of Nottinghamshire in 1936, Chairman of the Annesley Parish Council, and Chairman of the Broxtowe Divisional Conservative Association. He was awarded the OBE in 1951 for his work as Chair of the North Midland Region Price Regulation Committee, and his wife Daphne was also awarded an OBE, in 1958, for her charitable and political work.

Annesley Hall Struggles On

The final years of Mary Anne's life heralded great changes for the British economy, which would have undoubtedly affected the Chaworth-Musters' fortunes. The economy was impacted by the General Strike in May 1926, which involved most organised labour forces and lasted for nine days. The economic unrest continued for several years and was worsened by New York's Wall Street crash in October 1929, when those who had invested in US shares suffered.

At the end of 1931, Britain devalued its currency when it left the Gold Standard. The value of Sterling fell by a quarter, income tax had been raised again, and there was a reduction in public sector salaries, including the pay and pensions of armed forces. The agricultural depression continued up to start of the World War II, meaning reduced income from land for major estate owners, including the Chaworth-Musters. The family had also ceased to be Directors of Annesley Colliery in 1925, when it was bought by the New Hucknall Colliery Company.

The new owners invested a significant amount of capital into Annesley as part of a major modernisation scheme. In 1947, the National Coal Board was formed, and Annesley became one of 18 collieries based in the NCB's East Midlands Division. Records show that in 1896, Annesley employed 1,307 people, in 1923 it was 1,042 and in 1947 it had dropped to 888 people. Production wound down in the 1980s, after the miner's strike, but was re-established in the mid-1990s when the pit was bought and operated privately. Annesley Colliery finally closed in January 2000, bringing local mining to an end after 132 years in operation.[50]

---

50. David Amos, www.miningheritage.co.uk

When Jack ceased to be a Director of Annesley Colliery, this probably also ended the licensed payment per ton of coal to the family that had been in place since 1868. A local mining historian, David Amos, states that the family received a royalty on every ton raised until the mines were nationalised in 1947, when he claims the Government paid the Chaworth-Musters significant compensation.

This may not be the case however, as the Land Registry deeds for Annesley Hall show that in 1933, *"mines and minerals with ancillary rights"* were conveyed (sold) to The New Hucknall Colliery Company by Jack, John Baldwin Young (Rita's husband), Colonel Bertram Abel Smith (who lived in London and Leicestershire), and Harold Hunter Christie QC (a Sussex-based lawyer). These were presumably fellow Directors of ACC. If this was the case, then it is unlikely that the Chaworth-Musters received compensation in 1947, if they had already sold their mining and mineral rights. If so, the family would have narrowly missed out on a significant payment.

Whether or not Jack's income from coal ended in 1925, 1933 or 1947, it would be considerably less than that received from 1870-1918, as the coal resources were much depleted. This, combined with a reduction in agricultural income at much the same time, would have been a heavy blow in the 1920s, especially as Jack is likely to have paid significant death duties in 1921 on his father's death.

But it could have been worse. After all, Jack managed to keep Annesley estate mostly intact, whilst many major country houses were closed, the owners moving to smaller houses, hotels, or boarding houses. However, by 1938, money was clearly getting tighter, and Jack sold the long-held family seat of Wiverton Hall (along with its estate of 2,170 acres) to the Crown and it was lived in by a World War II Major-General.

Jack sold the last of the family's property (apart from Annesley and its Park) in Edwalton in 1950 and had, by then, replaced much of Annesley Park with plantations of conifers, probably to reduce gardening costs and to try to generate an income. This meant that the groomed elevations, carefully planted avenues of trees, the deer park, and the remains of the Norman motte and bailey gradually disappeared in a dense forest of spruce and firs.

Annesley Park was altered further in the 1960s when the grounds were split in two by the new M1 motorway, for which the family was paid under the Land Compensation Act 1961.

Mechanised farming gathered pace and was centralised, and most of the remaining small tenancies came to an end. Disused farm buildings were demolished as the land was sold off or came under the central Home Farm. Nowadays, these buildings would probably be sought after for conversion into rural, residential homes but in the 1960s, this was not yet in vogue, with most couples wanting new homes with all 'mod cons'.

In 1960, Jack and Daphne's second son Robert (their heir, John, having been killed in 1943), took over the running of Annesley, although Jack (aged 70) and Daphne continued to live there. Signs that money was increasingly tight are revealed by the fact that the large staff had been reduced to just one, Mrs Fisher, the cook, who had been with the family for decades. Jack died at Annesley in March 1970, aged 79, having conveyed the Hall and Park to his son Bob in 1968. Daphne left Annesley on Jack's death to live with her daughter and survived him by three years, passing away in January 1973, aged 77.

The Annesley Link Is Severed

Continuing the story of Annesley Hall, the new owner, Robert Patricius Chaworth-Musters (1923-1992), was known as 'Major Bob' or Bobbie. He retired from the army and ran the remaining estate at Annesley for a further three years after his father passed away, but it had become too expensive to maintain, was cold and too large for Bob and his wife Diana. On 26th April 1973, he sold Annesley Hall and Park to the Football Association. Just prior to this, on 20th-22nd March 1973, London auction houses sold off the Hall's contents, including the best furniture, rare porcelain and what was probably the finest private collection of stuffed birds in the UK. It must have been a sad day for Bob and his surviving Uncles and Aunts when the house, which had been in the family for hundreds of years, passed out of their ownership and the family's connection with Annesley was severed.

Sadly, Bob's wife Diana also died in 1973 and he later remarried and moved to Felley Priory. Felley had been in the Musters family since 1822 via John Musters, who married Mary Ann Chaworth, although the family had never lived there.

Bob died unexpectedly in 1992, aged 68, and the direct male line of Chaworth-Muster inheritance ended with him. His only child, daughter Venetia and son-in-law Thomas Brudenell lived there with their daughters Sophia and Victoria. Venetia sadly died only a year after her father, in 1993, and Thomas remarried and lives at Felley with his second wife Amanda.

The Football Association apparently intended to use Annesley Hall and grounds as a soccer training centre but were unable obtain planning to divert the footpaths which pass through the estate. As a result, they never used the Hall and sold it to Staffordshire property developers, Bargate Properties in August 1977. Bargate in turn, sold it to Derbyshire-based residential property developers, Dennis Rye Limited, who passed it to a sister company East Midlands Developments Ltd, in whose hands it remains.

The new purchasers carried out extensive internal alterations and removed many of the 17th century fittings, although it was never occupied. The fine balustrade from the terrace was stolen in 1995 and the roof and interior structure of the Hall were extensively damaged by fire in 1997. In 2005, the television show *Most Haunted* visited the Hall and spent a night exploring the crumbling interior in an (unsurprisingly, unsuccessful) search for the ghosts of 'Elizabeth' and 'William'.

Trying to protect the Hall, in 1986 the 13th-century park, what remained of the 17th-century terraces, 19th-century buildings and walled gardens were Grade II and II* listed. In 2009, English Heritage put the building on the 'Buildings at Risk Register' as of 'high vulnerability and deteriorating'. Although it remains on the register, the condition has been upgraded to stable.

On 16th May 2015, a second fire (suspected as arson) severely damaged two of the three floors at the Hall. An article in the *Mansfield and Ashfield Chad* on 8th July 2015 quoted Stephen Rye (the owner's son and director):

> *We are very serious about our plans for Annesley Hall. We have had ownership of the building for a number of years and now we want to do something about it. We have put a lot of funds into Annesley Hall, and we were talking to Ashfield District Council about it even before the fire. I am happy to let people know about our plans at the right time.*

However, nothing happened, which infuriated locals keen to see the landmark given a new lease of life. An article on *Nottinghamshire Live* of 27th May 2020 reported on the frustration of various local groups, quoting the groundsman Paul Genders:

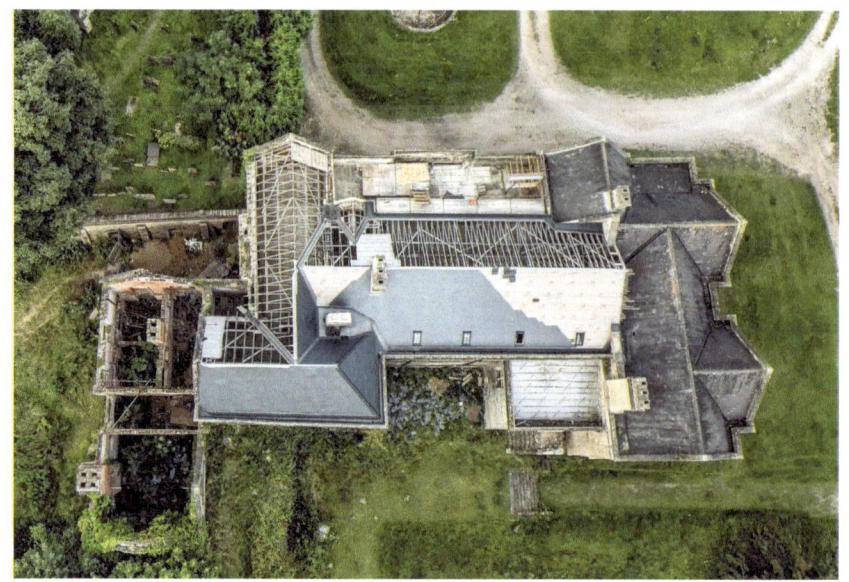

*Annesley Hall, September 2021,
courtesy of photographer Ken Hawley*

I'm devastated because it has got such a lot of potential and is a stately home with a lot of history connected to it.

Owner, Dennis Rye, died aged 87 in 2021. The companies are now run by his son, Stephen Rye. There were rumours that the stable block was to be turned into a pub and restaurant and some windows were repaired and a temporary staircase were built but nothing further happened. However, more recent photos in 2021 show the main building as having been mostly re-roofed. Stephen Rye commented on the photos on his Facebook page: *"We are on the way. It's been hard work to get to this point"*, so hopefully the Hall is on its way to being restored in full, although what it will become is unknown.

The Story Ends

The Chaworth-Musters' history can be traced back to the 1400s, but the family's heyday was undoubtedly in the 1850-80's, at the height of the Victorian era. Boosted by land and coal, the Chaworth-Musters were substantially wealthy and among the elite of UK landowners at the time, though were straightforward 'greater gentry' rather than aristocratic.

Perhaps the 1850's generation overspent – on general living and in their philanthropic desire to do their best for their estate and mine workers – building houses, schools, village amenities and a new church.

Finances were further stretched when the agricultural depression of the 1870s hit, reducing income from land, followed by successive governments raising income and land taxes. Patrick and Mary Anne appeared to try to stem the flood of expenses and reduce costs but, in hindsight, maybe the family's best was already behind them in wealth terms. This may well not have worried the couple unduly, as both seemed to prefer a simpler lifestyle based around the countryside and family, but they still had properties, land, staff, and a large family to provide for.

The Great War changed everything for the family. The couple suffered the loss of three sons (including their heir), a son-in-law and a nephew – all loved and greatly missed. Patrick's health suffered from the loss, and it was felt to have unduly shortened his life.

The economic uncertainties of the 1930s and 1940s diminished the family's wealth further. Their heir, Jack, was principally an army man and was possibly not trained in modern estate and business management. When he inherited in 1921, the family's fortunes were much reduced, whilst costs were still high.

Jack leased Annesley Park to the Forestry Commission in 1942-1944 but Annesley House was neither grand nor large enough to be turned into a visitor attraction, as many country houses were in the 1950s and 1960s. So, he perhaps felt that the only feasible option in 1973 was to sell. Even then, the family home suffered further misfortune.

The wealthy Football Association could have preserved it and the subsequent developer owners could have changed its use to a smart hotel or apartments (as has happened with West Bridgford Hall, a former family property). But, sadly for the Chaworth-Musters, this wasn't the case, and the house continues to lie semi-derelict. The desolate Annesley Hall is a sad memorial to a once-great local family whose wealth declined with the changing economy and who were ultimately broken by war and loss.

ACKNOWLEDGEMENTS

I first came upon this story whilst researching the subject of Victorian servants and I'd like to thank author Jeremy Musson for name-checking Patrick and Mary Anne in his book *Up and Down Stairs: the history of the country house servant*. On enquiring about the pair, he kindly sent me an extract from PTA Musters' book on the Chaworth-Musters. That got me hooked!

Thank you to Patrick H A Musters, PTA Musters' son, who gave permission for me to quote extensively from his father's very impressive work. After that, I contacted family members Richard Toller, George Hanbury and Barbara Chaworth-Musters, who helped where they could.

One of the family's contacts was David Amos, a local historian whose very good websites and books informed my work. David, in turn, pointed me towards Sue Hardy, a researcher for the Annesley Old Church project, who gave me a tour of the church site and Annesley Hall (viewable only from the boundary wall), loaned me out-of-print books, and kindly sent me a wealth of facts about the family. Sue put me in touch with distant family member Daniel Sandars, who took time to answer questions and outline his thoughts and opinions on the Victorian family. Many thanks to you all.

The team at the University of Nottingham, Manuscripts and Special Collections were all immensely patient in retrieving information from the family collection, answering queries, and providing copies of material during my many visits and follow-up emails. Special mention to Jayne Amat of the Nottingham team, for her diligent photo research. Similarly, my thanks go to Maja Frønes, the Manager of Surnadal museum in Norway, who went out of her way to locate information on the family's life in Norway from 1883-1888.

Apart from a fairly broad reading list, not surprisingly, I made extensive use of the internet. Two websites are worth a special mention. Key among them is Chris Baker's *The Long, Long Trail*, which is a simply astonishing personal endeavour covering every battle, regiment, and theatre of operation in World War One. Next up is Andy Nicholson's excellent *Nottinghamshire History* website, which provided material on Leonard Jacks, the Thoroton Society and coverage of most of the Chaworth-Musters' properties.

Finally, loving thanks to my partner, Tim Ayris, for his patience and support as I drew five (very stop-start) years of research and writing to a close.

Nicola Webb
March 2023

Reading List

Family History

Andy Nicholson, *Nottinghamshire History*,
   http://www.nottshistory.org.uk
Canon Frank Lyons, *Hills of Annesley*, published in sections in
   Annesley Parish, 1975
David Amos, *A Brief History of Annesley Colliery 1865 – 2000*, 2015
Denis R. Pearson, *Annesley through the Ages*, 1995
John Bateman, *The great landowners of Great Britain and Ireland*,
   1883
Leonard Jacks, *The Great Houses of Nottinghamshire and the County
   Families*, 1881
Lina Chaworth-Musters, *A Cavalier stronghold: a romance of the
   Vale of Belvoir*, 1890
Norfolk Record Office: personal and family correspondence and
   papers of the Hamond and Chaworth-Musters families, 19th
   century, in the Hamond of Westacre collection (HMN5/95-99,
   216-236)
Patrick T.A. Musters, *The Musters: a family gathering*, 2nd edition,
   2001.
University of Nottingham, Manuscripts and Special Collections,
   Chaworth-Musters papers 1538-2004
W.P.W. Phillimore, *County Pedigrees Nottinghamshire, Volume 1.*

Working History

Alan Beale, *Database of fatalities in the coal fields*,
   http://www.healeyhero.co.uk
Audrey Deal, *Straw Plaiting: The Victorian Country Child*,
   http://www.audreydeal.co.uk
Carole Llewellyn, *Women of straw*, 2016

Dave Harris, Coordinator, Midland Railway Study Centre, Midlandrailwaystudycentre.org.uk
David Amos, *Nottinghamshire Coalmining, Annesley Colliery 1865 – 2000*, http://www.ournottinghamshire.org.uk/ and Miningheritage.co.uk
Frank E. Huggett, *Life Below Stairs: Domestic servants in England from Victorian times*, 1978
Jeremy Musson, *Up and Down Stairs: the history of the country house servant*, 2009
Kate Clarke, *Women and domestic service in Victorian society*, The History Press
Lucy Lethbridge, *Servants: A Downstairs View of Twentieth Century Britain*, 2013
Noel Streatfeild, *Tea by the nursery fire: A children's nanny at the turn of the century*, 1975
Pamela Horn, *The rise and fall of the Victorian servant*, 1975
Pamela Sambrook, *Keeping their place: domestic service in the country house 1700-1920*, 2005
Pamela Sambrook, *The country house servant*, 2002
Pamela Sambrook, *The servants' story: Managing a great country house*, 2016
Tessa Boase, *The Housekeeper's Tale: the women who really ran the English country house*, 2014
The Durham Mining Museum, http://www.dmm.org.uk/
On Behalf of the People, https://www.coalandcommunity.org.uk/
Veronica Main, Hatplait.co.uk
Wendy M Gordon, *Mill Girls and Strangers: single women's independent migration in England...*, 2002

Leisure Society

Adrian Tinniswood, *The house party: a short history of leisure, pleasure and the country house weekend*, 2019
Adrian Tinniswood, *The long weekend: life in the English country house between the wars*, 2018
Børge Solem, *Norway Heritage*, http://www.norwayheritage.com/
Catherine Bailey, *The Secret Rooms*, 2012
Eleanor Gordon and Gwyneth Nair, *Public Lives: Women, Family and Society in Victorian Britain*, 2003
Evelyn Waugh, *Brideshead Revisited*, 1945
Fjord Norway, https://www.fjordnorway.com/

Flora Thompson, *Lark rise to candleford*, 1945
Mark Girouard, *Life in the English country house*, 1993
Morten Harangen, *Victorian salmon fishing*,
    http://mortenharangen.no/
Nordmøre Museum, https://www.nordmore.museum.no/
Pamela Horn, *Country House Society: The Private Lives of England's Upper Class After the First World War*, 2015

Victorian Period

A N Wilson, *The Victorians*, 2003
Geoffrey Best, *Mid-Victorian Britain 1851-75*, 2008
Jeremy Black, *A Brief history of Britain 1851-2010*, 2011
Ruth Goodman, *How to be a Victorian*, 2013

The Great War

Chris Baker, *The Long, Long Trail*:
    https://www.longlongtrail.co.uk/, 1996-present
Everyman, *On the front line: true World War I stories*, 2009
George Coppard, *With A Machine Gun to Cambrai*, 1969
Imperial War Museum, *Lives of the First World War*
John Mackenzie, *British Battles.com*, https://www.britishbattles.com/
John Sadler & Rosie Serdiville, *Tommy at War: 1914-1918*, 2013
John Sadler & Rosie Serdiville, *Tommy: The British army in the trenches*, 2017
Keith Gregson, *A Tommy in the Family*, 2014
Max Arthur, *Faces of World War One*, 2007
Michael Hanlon, *Roads to the Great War*,
    http://roadstothegreatwar-ww1.blogspot.com/
National Army Museum, https://www.nam.ac.uk/
Peter Hepplewhite, *True stories from World War I*, 2014
Rosie Collins, *Radcliffe on Trent WWI Group*,
    http://www.radcliffeontrentww1.org.uk/
Stephen Berridge, *Lightbobs*, http://www.lightbobs.com/
Stephen Bull, *Trench – a history of trench warfare on the Western Front*, 2010
The Wartime Memories Project,
    https://www.wartimememoriesproject.com/
Trevor Torkington, *WW1 Lives*, https://ww1lives.com/